Sacrifice

The Final Chapter

Ron Farina

Commissioned by
Duke Leopold d'Arenberg

Published by Lagrange Books, an imprint of Oren Litwin
Visit our website at https://lagrangebooks.com
Contact us at editor@lagrangebooks.com.
Sponsored by the Arenberg Foundation.
Visit our website at https://www.arenbergfoundation.eu

This is a work of creative nonfiction. Some dialogue has been reimagined for narrative purposes. Some events have been dramatized, but are presented substantially as they were described to the author.

Cover design by Deranged Doctor Design:
https://www.derangeddoctordesign.com

Map of Southwest Asia by United States Central Intelligence Agency: https://www.loc.gov/item/2001623732/.

Map of Iraq by United States Central Intelligence Agency, Cartography Center: https://www.loc.gov/item/2003629862/.

Map of Afghanistan by United States Central Intelligence Agency, Afghanistan Administrative Divisions: https://www.loc.gov/item/2009575509/.

Photos of, or concerning, the subjects of the book were provided by their families and friends. We thank them warmly for their permission to use the images, and their courage.

Because everyone needs to know.

PRAISE FOR "SACRIFICE"

The word "sacrifice" is often invoked when honoring veterans' service and military families. But rarely, if ever, has the full lived experience of what this word really signifies—the dread, grief, awe, and redemption—been captured so beautifully and faithfully as in Ron Farina's *Sacrifice*. The book not only profiles in vivid detail those who sacrificed their lives in service to our country but also tells the stories of the friends and family members they left behind. These are stories without end. No one touched by them will ever experience "closure." But these are *our* stories, which we, as American citizens, have a responsibility to know and appreciate. My wish is that every American reads *Sacrifice*.

—Todd DePastino
Executive Director, Veterans Breakfast Club

Ron Farina's latest book, *Sacrifice*, holds nothing back in its powerful storytelling. From lost brothers and sisters to sons and daughters, each story introduces us to brave men and women and their families. It also gives all non-military people a real and sometimes disturbing look at what our armed forces go through, protecting not just this nation but protecting themselves and their brothers and sisters in countries of conflict around the world. And the heartbreaking roles carried out all too often by the military, sent to families to deliver the news no one ever wants to receive, the death of a family member. *Sacrifice* is a book that makes no apology for ripping open the reality of what it means to be in or connected to the military. For all those lost, for all those now and for all of those in the future, we thank you for your sacrifice.

—Brian Scott Smith, broadcast journalist

Tears streamed down my face as I read the story of Helen K. Pedersen and her son, Special Forces, West Point Captain, Andrew Pedersen-Keel. Helen and I became friends, *soldier moms and soldier sisters,* when our sons were classmates at West Point. Andrew's death on the battlefield, the experience at Dover Air Force Base, where his remains arrived from Afghanistan, and the days leading up to his burial at Arlington National Cemetery were the most impactful weeks of my life. Those days, days that I was part of, shaped my life in unimaginable and unwanted ways. When you read this story and the other stories in this collection, you'll understand.

—Barb Day
Soldier Mom. Soldier Sister.

We owe it to the .4% who serve our country and fight our wars to know their sacrifices and struggles. And that includes the families and loved ones left behind by those who pay the ultimate sacrifice. Ron Farina doesn't simply tell their stories; he brings us into them. As the parent of an active-duty Navy SEAL, this book hits close to home. The turn of each page brought out new emotions; all different, all too real. These stories are about loss, and all the lives impacted when a soldier dies serving our country. Ron opens our eyes to the pain, chaos, respect, anger, and love that surrounds every aspect of a soldier's death. And he does so with the same compassion and grit we've come to expect from his storytelling. It's his gift. *Sacrifice* should be required reading for ALL Americans.

    —Bob Vitale
    President of the Board, Sticks for Soldiers

News stories of American military lost or injured in service of our Country are often fleeting, replaced within days by newer news stories. It is our responsibility as individuals to remember, and honor the service and sacrifice of our servicemembers and civilian contractors as well as their families, loved ones, friends, long after the news stories end. Ron Farina's latest book *Sacrifice* accompanies the reader through these sacrifices in a way that is emotional, educational, and most importantly respectful. Farina's storytelling provides an emotional look into the specific acts of sacrifice—using each person's unique perspective to tell their stories. As an RN with the Fisher House of Boston I have yet to read a book that relays the stories of sacrifice we hear about each day as accurately as *Sacrifice* does. *Sacrifice* is, no doubt, a must read for each and every American!

    —Abigail Deluca, MHS, BSN, RN
    Director of Operations, Fisher House of Boston

In *Sacrifice: the Final Chapter*, Ron Farina's Vietnam war experience enables him to capture the essence of military service and sacrifice, not only by these inspirational men and women warriors, but also by the remarkable people left behind. *Sacrifice* profiles courageous Gold Star family members and friends caught in the wake of untimely and tragic loss, left to endure countless unanswered questions, unfilled dreams, and an unfathomable range of emotions. I know two of the families profiled in this book, Helen Keiser-Pedersen, her husband Bob, and Pat and Michael Parry. Overcoming their own grief, they vowed "to do good" in the name of their sons, Andrew and Brian. Helen and Bob established APK Charities in memory of Andrew. Pat and Michael established a scholarship at Brian's alma mater, Norwich University, donating over $2 million in scholarships and gifts. These are just two examples of the caliber of the families and friends of the fallen.

I found the book incredible. Having served on the ground during combat operations in Afghanistan, many topics hit very close to home. Our country must always honor and remember these true patriots, and their loved ones, lost in service and defense of our great nation.

—Brigadier Gen. Ron Welch (retd.), US Army
Operation Enduring Freedom Veteran

Vivid, haunting, and profoundly moving. Ron Farina's eloquent, captivating book carries the reader from the dark heart of the battlefield to the harrowing challenges friends and family encounter when their beloved one doesn't make it home. These heroes sacrificed their lives, but they are not dead. They have been and their existence is anchored in the meta-physical being. A comforting thought.

This is writing so powerful that it steals your breath. A great read.

—Dr. Viscount Mark Eyskens, Minister of State, fmr. prime minister of Belgium

Crest of the House of Arenberg

SACRIFICE

The Final Chapter

RON FARINA

DEDICATION

This book is dedicated to Stacia Jensen and all the families of fallen soldiers, everywhere. You sacrificed your loved ones, your gift to the world. This book is for you.

Go in peace.

In May of 2007, HSH Leopold, Duke of Arenberg, toured Walter Reed Army Medical Center. Days earlier, West Point Army Captain Drew Jensen, a mortar platoon leader, set out to recover a Bradley Fighting Vehicle damaged by a roadside bomb in Baqubah, Iraq. The captain's team, under small-arms fire, took cover and engaged the enemy. Captain Jensen spotted a lone soldier, one of his men, pinned down behind a vehicle by enemy fire. Abandoning the safety of his own position, rushing to try and rescue the soldier, the captain was struck by a single bullet. Shot in the neck, the wound would leave him paralyzed and unable to breathe on his own.

He received emergency treatment in Iraq, most likely at a battlefield combat surgical hospital, before he was evacuated to Landstuhl, Germany. Stable, alive, seriously wounded, he was flown to Walter Reed Army Medical Center.

It was there that Duke Leopold would meet the captain and his wife, Stacia. He'd visited wounded before, would visit them again, never certain of what to expect. The hellishness of the injuries is sometimes shocking. But this . . . this left the Duke visibly shaken. The wounded Captain lay fixed to machines keeping him alive, his young wife lying next to him, the extent of the injury almost inconceivable.

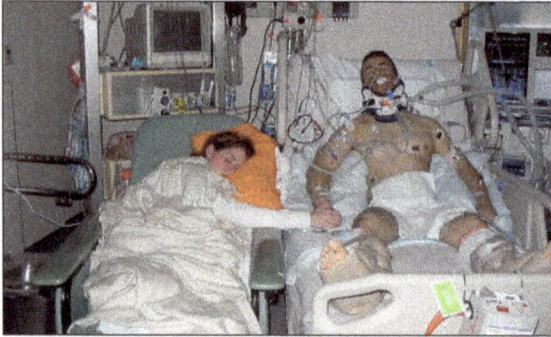

But that pit-in-stomach, knot-twisting feeling was quickly chased away. In the days that followed, Duke Leopold would be awed by Drew and Stacia's courage. During the few months they would have left together, Stacia and Drew discovered the strength to carry on in spite of the odds against them. They fought, side by side, shoulder to shoulder, doing everything possible to journey from the battlefield through a battery of rehabilitative treatments. Four months later, four months of trying, understanding that nothing would give Drew the ability to breathe on his own again.

In an act of medical kindness, doctors manipulated Drew's ventilator, positioned it so that he could speak. Drew had always been clear; he did not want his life prolonged by artificial means such as ventilators. He'd documented that in Army medical papers. And he whispered his decision to Stacia: he would leave the world on his own terms.

In September, four months after being carried from the battlefield, with Stacia by his side, nurses dialed down Drew's ventilator, honoring his wish, but not before Drew, able to talk through a manipulated ventilator, said goodbye. "Family, friends and acquaintances, thank you for your support," began his final recorded message. "Understand that I will miss *all of you, and to those who don't fully understand, I apologize."*

Stacia grieved. She'd been married to Drew for less than a year when the bullet tore through his body. They had plans. Children. A life together. All that changed in an instant. Stacia struggled. Grieving, she would learn, had its own agenda. Its own pace.

She would discover, like almost every family member of a fallen soldier, that grieving, well . . . it's a contact sport. It's real. Physical. Emotional. Exhausting. Turning inward, meditation, yoga, her own spirituality, that helped . . . some.

"Come with," her stepsister suggested, ready herself for a world-wide surfing trip. Stacia agreed.

At some point on the journey, the sisters made it to New Zealand, an island nation with a long love affair with surfing. Long coastlines, rolling Pacific swells, uncrowded beaches, and easy-going people. In Raglan, great surfing, clear blue waters, volcanic black sand beaches, Stacia felt different. Maybe she could stop running. Maybe this was a place to heal.

So she stayed, supporting herself, teaching yoga in Raglan and Coromandel, the latter on many surfers' bucket list. Healing herself until . . .

She began to heal the world.

Stacia started her own business, LillyBee Wrap, a company that makes and provides natural containers and food wraps made largely from beeswax, an alternative to plastic wraps and containers.

The company motto, "When intention meets action, we change the world." That is what Captain Drew Jensen and all the soldiers killed and wounded in Iraq and Afghanistan stood for . . .

Stacia and her son

The Other Side of the Door

Soldiers—scrubbed and combed, buttoned
Into perfect uniforms, shiny bars on shoulders,
Gold stripes on sleeves—
stand on the other side of the door.

Yesterday's breaking news with its queasy dread
Of something ill-fated scraped at your skin throughout the night.
You guessed—knew—that they might be here by morning. Now they are.

With each word—*Ma'am, on behalf*—hope dissolves into thin air.
The trained voice loses its disguise, sorrow slips past, and you—
You understand the soldier on the other side of the door.

Time passes. Grief is sly. The view shifts, and you make
Your own peace with it. Life begins to move—two steps forward,
One back. Out of nowhere sadness steals a minute—more.
And you remember the morning soldiers stood on the
Other side of the door . . .

War is awful. Nothing, not the valor with which it is fought nor the nobility of the cause it serves, can glorify war. War is wretched beyond description and only a fool or a fraud could sentimentalize its cruel reality. Whatever is won in war, it is loss that the veteran remembers.

— JOHN McCAIN

A nation reveals itself not only by the men it produces but also the men it honors, the men it remembers.

— JOHN F. KENNEDY

All that holds us together in the end are our stories.

— FREDERIK BACKMAN, *THE WINNERS*

AFGHANISTAN — Administrative Divisions

TURKEY

SYRIA

IRAN

JORDAN

DAHUK

ARBIL

NINAWÁ

SULAYMANIYAH

AT TA'MIM

SALAH AD DIN

DIYALA

BAGHDAD

AL ANBAR

BABIL

WASIT

KARBALA'

AN NAJAF

QADISIYAH

DHI QAR

MAYSAN

AL MUTHANNA

AL BASRAH

KUWAIT

SAUDI ARABIA

Persian
Gulf

International boundary
Governorate (muḥāfaẓah) boundary
National capital
Governorate (muḥāfaẓah) capital
Railroad
Highway
Road
Track
Airfield
Port

CONTENTS

BOOK THREE

BOOK FOUR: VOLUME ONE

BOOK FOUR: VOLUME TWO

BOOK FIVE

A FEW NOTES FROM THE AUTHOR

Although this book is a collection of stories about the families of fallen soldiers, I have included the story of a civilian contractor, Mike Doheny, and his family. Mike started working with Tetra Tech in 2005, after serving eight years in the Marine Corps. He had been in Iraq as a contractor since August 2007, but had served there twice before. He was part of the Coalitions Munitions Clearance program, which is responsible for disposing of captured ammunitions in Iraq. He was killed when an improvised explosive struck his vehicle in Iraq.

I use "soldiers" as a universal term for all branches of the military. No slight to any branch of the military is intended.

I use acronyms throughout the text. A glossary is included at the end of the book for easy reference.

PREFACE

On the day I began research for Sacrifice, Stories of the Families of Fallen Soldiers, *the temperature outside my window dipped below freezing. A cardinal, impossible to miss against an early winter snow, and bluebirds, chickadees, purple finches too, perched in trees, puffed up into little round balls of fluff to ward off the cold, waited for a turn at bird feeders in plain view from my window.*

Streaks of winter sun needled through storm clouds, breaking them apart, the threat of more snow disappeared with the fragmented clouds. I felt lucky, no, privileged, an aging veteran from a past generation, working to uncover and share the stories of a new generation of veterans and their families. Anxious, too, a familiar feeling that always tags along on the hunt for and discovery of information that ultimately leads me to people willing to talk to me. I know what I'm asking and it's a big ask.

For this book, those people, family and friends of fallen soldiers, would have to be willing to revisit their loss, their sacrifice, ultimately their grief and pain. Few have the courage to go beyond a first call. Those who did worked with me for months, hours at a time, answering my questions. When we weren't talking, we texted and emailed, sometimes every day, for weeks until we felt like we had enough to tell a story.

Recalling the past isn't a neat, question-and-answer process that moves along in a straight line. Recalling the past rarely moves forward that tidily. Memories do not drop into place that easily. But the connections get made. Randomly. Unsequenced. One memory leads to another, links information, and the story of a life begins to unfold.

I often doubted myself, questioned the wisdom of asking someone to revisit tragedy. That anxious feeling that tags along turned, often enough, into an uneasiness. I had more questions, more doubts. Would the message, this is what veterans and their families live through, be heard? Will people take a minute to read the stories? Will some good come out of all of this? Will I have asked too much?

But then I'm reminded of why I'm doing this—first for the caregivers profiled in Who Will Have My Back, *the first book in this trilogy. Then for the women in* Out of the Shadows: Voices of American Women Soldiers. *And now for the families—fathers, mothers, brothers, and sisters, husband and wives, children—in this book,* Sacrifice. *I can only hope that their stories will be read, heard, celebrated and remembered.*

———

Two years have slipped past my window since I began this book. Today, snow is on the ground again. The sky is grey, bloated with the threat of snow. I haven't seen the cardinal yet. He'll be here. He comes every day.

   —Ron Farina
   January 30, 2024

INTRODUCTION

Weeks before the end of World War II, in May of 1945, thousands of prisoners held in German concentration camps were liberated by American soldiers. Thousands of others, not so fortunate, died in death marches during those same final weeks.

Almost eighty years separate the story of the liberation of the camps from the end of America's wars in Iraq and Afghanistan. How does one connect these wars, eighty years apart, to the narratives that follow this page? The answer exists in a heartfelt thank you.

This book, *Sacrifice: The Final Chapter,* and the two before it, *Who Will Have My Back* and *Out of the Shadows: Voices of American Women Soldiers,* supported by HSH, Duke Leopold of Arenberg, are an expression of gratitude, a thank you to America, the American soldier, American veterans, and American families.

During World War II, Duke Leopold's mother and her family survived three Nazi concentration camps, rescued in the final days of the war by American troops. More than sixty years later in San Antonio, TX, the Duke met U.S. Army Colonel Al Metts. Metts, a young lieutenant in 1945, fighting for others in a European war, liberated the Duke's mother. The Duke himself wouldn't be living today without American intervention.

In those same final days of World War II, Duke Leopold's father was expecting a sure death in a Gestapo prison. The arrival of American troops allowed him to escape just before being shot, hanged, or beheaded.

These rescues, these gifts of life, have never been taken lightly by HSH Duke Leopold. They remain a legacy, a part of the Duke's family, something never to be forgotten, something to be honored, and celebrated. This book, *Sacrifice: the Final Chapter* is part of a lifelong thank you to America and a special thank you to America's Gold Star Families.

My personal involvement, coordinating the efforts that brought the stories of bravery, courage, sorrow, and sacrifice to the page, has been a privilege, an honor.

As a boy, I listened to my grandparents tell incredible stories about the Second World War. They never tired of the telling and I never tired of the tales, *all true*. They talked of how their region in Belgium was liberated by American and British soldiers. How that put an end to their constant hunger and latent fear. How, after four long years of uncertainty, their lives finally regained hope and perspective. How American service members brought with them not only food and freedom, but also new styles of music, canned beef, fruit drinks, and chewing gum. And how the Marshall Plan helped Belgium get back on its feet economically.

Motivated by the stories I heard, even as a boy, I decided I would take up the gun, become a soldier. My decision was born out of respect and gratitude for the American servicemembers who came to liberate us, and from the awareness that sometimes only a gun stands between good and evil. A gun. Not to shoot. Not to kill. Not to destroy. But to stop those who would do evil.

Hidden within the stories told to me by my grandparents,

past the bravery and courage of the American soldier, was the American soldiers' passion to protect the vulnerable, to defend democratic values, to stand up for the freedoms we have and will fight to protect, to live free, and to help others do the same.

Duke Leopold and I often ask ourselves, "Where does the US get such exceptional men and women, willing to sacrifice everything—even their lives? Where do those qualities of the good and noble arise in America to produce such an embodiment of our most precious qualities of sacrifice, loyalty, bravery, and patriotism?"

We think that it is at the dinner tables, church pews, classrooms, and firesides of middle America that those latent qualities—your qualities—are forged. It is the distillation of those qualities in the cauldron of war which makes America so different from the rest of us, so much the best part of us. We are shamed by your sacrifice, by your fierce loyalties, by your stoic acceptance of unimaginable hardship.

So, you serve, and endure, and persevere and suffer—nameless and invisible to the wider world whose safety is your constant gift. Indifferent to public praise and private fortune, you carry the banner of civilization to foreign shores, and there, on some wind-swept, boulder-strewn parapet on the edge of chaos and barbarism, you plant that banner. Standing there, you turn and call to us in words that echo down through the ages—"Sleep soundly," you say. "Sleep soundly because no one will hurt you tonight."

We in Belgium know how lucky we are to sleep beneath the blanket of freedom and security America's brave men and women in the military provide, and we are grateful every day that you have the fortitude and dedication to give so much to make that happen.

American mothers, fathers, husbands, wives, sisters, brothers, you have given up a loved one for your country, and to help others who cannot help themselves, for a way of life that is free and without fear. That is something that cannot be repaid. What makes you all so great is that you give so much and do not expect anything in return.

Unthinkable tragedy has struck the families chronicled in this book. A cherished son or daughter, husband or wife, sister or brother has been lost. But life goes on, different now without that lost loved one. For some the grief is decades old, for others it is fresh. At the time of this writing, not even two years had passed since the final days of America's departure from Afghanistan. Eleven marines, a soldier, and a sailor were killed on August 26, 2021.

Sacrifice: the Final Chapter is a reminder for some, a new awareness for others, of the sacrifice families of soldiers must be prepared to make and do. It is a look into the everyday world lived in by the families of American military men and women. Families living every day with the knowledge that a loved one is in harm's way. Families dreading a knock on their door that means the end.

Once more, I'm honored to have played a part in bringing this book to the reading public. I know grief and tears will come, memories of your loved one will ebb and flow, but you carry on. Thank you for your bravery, your strength in the face of the ultimate loss, the gift of your soldier to the world.

Thank you, American family.

Roger Housen

Colonel (retd.), Belgian Army

BOOK ONE

PART ONE

FROM THE OTHER SIDE OF THE DOOR

OCTOBER 5, 2007

By early October, as nights grew longer, pushing their way deeper into mornings, the City of Madison, Wisconsin, shuffled off to work in the dark. In Iraq, another day limped toward midnight, and the world turned.

An alarm, set to wake Army Sergeants Leanne and Ed Trottingwolf by 0530, glowed in the dark. Leanne blinked, cleared her eyes of sleep. The blurry display came into focus. *0510.* Close enough. She pulled her arm from under the blanket, reached over her husband, and slid the button to off, spoiling the alarm's chance to jolt them awake. Back from Iraq for almost a year, accustomed to predawn reveille, Leanne and Ed remained early risers.

Ed felt Leanne's reach and stirred. "Time?" he whispered.

"Almost. We've got a few minutes."

"It's Friday."

"It is. I'm ready for the weekend."

After showers, breakfast, coffee for Ed, they closed the door behind them. The day, summerlike for early autumn, was the warm-up act for record-breaking heat.

Ed slid into the driver's seat of a blue Chrysler Town and

Country van. He fitted a key into the ignition. Leanne, already in the passenger's side, buckled up. Ed turned the key. *Gracie* greeted them with a mild complaint then settled into an obedient idle. Ed gave her a minute to warm to the task. He fit a thermos of fresh coffee between the seats. Snug. Already on a second cup, he'd empty the thermos over the course of the morning. Leanne never understood the allure.

Before sunlight chased the night sky into full retreat, Ed parked the van. Leanne unbuckled, turned, slid off the seat, waited for her toes to touch the ground. Ed, already around to her side of the van, took her hand. They walked into the 7302nd Medical Training Support Battalion building. The Battalion's mission centered on the training of medical personnel assigned to combat support hospital units (CSH) in upper Midwest states, units that would almost certainly deploy to Afghanistan and Iraq. Leanne and Ed had been deployed to a similar CSH, the 344th at Abu Ghraib.

Duties at the 7302nd, especially for full time personnel, were fairly routine. For Leanne and Ed, the day ahead looked much like the day before—process requests, fill out forms, update personnel files, coordinate training lanes, order supplies—*same old, same old*. But not every day held the promise of routine. A bittersweet duty, notifying next of kin of the loss of a family member, a task soldiers accepted as a sacred honor, was the polar opposite of routine.

Everyone knew the score. Everyone understood.

As senior NCOs, Leanne and Ed stood at the head of a queue of soldiers trained for the duty. Senior NCOs were the most likely to be called upon to deliver the news of a loved one's death or injury. Leanne and Ed hoped they'd never see the day. But they knew that if the task fell to them, they'd call on their God for strength, and answer the call. They'd moved through their first year at the 7302nd without incident, almost forgetting the eventuality, the tap on the shoulder, the tag-you're-it moment lurking in the shadows.

Inside the building something felt different, not wrong, just off, left of center. The facility, usually quiet this early in the day, felt electric. Lights on in every office. More staff than usual already here. Leanne wrinkled her forehead, paused, tilted her head, looked around trying to decipher the unexplained, the uptick in activity this early. Morning muster not until 0800. Ed caught her stare. Void of an answer, just as puzzled as his wife of just six months, Ed shrugged his shoulders. The smell of coffee wafting from the small mess heightened his unease. *Okay, that's not right—I usually make the first pot.*

The XO, Lieutenant Colonel Olson, sat at his desk. His hunched shoulder squeezed a telephone handset against his cheek, holding it captive. His pen raced across a note pad in front of him. He didn't look up. Leanne and Ed made their good mornings to another soldier, Sergeant First Class Nelson, a Vietnam veteran.

Nelson, Leanne, and Ed barely settled into a shared office. Another sergeant already there nodded to them. A shadow appeared in the doorway. Olson stepped into the noncom's office, greeted by a collective "Good morning, sir." Not the classic military bark of subordinates, definitely a salutation of respect, but tinged with the warmth due a favored superior.

"Good morning," Olson said, pausing, looking at each of his sergeants, scanning faces, making decisions. "Listen up, Madison has lost a soldier, a young woman, a medic, killed in Iraq. We've got the duty. We have to notify the family and we have to do it quickly, before reporters get hold of the story."

Leanne and Ed stiffened at the news, looked at Olson, ready for whatever order he'd issue. Nelson rose from his desk, ready too. The other sergeant backed up, suddenly pale, hands shaking. His face went flat, a blank screen, locked—password protected. Leanne understood. This was not something he wanted any part of. She stepped forward.

"I'll take it, sir," she said, "I'll do it. I'll notify the family."

"Alright. Good," Olson said. "I'll determine who to assign

as CAO, later. Whoever it is will take over once the family has been notified. Master Sergeant Trottingwolf, you're the Notification Team Officer," he said, looking directly at Leanne. "One more thing, the Chaplain isn't available. You'll have to do this on your own."

Leanne swallowed hard. *Alone? No way. Never done this before. Sure, I've got the training, but alone, no, oh no, nooooo. Think Leanne, 'cause you're not doing this by yourself—think! Ed! Ed's going to have to do this with me. He will. I know he will.*

"Sir, let Ed accompany me in place of the Chaplain. We'll do it together." Olson looked at Ed, querying. Leanne turned to Ed. A moment of uncertainty passed quickly. Ed looked at Leanne, his nod of affirmation confirming the request.

"I'll go, sir," he said. "We'll do it together."

"That's fine Sergeant, but you two have got to move out. The family has to be notified before the news breaks. You need to go in Class A dress. You can take the company vehicle. Report back here for final briefing, I'll have the rest of the information you'll need. Questions?"

"No sir, not for now," Leanne and Ed, voices in perfect unison, replied, "but we'll take our van."

"Alright, just get going."

Conceding a huge head start to time on the other side of the world, Leanne and Ed moved quickly. Prepared for this exact moment, spurred into action with news media only two steps behind them, they hurried to the van. Ed thrust the key into the ignition. *Gracie* seemed to understand and roared to life, her response to Ed's foot, heavy on the pedal. The first of October's leaves, already brown and curled on the ground, scattered in the blast of the van's exhaust. Ed's foot barely tapped the brake pedal. Taillights blinked. Ed rushed the van back into morning traffic.

At home, they bolted out of opposite sides of the van—rushed inside. Their dress uniforms, cleaned, pressed, secured in garment bags, hung in a shared closet, reinforcements waiting for orders. Leanne and Ed laid the garment bags on the bed they'd left just an hour earlier. The rasp of the zippers racing down the face of the bags, an eerie scratch, rent the silence.

They dressed without thinking. Meticulous. Ed draped a tie around his neck, deftly threading and looping it into a perfect Windsor. They inspected each other. Leanne pinched the knot of Ed's tie, a tight triangle, between her thumb and index finger, centered it perfectly. They donned berets, slightly off center. Corfam high-gloss shoes.

Ready.

A quick return to the 7302nd. Final briefing. Filled in on the particulars. Roll out. Ed, confident. Knowing to head north. Thirty minutes to Portage Road. Never been. Find it.

"Don't speed."

"I won't," Ed said, looking left, right, inching *Gracie* onto the street.

10:00 a.m. Heavy traffic gone. They pick up speed. Buildings blur. Trees thin. Ed passes a few slower cars. Air rushes through an open window buffeting Ed's beret. He slides the window shut. His foot goes heavy on the pedal. Too fast. He backs off. The sky above—clear. Twenty minutes more.

Leanne looks over to Ed. He catches her stare, acknowledges, turns back to the road.

———

DOUBT CLAWS AT LEANNE. *I've never done this before. Ed too. What if no one is home? How will we find them, the mother and father? Let me go over the words again. 'Sir, the Department of the Army. . . wait— what if it's just the mother, both parents . . . my speech . . . it's supposed to be as natural as possible. It's my job, not Ed's. I'm senior NCO, the Notification Team Officer. Can't read it. Play it back again. Again. Okay, I think I've got it. What else? I'm supposed to confirm that I'm speaking to the next of kin, ask if we can come in, encourage them to sit. Why?*

Why is that so important? Is it in case one, both of them collapse, does that happen? I guess so, right? Shouldn't we have a medic with us? What else? I think, um, should we . . . are we supposed to wait until both parents are present? How's that going to work, I mean whomever it is, they're going to know why we're here—

"Ed, I'm going to call Pastor. I want to see if he has any advice, words, maybe just a prayer for us to find the strength to do this right, to offer heartfelt compassion. This has got to be the worst thing that can happen to parents. We have to get this right."

"Alright, call my dad first, can you do that? Use my phone. I want to talk to him. He'll, well . . . I just want to talk to him."

Leanne punched in the numbers and handed the phone to Ed, then called Pastor.

"Pastor, Leanne Trottingwolf."

"Leanne, hello," Pastor said. "How are—"

"Pastor," Leanne said, interrupting him, explaining, wishing they could pray together. "We need strength, grace to do this well. Pray for us."

"Leanne, you and Ed can do this. Remember the words of Psalm 23, '*even though I walk through the valley of the shadow of death, I will fear no evil, for you are with me; your rod and your staff, they comfort me.*' Leanne, you don't need to fear the task ahead. God is with you. His presence gives you strength. You will do this with grace and dignity. I know you will. You and Ed are the right people for this task. Go with God."

"Thank you, Pastor. Thank you," Leanne said, turning her eyes to the road ahead, listening to one side of Ed's conversation.

"Yeah. Yeah, I know."

"I will, I will, Sonny," Ed said. Ed's father, Edwin II and

Ed, Edwin III, called each other "Sonny," a private joke between father and son. Edwin II sometimes used his Cherokee name, Wahoo, Screech Owl.

Leanne watched Ed listen to his father. She marveled at the relationship. Both men leaned on something greater than father and son, something different. Leanne could see it, had seen it the day she met Screech Owl. She could only imagine what Wahoo would be telling Ed. She knew Ed would gain strength and wisdom from his father's spoken words. It was, she knew, a Cherokee thing.

Ed set his phone down. He white-knuckled the steering wheel.

"You okay?" Leanne asked.

"Yes. I just needed to hear his voice. He is a strong man."

THE ROAD CURVES. Ed's foot comes off the pedal, *Gracie* slows, glides through the long arc of the road. Leanne feels the gentle shift in speed, *Gracie's* slight lean into the curve. Leanne sways with the momentum.

Twenty minutes gone. They've got to be close. They're silent. Ed sees the street sign up ahead. The turn comes up fast. He starts to brake. Turns. Leanne spots the house, *2601*. The numbers, big, black, stand out against the sand-colored exterior. Ed drives by, turns back, comes up on the house again, ready to pull over. Off-white trim blends softly with the main color of the house. Well kept. Grass mowed. Clear of fallen leaves, the early season deserters raked and bagged. Walkway neatly edged.

"Don't stop in front of the house," Leanne says. "Park down the street so *Gracie* is out of sight. It might not matter once someone sees us in uniform; there is no way to hide why we are here. But this will give us another minute."

Ed eases to the side of the road. *Gracie* rubs a foot against the curb. Leanne and Ed sit. They reach for each other's hands. Pray together . . . *Amen.* The street, quiet and empty, looks abandoned, almost everyone gone off to work. School. Leanne and Ed walk, braced and soldierly, masking their own uncertainty, the picture of military bearing. No one follows. No media trucks. No onlookers. Time, still on their side. They walk in step. Shoes tap out a soft cadence against the pavement.

They reach the mouth of the walkway. Stop. Look toward the door. Fifty feet. The longest walk of their lives. Step up to the door. The house looks quiet. No movement inside or out. A chickadee, perched on an outside light, has a lot to say, then flies off. Leanne tucks her fingertips into her palm, raises her hand, ready to knock, hears a dog bark.

PART TWO

THE SOLDIER

She felt like she hadn't slept in days. She barely had. R&R at home in Madison, late nights with old friends, her birthday, time with mom and dad—two weeks that had been anything but restful. She wouldn't have had it any other way. Now, on her way back to the war, Army Corporal Rachael Hugo gave in to the seduction of sleep. She fluffed a flight pillow against the airplane window and closed her eyes. The thrum of the commercial airplane's engines lullabied her to a sleep that took her right through to sunrise in Kuwait.

Not long after she boarded the airplane, she'd won the window-shade battle. *Down.* The private sitting next to her wanted it up. Rank, no matter how slim the margin, had its privilege. Hours later, on the other side of the world, she slid the window shade up. She looked out at the cloud cover that hid Kuwait. The rising sun streaked the sky. Clouds blushed crimson.

The private stirred. Just in time. Rachael wanted out of her seat.

Inside the airplane lavatory, she splashed water on her face, looked in the mirror, eyes puffy. Unfettered shoulder length hair framed her face. Knowing that she couldn't wear it like that once she left the airplane, she deftly twisted it into a knot.

Two days earlier, she'd said her goodbye to Ruth, her mother. Her father hugged her. "Be safe," Kermit Hugo said.

"I will, Daddy," she replied, flashing a smile, secretly masking her concerns about Iraq, the world she'd have to live in for another six months. "I'll be home by Christmas, this time for good."

Kermit Hugo had nodded.

"Mom," Rachael said, turning back to Ruth. "Be ready to do some shopping when I get back. I'll be so ready to get out of this combat uniform. I'll probably do some online shopping while I'm deployed. That way I'll have something to wear as soon as I get home."

"Well, don't spend all your money shopping on line. Get back and we'll do some shopping together."

"Okay," she said, but online shopping half a world away, abstract, tugged at the girl in her. The idea of liberating herself from the unflattering combat uniform, donning "civvies," proved difficult to resist.

She made it back to her seat, beating the fasten-your-seat-belt prompt. The airplane slipped through the cloud cover, pulling sunlight with it. Kuwait stretched out below, bathed in the early morning sun. She'd be on the ground soon. Hop a flight to Baghdad. From there hitch a ride to FOB Summerall. The FOB, her home for six more months, would become hot as hell in another month. By mid-summer, not even winds blowing across the desert could cool the soldiers stationed there. Before Saddam built a military airbase there, the land belonged to God and wandering nomads.

Days, she knew, would be a mixed bag of ups and downs. She also knew she'd have a decision to make once she redeployed. Stay in, or rejoin the civilian world. She loved her job, combat medic, and she loved the Army too, but she had a restlessness all her own. She pushed that out of her mind.

Anxious to get back to her unit, she went off in search of the first flight she could jump on, hoping for a short stay in Kuwait, not a repeat of the month's long, mind-numbing staging back in December of '06, her first Christmas away from home.

Luck!

A sick soldier became an empty seat on an airplane leaving later that morning. *Empty seat, ha!* Canvas webbing waited for her and the other soldiers, who'd cram together inside the Spartan-like C-130, the military's no-frills, work-horse airplane.

After a quick breakfast, the DFAC open 24/7, she shuffled onto the C-130. She dressed in full battle rattle, Kevlar, M4 rifle hanging from shoulder to waist, a Beretta M9 pistol strapped to her thigh. She wore a soft vest. The courtesies of old wars, Medic and Red Cross insignia, ignored by insurgents, made combat medics easy targets. Armed like infantry, medics fought to protect wounded soldiers, themselves too.

Inside the airplane, she dropped onto the canvas, unslung the M4, rested it by her side, and settled in for the short flight into Baghdad. The unfolded buttstock of the M4 slid forward. She tucked the weapon closer to her side. The touch of the cold steel felt familiar, pushing her into a mild, melancholy muse.

SHE'D GROWN up close friends with rifles, hunting side by side with her father and uncles most weekends during hunting seasons. The first time she had game in sight, enough for a meal or the wild game jerky Kermit had been taught to make by his father, she hesitated, didn't pull the trigger. The rabbit nibbling on woodland aster, hearing movement, darted off and disappeared in the underbrush.

But Rachael became a good hunter. She had good aim, and a steady hand.

On a late fall morning, on another hunt with Kermit, their breath a plume of steam against the morning chill, Rachael, her dad, and the dogs, walked into the woods in search of small game. Frost collected on the toes of their boots. One of the dogs stopped and chewed at a ball of ice knotted between its toes. Father and daughter waited close to a narrow, worn pathway, most likely a rabbit run, a ribbon in the frost-covered grass. Rachael moved downwind.

The dogs picked up a scent. A rabbit, alarmed, raised up, froze like a statue, its nose quivering, searching the air, then ran toward Rachael. Kermit yelled, "Here it comes!" Rachael raised her rifle. She remembered what she'd been taught. Squeeze, don't pull. Keep the rifle steady. Smooth motion. Breathe and exhale slowly. Don't pull, you'll make the rifle jerk, miss high.

Boom!

Crows, jolted by the blast of the Winchester 1300, leapt from treetops, cawing angrily, chastising the two hunters. The rabbit jerked awkwardly, spun, then flopped on its side. The dogs charged toward the fresh kill, bellowing and howling. They circled the rabbit, continuing their wild celebration. Kermit caught up with Rachael, called the dogs off. Well trained, they surged together, milling and pushing their way toward the rabbit, sniffing, whining, their blood lust unsatisfied. Kermit looked at the rabbit. "Nice shot, Rach," he said. "You got him."

Rachael beamed, did a little dance, stomped her feet, fist pumped with her free hand. "Yes. Yes! I got him. Popped him!"

"You did," Kermit shouted, celebrating almost as exuberantly as Rachael. "Hell of a shot. Look again, look, a clean head shot, none of the meat is spoiled. Geezus, Rachael, that's a great shot. Gut him, he's your kill."

She found a clean patch of grass to gut the rabbit, careful to keep the animal clear of dirt and mud, then slit open the belly, scooping out the innards, taking care not to burst the bladder, bowel or intestine. She wiped a bloody knife on the still-frosty grass, then rubbed her hands through a cleaner patch, the frost melting against her warm flesh, cleaning the blood away as she rubbed her palms and fingers together.

Over the years, father, daughter, dogs, an occasional uncle too, became a team. Whatever they shot, they ate. Squirrel stew, roasted rabbit, and jerky, occasional game birds too. They hunted together every season until Rachael deployed. Before she left again, she'd made plans with Kermit to hunt together when she got back. She'd be home in the middle of the next season.

WITHOUT WARNING, the airplane suddenly plummeted into a steep dive, lifting Rachael from the canvas, pitching her forward, shoulder straps keeping her from tumbling. She fought a wave of nausea, her stomach rebelling against the sudden drop. It didn't matter that she'd strapped in, secured her body; her insides, caught in the free-fall, floating sensation, felt like they were free to move about the cabin, *Keep morning chow down girl. Keep it down. Did you forget that the pilots drop out of the sky when landing at Baghdad? Can't risk the slow descent. Too dangerous. Swallow. Take deep breaths.* The airplane bumped once; the wheels screeched in protest. The roar of the engines reversing the airflow filled the inside of the C-130. Slowing to ground speed, the pilot taxied away from the runway.

Rachael's stomach quieted.

No need to wait for ground REMFs to unload the airplane. Knowing that she'd return, she'd left most of her gear in her CHU at FOB Summerall. Now, with just a little more luck, she'd find a supply truck or, better yet, a squad from her unit on its way back to the FOB. She'd hitch a ride and report in. Six more months. What waited ahead? Anything could happen. She learned that early on, just two months into her deployment.

A SQUAD, not hers, had an early morning mission. They'd readied four Humvees, a typical rollout tactic. Fueled and armed, the squad, four soldiers to a vehicle, but short a medic, formed up. A quick final inspection and they'd move out. Rachael got word that they planned on rolling out without a medic. She hurried to the assembled squad.

"Staff Sergeant, wait," she said. "I'll roll out with you guys."

"You're off duty, Hugo. Stay inside the wire."

"I got nothing going on, Staff Sergeant, day's clean, and you need a medic."

"Alright then, get your gear. Mount up in the last Humvee."

"Roger that, Staff Sergeant," she barked back. "I've got a 'Unit One Pack' ready to go."

Outside the wire, turret gunners scanned roof tops, windows, alleyways between buildings, looking for anything out of the ordinary, or anyone with bad intentions. The lead Humvee's vehicle commander never saw the fresh patch on the roadway. No one saw the spotter, cleverly hidden. The blast lifted the almost seven-ton Humvee into the air, then body slammed it against the ground. The Humvee burst into flames. Smoke, the smell of burnt rubber, explosive, and the stink of charred flesh billowed above the Humvee. A hail of small arms fire erupted, a lethal violence raking the convoy. Bullets plunked against the Humvees. Turret gunners returned fire. The Staff Sergeant, engulfed in flames, on fire, being burnt alive, fell from the Humvee, his screams heard above the gunfire. Through the smoke and dust, Rachael could see him thrashing on the ground.

Soldiers smothered the flames. Others returned fire.

Rachael watched. Her concern extended beyond the call of duty. She needed to do something for the soldier on the ground and fast. His screams, louder than the clatter of battle, roused her to action. *He's dying. I'm here to save him. That's why I rolled out with these guys. I might be his only chance.*

"I've got to help him," Rachael shouted at her vehicle commander.

"Negative. Wait until the firefight is over."

Rachael didn't lean toward hesitancy; instead, always ready, she jumped into action. "Sergeant, I'm going after him." Rachael said, her words punctuated, a period, not a comma, ended the conversation. A look of resignation spread across the faces of the other soldiers inside the Humvee. Rachael stared at them, determined, defiant. She knew she couldn't stay and watch the soldier die. This is what she was trained for. But there was more—Kermit had taught her that there's more to life than yourself; always be ready to give back, to help others. *I will daddy, I'll help.*

"Cover me," she shouted, then left the Humvee, running to the Staff Sergeant. She knelt beside him, read the pain, torment twisting his face. Bullets ricocheted all around her. *Morphine, calm him down, ease his pain, can't get an IV going with him thrashing all over. Should have stopped moving so wildly by now. Another. Hit him again. Ah, better already. Start the IV. Talk to him. God, he's burned really bad, so much of his body.* She tended to him. Every touch as gentle as possible, but there's no place for gentle on the battlefield. The pain alone was killing the Staff Sergeant. She did what she could to stabilize him. He needed an evac now. *Keep him alive, Rachael, keep him alive.*

She watched the Blackhawk lift off, flying the Staff Sergeant to the closest CSH. She'd bought him enough time. Doctors would finish the job she started, saving his life. Inside the Humvee, on the way back to the FOB, Rachael, worn out, the flow of adrenaline ebbing, closed her eyes, letting a numbing fatigue buffer the journey back to safety.

IN THE DAYS that followed the attack, Command Sergeant Major Kevin Nolan took note of Rachael's actions, her life-saving efforts. He tucked the information away. More aware of her now, he realized that her daily performance exemplified excellent soldiering in almost everything she did. *Look at her, off duty and at the clinic. She's high speed. Like to have more like her.* Nolan decided to award the unit Coin of Excellence, more commonly referred to as a Challenge Coin, to Rachael. He caught up with her outside the aid station on FOB Summerall.

"Corporal Hugo," he called out, "a moment."

Rachael turned from the soldier she was with, reported to the sergeant major, concern at being singled out.

"I wanted to congratulate you on the way you conduct yourself, Hugo. You're a credit to the unit," he said, offering his hand. When Rachael reached out and shook the sergeant major's hand, she felt something pressed against her palm. Surprised, she almost fumbled the medallion-sized coin the sergeant major slipped into her hand. In a moment of under-standing, she recognized what she'd been given. Call it what you would, a Coin of Excellence or a Challenge Coin, the honor, a tradition some say dates back to World War I, invited Rachael into an exclusive band of brothers.

ON HER LAST NIGHT HOME, sitting around a firepit with Kermit and Ruth and a few other friends, Rachael sat next to her father. Between swallows of beer, she leaned over to him, took his hand and pressed the Challenge Coin into his palm, just the way Sergeant Major Nolan had done it.

"Daddy," she said. "I want you to have this."

Kermit opened his hand, looked at the coin, crossed pistols centered in a circle of bronze above the unit emblem stared back at him. "What's this?"

Rachael explained.

"I can't take this, Rach, this belongs to you."

"Then keep it safe for me, Daddy, until I return."

The remaining months at FOB Summerall dwindled. Her tour aged. Mostly uneventful. Time to go home drew near, a time soldiers grew leery of. She rolled out on a mission to train Iraqis, turn them into a civilian police force. Back seat. First Humvee in queue. Squad leader's choice. With luck, home for Christmas. But Luck, fickle and deceiving, a trickster with something still to say, would hold her tongue only so long.

PART THREE
NEXT OF KIN

IN HIS KITCHEN, KERMIT HUGO SLID THE EDGE OF A KNIFE across stalks of mushrooms large enough to hold the diced onion and chopped crab mixture he'd prepared for a filling. He cored the last bit of stem from the mushroom caps, ready now to stuff them. He'd bake the mushrooms, a tasty part of his lunch. Almost eleven, plenty of time. Second shift starts at three. He'd leave the house around two-thirty.

He placed the meal into the oven, 350 degrees, thirty minutes, checked his watch again. Ruth, already at work, would probably be on a break. He called her. While they talked, Mister Two, one of Kermit's prized dogs, uncoiled himself, sat up, stretched, shook his head with a loud flapping of his ears, and sniffed the air. He listened to the coded message from outside the door. Something invisible waited on the other side.

Leanne's first knock, muffled by the dog's barking, went unnoticed by Kermit. Leanne waited, knocked again, stepped back. The dog barked a second warning.

"What's up, Mister Two, you hear something?" Kermit said, shifting the phone to his left hand, setting the oven timer with his right.

"Ruth, hold on a minute, I think someone's at the door. Let me check," he mouthed into the cell phone.

"Who would be there now?"

"I can't tell with Mister Two's barking. Hold on."

He held the phone close to his chin, walked to the front of the house and peered through a big bay window off to the side of the front door. *Nothing.* He leaned deeper into the hollow of the window. *Don't see—wait—that looks like gold chevrons, a lot of stripes, three up, three down. High ranking NCOs. Look at the stripes! Looks like two soldiers. What did Rach tell me? "Dad,"* she'd said. *"If something happens, if I'm wounded, the Army will assign what they call a CAO, they'll call, or the Red Cross will call. If, well . . . if I'm killed, a notification team will come to the house, officers or high-ranking NCOs." High ranking NCOs. Oh no. Don't be what I think this is, but what else can it mean, two soldiers at my front door in the middle of the morning?*

"Ruth, it looks like two soldiers at the door. I can see sergeant's stripes on their uniforms. Maybe you'd better come home. This can't be good news."

"What? What did you say?"

"There are soldiers here," he said again, keeping his voice calm, trying not to unnerve his wife. "Come home."

"Is it, do you think—"

"I don't know," he said, "but why else would soldiers be at our door?"

"No. No, not Rachael, not my baby girl!" she screamed, her voice a rising glissando. "NooOO**OO**!"

"Calm down, Ruth. Come home. Be careful," Kermit said again, tapping his phone, ending the call, moving to the door, Mister Two behind him. He fumbled with the door, pulled it open. Two soldiers stood—silent and motionless. Kermit felt the gorge rise in his throat. He swallowed, fought hard against the caustic burning billowing from deep inside of him.

"You two," he said, the words filling the space between

them with sorrow, "you two don't mean to tell me my daughter's dead . . . killed? Is that why you're here?"

"Sir," the soldier with more stripes, a woman, said, "I'm Master Sergeant Leanne Trottingwolf, this is Sergeant First Class Ed Trottingwolf, may we come in?"

Kermit's stomach mutinied, turned sour, knotted and angry, twisted with pain. He fought against the sudden urge to vomit. He needed a moment, knew if he tried to move, he'd topple into the two soldiers. He found a voice, not his, not the smooth tenor, instead some atonal rasp. The words snagged on his pain, caught in his throat. He sucked in a deep breath, forced himself to speak. "Okay, yeah, come in," he said, stepping aside, inviting the soldiers into his home.

Mister Two sniffed at their legs. Satisfied that they were no threat, he retreated. Kermit followed. Lightheaded, fearful that he'd pass out, he stopped, took in a deep breath . . . steadied himself. The soldiers turned. Silence. A too-long stare. Kermit went first.

"I'm asking you again," he said, his hoarse voice breaking, "are you here to tell me my daughter's dead?"

"Sir," Leanne said, "Is your wife—"

"She's not here," he said, interrupting Leanne.

"We can go get her if you'd like, she doesn't need to drive."

"She's already on her way."

"Alright, sir, we'll wait until she's here."

"No, you won't." Kermit said, surprising Leanne and Ed. "I'm not waiting for you to tell me what I already know. You're here, so tell me now what you came to tell me."

Taken aback by Kermit's insistence, Leanne hesitated. She looked at Ed. He closed his eyes and bowed his head, prayed for the answer. When he looked up, Leanne stared back at him. He nodded, wordlessly confirming for Leanne what her heart had already told her. *Tell him. With the grace of God, tell him —now. Don't add to his pain.*

"Sir," she said, halting for a moment, her shoulders trembling, her eyes damp and glossy. "Sir," she said, beginning again. "I'm here to inform you that your daughter, Corporal Rachael Hugo, died as a result of injuries suffered in an attack during a routine mission in Bayji, Iraq on October 5th . . ."

The words, sterile, officious, slapped at Kermit, an invisible blow, exploding in a starburst that set his face on fire, blurred his vision. Each word Leanne spoke shredded Kermit's last bit of hope, the wish for a different answer than the one he'd known was coming.

Leanne's voice slowed, softened to a whisper. "On the behalf of the Secretary of Defense, and a grateful nation, I extend to you and your family my deepest sympathy for your great loss."

Overwhelmed, her grief genuine, Leanne lost the battle with tears. Ed, too. Kermit, wrestling with his own emotions, brushed his sorrow aside, brought Leanne and Ed deeper into the house. "Are you guys okay?" he asked. "Can I get you anything, water?"

"No, we're fine, Mr. Hugo."

"My wife should be home any minute. Sit, please. I'm going to make a few calls while we wait for her."

Kermit called his mother. His father, a practical man, had been gone since 2002, ravaged by lung cancer. Kermit never fully understood his father's early life, the details sketchy. But Richard "Dick" Hugo believed in the value of a man's hands. Knowing how to carpenter, plumb, and wire carried him through a life that supported his family and ensconced them in their own home in Fitchburg, Wisconsin.

Fitchburg, that's where Kermit grew up. Back then Fitchburg was close-knit. Everybody knew everybody, including Dick Hugo, volunteer firefighter, and a man who believed in the importance of giving back to the community. If someone needed help, Dick Hugo was always quick to lend a hand.

He kept his son close, taught him to hunt and fish, spent

plenty of time with him. Kermit apprenticed under his father's tutelage, learned, just like his father, to navigate through life by the magic of his own hands. By the time he turned twelve years old, Kermit knew enough to work side by side with his father, framing, siding, and roofing a shed almost the size of a small barn. When they completed the shed, standing back, side by side, his father slipped a beer into Kermit's hand. Kermit grew into a man all his own.

If he'd thought about it, Kermit had done much of the same with Rachael. It had been easy, natural, just like growing up with his dad. She was curious. She learned quickly. And Rachael had become her own woman.

KERMIT CALLED HIS BOSS, apologetic. "I'm not coming in today," he said. "Rachael was killed in Iraq. There are soldiers here. I'm waiting for Ruth to come home. It's gonna be harder on her."

"Kermit, for God's sake, man—don't worry about work. Do what you need to do. Take all the time you need. What can I do?"

"I don't know, I really don't know. We're waiting on more information, you know, find out what happens next."

"Kermit, go. Go do what you need to do, and don't worry about anything here."

Before Kermit decided on who to call next, Ruth blew through the front door, a tornado roaring wildly into the room. "What's going on?" she shouted.

"Ma'am," Leanne began—

"Don't ma'am me," Ruth screamed, the shriek coming from somewhere deep inside of her. "Don't say another word. I'll kill you. I will," she swore. Agitated, her blood up, she charged at Leanne.

Ed stepped in front of his wife. Kermit's strong hands shot

forward. He grabbed Ruth by the shoulders, spun her around. He knew his wife, fiery, passionate, quick to anger, a woman bent on having things her own way. And he knew that in her anger she'd lash out at everyone and everything around her.

"Stop. Stop!" he said. "Knock it off. It's not her fault, do you understand? It's not her fault," he repeated, while Ruth flailed wildly, windmilling her arms, trying to break free, anger the sole extent of her ability to cope.

Kermit held her. He wouldn't let go until he felt certain she'd behave. She could continue to fight. She'd lose. She knew it. She settled down. No match against Kermit's strength, she collapsed against him.

He felt the change in Ruth. Her sharp, hard breathing, frantic, coming in staccato bursts, calmed. He turned to Leanne and Ed.

"Are you two, okay?"

"Yes, Mr. Hugo."

"Alright," he said. Ruth, for the moment, settled by his side, a tinder box with a short fuse.

Kermit capped his own emotions. *Too much to do. Keep Ruth calm. Get answers. What comes next? Where is Rachael? How did she die? How do we get her home? People—I've got to tell more family. Ruth will want to make calls. What about these soldiers?*

As if she'd read his mind, Leanne spoke up. "Mr. Hugo," she began, only to be stopped.

"It's Kermit, call me Kermit," he said.

"Mr. Hugo, Kermit, ma'am," Leanne began again, looking at Ruth, every word the strike of flint against steel that could spark Ruth's emotions, setting her ablaze again.

"A CAO, that's a casualty assistance officer, will take over after we leave. He'll have the answers to most of your questions, run interference with news outlets, begin to make arrangements to get Rachael home, everything that needs to be done—he'll see to it. He'll be available to you until Rachael is home and stay until there's nothing else that you need."

"That will help," Kermit said. "We've never done anything else like this. I'm not sure what to do—exactly."

"We'll wait with you until the CAO gets here, if that's okay? We can help with calls if you'd like. Are there some calls beside family that you need made? We can do that. Anything that we can do? We're here," she said, without pretense or false earnestness.

Leanne and Ed stayed long after they should have, hours longer. Unruffled by Ruth's outburst, they deftly navigated around her anger. Weeks later, Kermit would play back the morning, grateful that Leanne and Ed had been the ones chosen to deliver the news. Genuine. Heartfelt. Impossible, Kermit thought, for anyone but Leanne and Ed to have handled the morning the way they had—with such grace.

Later that night, Kermit tossed the mushrooms into the trash. He thought about sleep. No chance. The mushrooms made their way to a compost heap where they'd wait for spring, midwife to next year's garden.

"SERGEANT NELSON," Lieutenant Colonel Olson said. "I need you to take over as CAO for the Hugos. Are you up for it?"

"Yes sir, but what—"

"No time to explain, get into a dress uniform and get out to the Hugos'. I've got all the details, let me brief you, then go."

"Yes sir."

Nelson arrived at the Hugos'. He relieved the Trotting-wolfs, then sat with Kermit and Ruth. "I'm as sorry as anyone can be about your daughter, Rachael," he said. "I'll do my best to explain what happens, and to take care of everything. First step, I'll get Rachael home."

Questions, some more pressing than others, nagged at Kermit. What had happened to Rachael? How did she die?

Did she suffer? Sergeant Nelson didn't have the answers. Command Sergeant Major Kevin Nolan did, but he was in Iraq. A day or two later, Kermit and Nolan connected. That's war in the digital age. The Sergeant Major told Kermit what he knew.

THE MORNING of October 5th in Iraq, a squad of soldiers, four Humvees, four soldiers in each vehicle, rolled out on a routine mission, a full day training up Iraqi police recruits. Nothing unusual about that by 2007. Rachael, at the request of the squad leader, rode in the first Humvee in queue.

Ten mikes out from a joint security facility, the intended destination, they rolled through the streets of a small town. Not the first time. There are only so many ways in and out of a FOB and to a routine destination. *Routine.* Insurgents favored routine. Counted on it.

They watched from the window of a two-story building, waiting for the convoy to reach a wired IED buried in the road the convoy used to pass through the town, a road lined with cracks, a patchwork quilt of crudely repaired potholes, loose gravel, and roadside rubble.

Wire that ran from the window to a utility pole snaked its way through a crack in the pavement. Sometime during the night, under cover of darkness, the bomb maker stripped the plastic coating from copper wire. He twisted the bare strands together with the leads from four 155mm artillery rounds buried beneath the road's surface, cleverly disguised as just another patch in the road.

Neither the driver of the Humvee, nor anyone else, saw the wire or guessed that the patch, maybe a little cleaner, newer, than the others, wasn't anything more than the dozens of patches that pockmarked roads everywhere in Iraq.

The convoy, unsuspecting, rolled toward the death trap.

In the instant that the lead Humvee fitted itself above the bomb, the spotter, his hand steady, his fingers curled around the detonator, pushed his thumb down on a nickel-sized button. Windows of nearby buildings shattered. Dust and smoke billowed high above the convoy. Fragmented steel pierced the Humvees. Chunks of pavement rained down on everything.

The turret gunner, a big soldier who everyone called "Big Mac," blasted by the explosion, jack-in-the-boxed out of the turret. His body, splintered bone and ripped flesh, lay on the ground in a crumpled heap. He was alive. Barely.

A soldier in the passenger seat shoulder-blocked his door, smashing it open with a force that spilled him onto the ground. He came up firing his M4. Rachael's door, armored, but no match for the force of four massive artillery rounds, its thick hinges fissured by the blast, hung at an odd angle. Rachael, tossed around like a rag doll, bounced and ricocheted against the roof of the Humvee. Ripped from her seat, she toppled through the partially dislodged door.

Unconscious, severely wounded, bleeding badly, still tethered to the Humvee, her foot tangled in the webbing of a map and gear holder. Half in, half out of the Humvee, she dangled in harm's way. Limp, motionless, suspended just a few inches above the ground, she lay exposed to small arms fire. The driver, his door mangled shut, crawled through the Humvee and scrambled over Rachael, falling onto the street. He rolled, bounced to a kneeling position and returned fire.

Inside the Blackhawk carrying her to a CSH at Camp Speicher, Rachael opened her eyes. Soldiers looked at her. For a second, just a second, she looked back, held their gaze. Then . . . her eyes slowly disappeared, rolled back beneath eyelids that fluttered—closed. Somewhere in mid-flight, her heart stopped beating.

"Thanks for telling me that, Sergeant Major," Kermit said after hearing the whole story. "Thanks."

UNDER THE COVER OF DARKNESS, reporters, well-wishers, the curious, those that swarmed outside Kermit's front door during the day, disappeared. Nelson, too, gone home, done for the day, gave Kermit a moment of silence. Nolan had said the quiet part out loud, answered the question that every parent of every lost soldier has, "What happened to my child?" He hadn't eased Kermit's pain as much as he'd filled the void with the recount of the attack. Kermit had always understood the danger facing Rachael, but it had remained an abstraction, something he thought about on occasion, usually with absent-minded detachment. Now he realized with a finality that had masqueraded as disbelief that Rachael was gone.

Gone! At peace. She has no worries anymore. Her sacrifice is complete, over. What now? How do we carry on, live without her? Ruth will not accept this. I gave Rachael my blessing, first to enlist, supported her when she deployed, told her I was proud of her. Now this. Ruth will need to blame someone, that's how she'll cope. It's not anyone's fault. It's war. Soldiers get killed in war. I knew this could happen. Still, I always thought she was coming home. How else could I have sent her off to war? Not without hope that she's coming back. What's next? Who teaches me and Ruth to live with this. Where's the manual? How? How do we do this?

MANY OF THE immediate answers to Kermit's questions rested with Sergeant First Class Nelson. The pain of dealing with the loss of Rachael, almost insurmountable, would have been too much if everything had fallen on Kermit's shoulders.

Nelson distanced himself from his own emotions, tucked them into a box that he'd open later. For now, he carried out his mission. He buffered the Hugos from a macabre dance, a sad waltz with the disturbing, merciless details of bringing their daughter home, burying her. He sifted through requests from news media, protecting the Hugos without them even knowing it.

Some details, no matter how sad, no matter how indelicate, demanded a decision. Nelson sheltered Ruth and Kermit from as much as possible. The mundane, the obligatory, the things that didn't care about sadness and pain. The cold reality of Rachael's remains on the other side of the world—an undertaker. Forms needing completion, signatures. Would Rachael, *would they be able to see her one last time, an open casket?* A casket. What parent thinks about picking out a casket for their child? The parents of soldiers? Maybe. Kermit had never thought about it.

"Ruth, Kermit, I know Rachael will be home soon," Nelson said. "I'm sorry, but I have to ask. Have you thought about a casket? Do you know what you'd want for Rachael?"

"Real wood," Kermit and Ruth said. "Real wood. Cherry. Something warm. Traditional. That seems right for Rachael."

UNABLE TO MEET the airplane carrying Rachael to Dover AFB, Kermit and Ruth waited for her arrival back in Madison. Rachael's airplane landed near mid-day. The airplane, a private charter (Rachael always loved to make a big entrance), taxied to a private location on the open tarmac. A waiting honor guard, the 79th, the unit Rachael served with, trained with, belonged to, stood ready to receive one of their own. The cargo door opened, revealing Rachael's flag-draped casket.

The guard stepped forward, rolling a gurney. The wheels wobbled indelicately. An electric motor whined mechanically as the gurney scissored upward to reach the waiting casket. The guard, white gloved, solemnly slid Rachael onto the gurney, moving her with dignity to a waiting hearse.

Ruth's knees buckled. Kermit caught her, kept her from falling. She audibly gasped. Raised a hand to stifle her shock. She cried openly. Kermit fought the tears that welled in his eyes. The stoic soldiers, an honor guard sent all over the country, couldn't hold back. Tears normally absent from their faces flowed freely.

The convoy, Rachael's last, formed up. Police escort in the lead. Patriot Guard to the rear, at the six. Rachael, this time tucked away safely into the middle. "I want to stop at the house before we get to the funeral home," Kermit said. "I want to take Rachael home one last time." The procession detoured. They neared the house. American flags, a sea of them, washed over the grass, planted there earlier by the Patriot Guard. Kermit and Ruth, silent, each with their own thoughts, waited.

Home. This was Rachael's home.

The procession moved on to the funeral home. Kermit and Ruth would have the weekend to privately grieve. They moved through the days in a haze of grief, barely knowing what to say to one another. Kermit felt sad, scared too. Scared that the loss of Rachael would break Ruth, sad that Rachael's death would change their lives—forever. Even more sad, when he grappled with all that Rachael would never have. Never know.

On Monday, at the Army Reserve Center, red-eyed and exhausted from too little sleep in too short a time, Kermit and Ruth faced the public. Reporters jockeyed for position, trying to get as close as they could. "Rachael," Kermit said, pausing, looking out at reporters, soldiers, friends, family, the governor, all gathered.

"Rachael," he started again, "saw a lot—death, destruction, despair while she fought for the country. She saw good things too. No matter what, she always kept her head held high. That's who she was. In one of her emails to me, really early on in her deployment, she wrote that she loved what she was doing. 'This is what I choose to do, and being a medic is what I live to do,' she wrote in that email."

"She'd found her purpose in life, helping others," Ruth said. "All she wanted was to serve her country. We traded emails about her coming home, shopping for clothes, I even told her not to spend too much money, but she was really excited about coming home, dressing up."

"She was more than a daughter," Kermit added. "She was . . . she was wonderful. We did so much together. I'll miss that. I couldn't ask for anyone better."

BEFORE CALLING HOURS, a private wake, the night before Rachael would be buried, Kermit and Ruth faced another decision. Open or closed casket. They'd first need to see their daughter.

"Wait," the funeral director said. "Wait here, we'll get Rachael ready for you."

Motioned into the room, not knowing what to expect, Kermit and Ruth approached their daughter. Kermit's chest ached. His legs felt heavy. Each step forward an effort of will. Ruth, her face pinched, her eyes burning with sorrow, moved with him. Soft carpet felt like quicksand. A few feet remained. Close now. They can see her. She's . . .

She's beautiful. Asleep. For all the world she looks like she is just sleeping.

In the morning, the Patriot Guard escorted Rachael's funeral procession. With her mission accomplished, relieved of duty, Rachael could stand down, rest forever. A covey of doves, released, spiraled into the sky. A lone dove stayed perched on the roof of the mausoleum, silent, watching over Rachael until her coffin was slipped into a sarcophagus, high above the ground.

DREAMS STARTED THAT NIGHT. In his sleep, Rachael talked to Kermit. In the dream, he talked to her, too. "Rachael," he said, "You can't be here, you're gone."

"But I am here, Dad. I am here."

"I feel you near me. I can see you, hear you. You're not real."

"I am, Dad. And I'm okay. It's okay. I'm here . . ."

Kermit fought through the thick fog of the dream, roused himself. Rachael slipped away. For the first time since the news of her death, the chokehold of sadness took full control. Tears wet his pillow, streamed down his face. He looked at Ruth, stifled a sob, and swallowed hard, unable to hide his grief any longer, hoping not to wake his sleeping wife.

"Yes Rachael," he whispered into the night. "You're here. I know it now."

IN THE DAYS, weeks that followed, the people who cared, who had honored Rachael, had consoled Ruth and Kermit, went home, back to work, back to lives of their own. A silence settled over Ruth and Kermit. Lost in their own private grief, they hardly knew what to say to each other.

A year of firsts followed, firsts without Rachael. First Thanksgiving. First Christmas. First hunting season without Rachael. Her birthday. A year passed. Two. Kermit moved through life in a fog, survived the days on muscle memory. Autopilot. He went to service after service for other fallen soldiers, not certain what he was hoping to find. He volunteered with different groups supporting veterans and their families. The demands of the volunteer work filled his days, kept him from thinking about Rachael. He championed different causes for veterans and their families, worked on a

Blue Star Family project as far away as Massachusetts. He proposed and succeeded in changing Gold Star Mother's Day to Gold Star Family's Day. President Bush passed on the request to Barack Obama, who formally proclaimed the last Sunday in each September as Gold Star Family's Day.

The answers, the distractions he was looking for, weren't there, only reminders. Each time he saw a flag-draped casket, looked at tear-filled eyes, flinched at rifle salutes, it felt like Rachael was right in front of him. Every service snatched him back to the day he buried Rachael. After a few years, he stopped. Too much, just too much.

Ruth struggled openly, her face a mirror of the pain she felt. Her smile, the soft expression she sometimes wore, fell away, replaced by a haunting emptiness. She spun an intricate web of anger and sorrow, a web of grief that held Kermit captive too. She still blamed him for Rachael's death. She'd always blame him, even when it almost drove them apart. "You encouraged her to go. You killed her, my daughter," she said, too loud and too often, until the threat of divorce became real. They found a way to work it out, staying married until Ruth died. *Cancer.*

———

October 5, 2022

Small game hunting season opened in late September. Not long after Rachael's death, Kermit skipped a season; one became two. He lost interest. Maybe without Rachael, hunting wasn't the same, maybe. Who's to say? Dust has collected on Kermit's firearms, a bow, and the Winchester that Rachael hunted with. The sea of flags that blanketed the front of his house have long been furled. The thunder of the Patriot Guard, a distant echo. And still . . . still not a day passes without wishing Rachael was here. The same questions scroll through his mind. Who would she be? A wife? A mother?

Nurse? Soldier? More than a daughter, his friend? In his dreams, she is all these things. In his dreams, he can believe, feel her presence, even to this day.

Sometimes, in a quiet moment, in a great room he built with his own hands, Kermit sits. The room welcomes him like an old friend. Pine planking neatly fitted, mitered, and angled, bathes the room in a soft honey hue. A wood stove, expertly chimneyed into a corner, fights off Wisconsin's cold winters.

And sometimes, in those moments Kermit might finger the Challenge Coin Rachael slipped into his hand, its heft a reminder of all she was. The grief never gets lighter. Kermit, a man, a father, found the strength to carry the weight.

Army medic Rachael Hugo, May 13, 1983—October 5, 2007

*Challenge coin presented to Rachael Hugo; left with her father,
Kermit Hugo, for safekeeping until her return*

Twelve-year-old Rachael testing for a rifle permit

Rachael Hugo

Sergeants Leanne and Ed Trottingwolf, the two soldiers tasked with notifying Kermit Hugo that his daughter Rachael had been killed.

Leanne in Iraq with local children.

Ed in Iraq. Leanne and Ed served together down range.

BOOK TWO

PART ONE
BROTHERS

Saturday morning in Broken Bow, Nebraska, seat of Custer County, not long after summer's end, long enough for his younger brother Bob to return from Colorado—*summers with his father, Myron Kugler*—Mike Doheny leaned from the top bunk. Head over the side, he looked down at Bob.

"You awake?"

"Yep."

"You sure about this?"

"Yep."

"We're gonna play tackle today, it won't be like other games."

"I know. Where we gonna play?"

"At the high school. Let's get up, eat, get going."

"What time's everybody meeting up?"

"Probably around ten."

In the days leading up to the Saturday morning game, long before texting, Apple was still something you ate, and teens had their own wireless network. Rumor, hook ups, word of a rendezvous, spread through an osmosis of clipped conversations in class, at lunch, or passing each other in the halls.

"Game Saturday."

"Where?"

"School field."

"Can we use the field?"

"Team has an away game. Nobody around to stop us."

"Okay, see you in shop."

"Later man."

Fist bumps and nods sealed the deal. "I'm in."

On Saturday morning, the abandoned high school field, unblemished yard lines and grass greened by Nebraska's early fall, waited for the ragtag group. They arrived in pairs, threes, a lone straggler, Mike and Bob. They wore Wrangler's or Levi's, sneakers; nobody had football shoes. Hooded sweatshirts buffered them against last night's chill, outwitting a sun disappearing behind moving clouds. They came together, slouch-shouldered boys, hands in their pockets, hoods framing faces, shuffling, bumping shoulders, digging a toe in the grass, waiting.

"Choose sides," Big Kyle shouted. "Supposed to be five on five, we're short one. Who's missing?"

"Anybody tell Dustin?" Blank stares.

"Now what?"

"I'm gonna play," Bob said, giving away four, maybe even five years, and about fifty pounds to the high schoolers.

"What are you, like nine?"

"Almost ten."

"You okay with this, Doheny?"

"Yeah, just go a little easy. Rules?" Mike said.

"Five-second count before you can go after the quarterback. Tackle, but nothing on the knees. No punts on fourth, gotta throw instead of kick. Call it, Doheny. I've got odds. Two outta three."

Hands shot forward, almost colliding. Fingers popped from closed fists. Shouts. Odds! Evens! Evens again!

"You get the ball first," Big Kyle said, nodding at Mike.

Bob, Mike, three others circled. Mike called the play. On three. They broke the huddle.

"Four! One! Three! Hike! Hike! Hike!"

One Mississippi. Two Mississippi. Three—Four—Five—three players rushed at Mike. Bob rose up from his half crouch, a head shorter than the opposing player. Arms crossed, he barreled into the boy in front of him, slamming his elbows against floating ribs. Mike let the ball fly. Missed. They huddled again.

Thirty minutes later, the scoreless skirmish escalated, an over-the-top seriousness to a pickup game of wanna-be jocks. Faces blur. Grass, torn and shredded, clings to players' faces, the back of their hands, sweatshirts, stains the knees of their jeans. A rich loamy smell, dirt loosened beneath the pounding feet, intoxicating, incites a blood lust. The hits get harder, tackles colored with mean intent.

Both sides form up, cohorts clustered along the scrimmage line, faces just inches apart. Plumes of steam, hot breaths against the cool morning air, fill the no mans' land. Mike takes the snap, fakes the pass, and shoots a gap in the line, gaining yards. Bob blocks the player in front of him. *Hard.* The play over, he joins the huddle. The bigger player glances over his shoulder, glaring at him. *Little shit is hitting as hard as everybody else. Take it easy on him, my ass.*

They give up the ball on downs.

Big Kyle gathers his group. They break the huddle, line up. Bob hits the ball carrier, tackling hard as he drives his seventy pounds into the bigger player, smashing his head into the bigger boy's gut, grinning when he hears him grunt.

In the huddle, the boy demands the ball again. Bob sees the handoff, sees a space, flies at the bigger player, his heart racing. *Got him. I'm gonna get him again.*

Perfect, the boy thinks, *little shit took the bait, just what I was hoping.* He tucks the ball against his hip, abandons the goal of gaining yards. Intent on teaching Bob a lesson he lowers his body, leads with a shoulder, launches himself like a rocket, driving his shoulder up and into Bob's nose. Bob, thrown backward, falls like a sack of grain tossed onto the bed of a pickup. His face explodes. Pain spiderwebs from his nose, through his cheeks, into his eyes in a flash of purple and white light. Blood splatters from his nose. Bob staggers, dizzy, trying not to fall, or cry. Failing on both counts.

Hands slip under his shoulders. Mike hauls him to his feet.

"You okay?"

"Yeah, I think so."

"Let me see your face. Does your nose feel broken?"

"I don't know."

"Then it's probably not. You'd know," Mike said, then turned to the other boy. "What the hell is wrong with you, man?"

"Hey, the kid's hitting hard too—"

"What? What did you say? The kid is my brother. His name is Bob. He's in fourth grade, you ass. You wanna hit somebody hard, try me, c'mon," Mike said, his voice flat, serious, his reputation outdistancing the other's nerve. Few, if any, wanted to tangle with Mike Doheny. He fought to win, almost always did, often leaving the other boy bloody.

"Game's over," Mike said, bending the others to his will. "You still wanna play, you do it without us. Bob, let's go."

"But, I still wanna—"

"Wasn't a question, little brother. Let's go."

They walked off the field and away from the school, two brothers, the bigger stronger draping an arm around the younger.

PART TWO

MIKE DOHENEY

BY THE TIME HE LEFT THE RANCH, IN THE FALL OF 1995, MIKE Doheny was ready to audition for life. For five months, May into September, days with hay, horses, cattle, fence-posts, and farm machines had occupied his time. The months of ranch life, Mike's first stop after a detour in a juvenile detention camp, plus retired Army Captain Kevin Cooksley's patience, worked their magic.

Kevin, fair, demanding, uncompromising, laid it out for Mike. Knowing and doing aren't the same thing. Knowing right from wrong isn't enough. A good life comes from the doing. Doing the right thing, that's what will entitle you to a better life. Not a guarantee, but a ticket to admission. The alternative comes with bad consequences.

"The choice, Mike," Kevin said, "will always be yours. You can stay here as long as you want, as long as you stay out of trouble. Ranching's hard son. It's not for the faint of heart, but it's honest work. There're not many places better to grow up on. Here, we draw a line around our own. That includes you now. That line will keep the fools at bay until you get it figured out, until you're old enough and mature enough to understand you don't need the approval of others. You can use your own better judgement to go through life. You'll learn that here, and know this, this is the one place you can always come back to."

Mike learned. Not without missteps along the way. Outbursts of anger, frustration, patches of resentment bumped against Kevin's stoical authority. Field after plowed field, bale after stacked bale of hay, Kevin stuck to a tutorial: what's worth doing is best done right the first time. Mistakes are something we learn from; you make one, own up, fix it. You can live a good life or make excuses, but you can't do both at the same time.

"On a ranch, excuses will get a calf killed, a machine broken down, a failed crop. Life isn't really so different," Kevin said. "You don't do what's right, life will grab you the wrong way."

Mike slowly changed from the begrudging student to the willing pupil.

Until the ranch, before Kevin, life had made Mike into something else. In all the ways one might imagine, disaster ran alongside his early life. His parents, Kathy and Patrick Doheny, like every young couple, not giving much thought to a life that quick-steps towards everyday struggle, married quickly. Almost as quick as it took to say "I do," kids, jobs, debts, the everyday crush of life smothered the thrall. A few more years, highs and lows, mostly lows, and the marriage broke apart. No one's to blame. The timeless riddle that is men and women—unsolved.

Kathy would marry again; that marriage—lasting just long enough for another child, Bob—fell apart too. A mother's love, hers, holds the family together. Long hours at low-income jobs keeps a roof over their heads, food in their bellies. She outwits the odds against them, keeping her children safe and loved, barters, strikes unlikely deals, even convinces the owner of a house ready for demolition to rent it to her for pennies on the dollar. She makes the old house a home for three years. A wood stove, chimneying smoke into cold Nebraska winters, devours wood faster than a hungry bear waking from hibernation. John, the oldest of Kathy's boys, tries to keep up.

Three years later, then low-income housing for a few more, Kathy's hard work pays off. She moves the family into a house of their own, a flat-roofed fixer-upper begging for mercy, but it's hers, and she makes it a home, a haven for her children. Few with more would understand, but to Kathy and her children, it's Alhambra.

John the oldest strikes out on his own. Amy, the only girl, will eventually find her own way. Fathers, Mike's, Bob's too, fade in, fade out, scenes from a bad movie script. There's always too much month at the end of Kathy's money. Life isn't easy. But Kathy, a lioness, protects her Pride. They survive.

MONTHS on the ranch and Kevin sees what Mike fails to see in himself, he's quick, smart, strong—and after something. As spring changes into summer, days longer, Mike looks up, catches the sun, grows into the better parts of himself. By summer's end he's changed into something else. *A breakthrough?* Maybe, but on the ranch, with care, and a season's long growth, everything stretches toward maturity.

Alone at night in his camper trailer, a privacy Kevin offered, Mike begins to see the better parts of himself too. He thinks differently. Trouble isn't a birthright, a legacy. Choices. Laying on his back, he dares to dream, but dreams, if you want them to come true, need a starting point.

School. The dream had to start there. But how? After what I've done, ransacking the school, they won't let me near the building. Kevin. What did he say? It's okay to ask for help. I don't know how. I don't know how...

A day later, he talks with Kevin.

"You don't know how, or you're too proud to ask for help?" Kevin said.

"A little of both, sir."

"I'll take you to the school. Told you I would. We ask if you can come back," Kevin said. "You show the principal you've changed, learned from your mistakes. I'll vouch for you. The whole family will. But hear me on this. If I vouch for you and he takes you back, I'll run you down if you mess up. It's my word I'm offering up for you. We agree on it?"

"Yes sir," Mike said, "but what about the guys I used to run with? You remember what happened the last time you brought me home?"

"Yeah, I do. Turned out alright, the way I remember it."

———

A FEW WEEKS after Mike came to the ranch, he had felt ready enough to go home, a visit, see his mother, maybe to say I'm sorry, or thank her for simple things, a mother's worry over a son, forgiveness for foolish mistakes.

Kevin readied his family. His wife, son, and daughters filled the backseat of the family car, a copper-colored Chevy station wagon with a diesel engine, a car that said middle-aged rancher, wife, and kids, a car like the one Chevy Chase drove in the movie *Family Vacation* but missing the pestering mother-in-law. Mike rode front seat, shotgun. They drove from the ranch to Broken Bow, near the block of homes that included Kathy Doheny's, the flat-roofed fixer-upper, a burl in a copse of houses that captured and protected her family.

A car filled with boys, boys Mike ran with, drove toward the Chevy wagon. Trouble.

"What's this, Mike?" Kevin said.

"It's them. I don't want them to see me," Mike says, then ducks down out of sight.

The car passes. Too close, within inches. Faces peer into the wagon, wraiths behind rolled up windows. Kevin drives past the house. Circles the block. He sees the boys up ahead. Rolling up on the house, the boys cross onto Kevin's side of the road, cross back, signaling their intent. *Intimidate.*

Young fools, wanna-be toughs, they miscalculate. They know nothing about Kevin Cooksley, former Army captain, paratrooper, husband, father, rancher. *A man.* Kevin faces off, easing the Chevy to the opposite side of the road.

"Husband," his wife whispers. "The kids are in the car."

On cue, the oldest daughter, louder, more anxious than her mother shouts, "Dad, they'll hurt you!"

The rest of the children offer shouts of concern.

"We're okay. Watch," Kevin says.

He keeps the Chevy on a collision course. Straight. *Steady. Not left. Not right. Straight. They'll blink.* They do, swerving well before the possibility of meeting the Chevy head-on, then accelerate and disappear. Kevin left turns around the block again, making sure.

"They're gone. Won't be back is my guess. Go see your mother. We'll say hello and pick you up later."

Mike, fearing that he couldn't come home, discovers that he still has a place under Kathy's roof. He returns to the ranch that night. For the next five months, under Kevin's tutelage, the line dividing right from wrong defined, Mike makes his choice.

BROKEN BOW HIGH SCHOOL, Kevin's counsel, and a mother's acceptance turned Mike into someone else. After the meeting with the principal, Kevin by his side, the stern warning understood, one misstep and it's over, Mike earned a diploma.

Almost half a year passed. Pizza Hut, a few other ill-fitting jobs, nothing close to the future Mike dreamed of. By December the idea of life in the military becomes more than an idea. The seed, carried on the wind, planted in the field of Mike's dreams, takes root. Kevin's counsel is like fertilizer.

"The military's a good place to build on what you've accomplished so far, a good place to learn and grow, if you think that's what you want. I can tell you this much. I watched a lot of boys turn into men in the military. It's a decision that you'll have to make for yourself. I can also tell you this. I never regretted a day of my time in the military."

At Christmas, Mike handed a gift-wrapped copy of his enlistment to Kathy. She wept.

THE MARTIAL DE rigueur of Marine Corps boot camp, close-order drill, physical fitness, rifle marksmanship, long marches, obstacle courses designed to put even the strongest recruit to the test, stirs a passion in Mike. The martial way, measuring yourself against peers, physically primed for challenge, the life, intoxicating, wakes something in Mike. Every fiber of himself comes alive.

After boot camp, he joins 3rd Battalion, 5th Marines, rising quickly through the ranks. Sergeant Mike Doheny in just two and a half years. Marine of the Quarter. Marine of the Division. Jungle Warfare Training Instructor.

Gung Ho. Squared Away. A Marine's Marine. High Speed!

But sometimes there is just no understanding the unexplainable, *just the wants and needs of the Marine Corps.* After reenlisting, just months before 9/11, Mike, a warrior with a war that was about to begin, found himself ensconced as part of a security detail at Kings Bay, Georgia, the nuclear submarine base. When the men he trained with, brothers, go off to war just months later, *Operation Enduring Freedom,* Mike is left behind. Requests for transfer, requests to deploy are denied. Every part of him aches to join the fight. The ache festers, grows into resentment. At the end of his second enlistment, having given the best he has to offer, Mike Doheny leaves the Marine Corps.

After the Corps, like a bruised boxer, Mike shrugged off the eight-count, raised his gloves, signaling to anyone watching that he was ready to fight. He'd trained himself to step into the ring. Iraq had become the roped-off canvas. SOC, a security defense contractor, a promoter in need of well-trained contenders looking for a fight, arranged Mike's first match, his second, and a third, too.

Mike bobbed and weaved his way through two SOC deployments and the thousands of ways to die in Iraq. When death finally caught up with him, it was quick.

For eight years, Mike served honorably, calling the Marine Corps home, then two more years as a civilian warrior—ten years—long enough to erase the legacy of troubles that had dogged him, burnishing his once-tarnished reputation. If only he'd lingered a bit longer, but life had other ideas.

Life ate Mike Doheny alive.

PART THREE

LONE SURVIVOR

On December 8, 2007, SOC Team Six left the Farm, the former site of Saddam's exotic zoo. They rolled out under a robin's egg blue sky. The sun, pushing back against the morning chill, had gained an edge. Even for December, the day warmed quickly. The convoy, eight vehicles, a mix of military and civilian contractors, navigated their way out of Baghdad and onto Main Supply Route Bismarck, MSRB. En route to a remote site to gather intelligence, their mission, to confirm an uptick in insurgent activity on a previously cleared area, forced the convoy through villages on the one day of the week that was best to avoid. Saturday. Market Day.

Billy Joe Johnson, in the gun turret of an up-armored F-350, had a bad feeling. He hated rolling through villages on Market Day.

While the convoy journeyed, Billy made small talk with Mike Doheny, Micah Shaw, and Steve Evrard, the three other civilian contractors sardined inside the F-350, lead truck in the convoy. Billy had met Mike Doheny five months earlier, in August. The two struck an almost immediate friendship, even though Mike refused to string together much more than a three-word conversation, or share pogey bait from a well-stocked footlocker. Once, when pressed, he relented and gave Billy a stick of gum. One stick. Just once.

Guy's funny about his pogey bait.

Billy turned his attention back to the road.

The route would take them through villages bustling with Market Day shoppers bartering in Baghdadi Arabic. When the convoy rolled into the first village, a throng of shoppers blocked the road, forcing the convoy to slow. Billy felt "eyes" on them. His mood changed. Call it a warrior's premonition, a "Spidey Sense." The crowded street made him uneasy. The mass could easily create a choke point, force the convoy to stop or alter their route, pushing them into a "fatal funnel."

Billy, positioned in the gun turret, scanned rooftops, windows, alleyways. Mike and the others looked sharp. They exited the village. A few klicks out, Billy looked down. Relief flooded over the faces inside the truck. Someone smart-assed the others. Everyone laughed.

Insurgents waited on MSRB. They'd positioned IEDs and set up a small arms ambush, hoping to get lucky, hoping to get the timing right, hoping that once the convoy rolls into the kill zone, the explosion will leave behind human debris—*human debris*. When the convoy becomes an easy target, a thumb pressed on a detonator button, or maybe a finger that hits send, the result is the same.

In the instant that the F-350, filled with ammunition, explosives, grenades, a rolling bomb, fit itself over the death trap, Billy felt the blast. *His world slow-motioned.* Torn loose from the gun turret, blown into a sky fountaining dirt and metal, blood and bone into a billowing cloud of smoke, Billy felt his body rise, felt the Kevlar he wore tear from his head, his vest ripped from his body. Sickening smells, burnt plastic, metal, gunpowder, charred flesh, seared his throat. A kaleido-scope of light, reds, oranges, blues, yellows, blinded him. He felt a sharp, barbed, hubcap-size piece of shrapnel harpoon his leg.

He rose inside the swelling mushroom cloud, rising to the uppermost point of the explosion until the blast spit him out with a force that sent him dozens of feet away from the Ford. He felt himself falling. The speed of the descent, coupling with gravity like a sex-starved lover, body slammed him into the ground. Every piece of his battle gear, all of it exploded from his body. He lost consciousness.

Torn apart and bleeding, nested into weeds and knee-high scrub, his eyes popped open. His lungs, compressed by the blast, fought back, vacuumed the air, sucking and swallowing, fouling his mouth with gunpowder, smoke, and dirt. Little air.

Water, how good would a taste of water feel right now? Small arms fire. I hear it. Can't feel my right leg—damn it's gone. My boots— goddamn it—those were my favorite boots, Marine Corps issue, my lucky boots, dammit! That pisses me off. Let me see if I can get up. I'm up. Down. I can't stand on one broken leg, too painful. Alright—what now? Find cover. Enough brush to hide in. Yeah, but your own guys won't see you either. Get back to the truck then? How? Crawl. On one arm? Yeah. You've still got one that works, that other one's bent backwards. No help there. How do I do this? Okay push up on the elbow, anchor, pull forward. It's working. Again. This is going to take forever. Got a better idea? Keep crawling; you've got to get closer to the road. Again. Push up. Anchor that elbow. Pull. Drag yourself. Again. That's it. Again. I can't. This is as far as I go.

I gotta stop, roll over. Noise. Radio crackling. Someone is running. Raise that arm, wave. He sees me. Sean Powers. Battle buddy from another truck. Okay, good, he found me. I'll be okay.

"I got you," Sean said, kneeling next to Billy.

"Guys in the truck, Sean, take care of them first. Just fix me up with a tourniquet. You hear me? Go. The guys in the truck are the priority. You going to move? Go! You gotta get the guys out of the truck."

Before Sean can answer, the radio comes alive. Through the static and crackle, Billy hears the team leader ask if there are any survivors in the truck. He sees Sean shake his head, can't hear what he says, doesn't need too. Understanding floods over him. *Billy Joe Johnson, me, I'm the only one still alive.*

Mike, Micah, and Steve traveling with Billy, still laughing at the smart-assed nonsense, the open nervous relief valve used by all soldiers, never knew what hit them. The truck with their bodies trapped inside continued to smolder.

Medics arrived, knelt next to Billy. Still in shock, the pain hadn't gripped him—yet. Billy knew it would. The medic staunched the major blood flow, started an IV. Eleven days later, Billy, eased out of a medically induced coma, opened his eyes at the military hospital in Landstuhl, Germany.

Those eyes told anyone who knew him what they needed to know. Billy Joe Johnson had the will to live. He fought back, regained a toehold—survived. Death, fighting a strong argument, lost.

PART FOUR

BOB KUGLER

DURING HIS YEARS AS A RESERVIST, AN ALMOST DECADE-LONG enlistment sometimes stippled with a few months of active duty, Bob, the once-outweighed, bloodied, nine-year-old football player, now twenty-five-year-old Marine Sergeant Kugler, flirted with deployments to Iraq. In 2007, he extended his enlistment when his reserve unit finally deployed. He landed in Iraq in early August.

Days later, just one hundred miles southeast of Baghdad, older brother Mike, the former Marine Sergeant Doheny, now one of the thousands of civilian contractors supporting the American military, settled into a containerized housing unit, a CHU, on Forward Operating Base Delta.

Bob and Mike worked the next five months in country, sometimes separated by no more than forty miles, never getting any closer. Mike, a civilian warrior, constantly in harm's way, rolled out on missions in support of the US military. Security details. Escorting VIPs. Intelligence gathering. Bob, stuck in a Marine Corps heavy equipment shop at Al Tequedum (TQ), frustrated with his rear echelon status, never rolled outside the wire.

In early December, the brothers scheme to see each other,

but the best laid plan fails. Mike, a few days in Baghdad on the Farm, the former site of Saddam's zoo, *lions fattened on the bones of anyone foolish enough to lock horns with the toppled dictator,* is close to TQ. If the brothers are ever going to connect, this is the chance. But duty calls, and before Mike can make the forty-mile trip from the Farm to TQ, the war pulls him and the team he is part of in a different direction. Selected for a mission that will take him away from the Farm, Mike and the team roll out, scuttling the one chance the brothers have to see each other.

Mike emails Bob, shares the bad news. The brothers swap a few more emails. Mike, in his final missive before rolling out, tells Bob about a young goat that he found, hungry and abandoned. Mike bottle-feeds the animal. Bob, in true Marine Corps fashion, cautions his brother on the risks of sexual intimacy with goats. They get a good laugh.

Their last.

AT TQ, just on the other side of sunrise, Bob left the gym. Cool December morning air nipped at his face, flushed from an hour-long predawn dance with dumbbells. The metallic slap of 45lb weight plates he'd slipped onto the long barbell—colliding—still echoed in his ears. His muscles tight from exertion, a welcome ache. The weightlifters' credo: "No Pain No Gain."

TQ, slowly waking, yawned. Marines, men and women, began to dot the pathways on their way to any of a dozen or more unit bunkers, but mostly headed toward the base mess hall—breakfast. Sunday menu—chipped, creamed beef on toast, more affectionately known as shit on a shingle. Bob skipped chow, moving instead with a deliberate cadence, focused on getting to the heavy equipment maintenance shop. He barely noticed the desert surrounding the airbase. Nothing like Nebraska. Just low scrub and sand. A lot of sand, too much when wind swept over the base, howling, fighting its way into the smallest crevices, the tiniest crack, fouling engines, weapons, and moods.

Sunday. No days off. Still though, it shouldn't be too busy. The shop up ahead, Bob quickened his pace, wanting to arrive before his crew, savor the few minutes of solitude, email home —maybe Mike too. Even better, maybe find a few welcome emails waiting in his inbox. Inside the shop, he nodded to Marine Corporal Welch, overnight watch, early morning riser —Bob wasn't sure which. He slipped into the one office boasting a computer and comms. He logged on. Waited. Password. Keystroked it in. Waited. *C'mon—ah, there it is.*

The screen blinked, settled, then stared at Bob. He scrolled through the inbox. Nothing from Mike. A few from friends. Happy to see the email from his sister Amy, he cursored. The arrow danced, settled. He clicked open the email. Joy turned to worry as he read each word. *Mike has been in an accident.*

Oh God, no! Wait man, don't jump to conclusions, maybe they rolled the truck, happens all the time . . . maybe he'd busted a leg, something like that. Keep reading. Yeah, yeah, that's it, he probably broke his leg.

He read more. *You need to call home, now.* Now! The word leapt from the page. Fear spidered through him.

Why call home if Mike's been in an accident? I can email him. Unless. Stop guessing. Call Amy. I don't have a number for her. She didn't leave one. Alright, think, Kugler. Mike's wife Melissa? Yes, Melissa. Her number is one digit off from Mike's. Got it. Call her. She'll know what's going on.

Bob used the landline in the bunker. In minutes, linked to the Offutt AFB switchboard, he waited for the connection, pacing like an expectant father. *Click.* Offutt operators patched him through to Melissa.

"Melisa, it's Bob."

"Hey, Bob," Melissa said, her voice a gentle whisper, a manufactured generosity to soften what she needed to say.

"Melissa, what's up, what's happened to Mike?"

"Bob—Mike's convoy—didn't—Mike—"

"Melissa, stop. You're breaking up. I can't understand what you're saying."

"Bob, can you hear me okay now?" Melissa said, after stepping outside.

"Yes, much better. I've got you now."

"Mike's convoy was ambushed, hit by an IED. Bob . . . Mike didn't make it."

"What? What did you say?"

"I'm so sorry, Bob. Mike was killed yesterday. He cared for you so very much. I know how important you were to him . . . I'm really sorry," she said again, her words colliding into one another, falling like dominos.

Bob's eyes filled with sadness. He tried to speak. A strange sound scratched past his tongue, rasped against his lips. He managed a coarse whisper.

"Melissa, I've got to come home. Let me see what I can do. I'll do whatever it takes," he said, then let the phone slip from his hand.

Unsteady, Bob felt himself falling. Out of control, he tried to steady himself, break free of the spell, but grief held him in a muscled grip. His shoulders struck the wall behind him. He slid to the floor, legs bent, knees toward the ceiling. Sitting there. Stunned.

"Sergeant Kugs, are you okay? Man, what's wrong?" Corporal Welch said, hands outstretched, moving toward Bob.

The corporal's words snapped Bob back. He squinted at the Marine, waved him off. Then pushed himself up, planted his hands on the desk in front of him, took a minute. "My brother's dead," he said, the words breaking against the silence, falling to the floor like pieces of broken glass. "He was killed yesterday. I've got to find Gunny Ortega."

"I'll go. I'll find him. You wait here."

Somewhere between the bunker and the mess hall, the

corporal almost bumped into Gunnery Sergeant Ortega. He explained. The two Marines quick-stepped to the bunker. Ortega found Bob still standing at the desk. The words tumbled out of Bob. "Gunny, my brother is dead, killed yesterday. I need to get home."

The gunny stared at Bob, took a few seconds to process, then jumped into gear. "Okay, okay, Kugler, let's get things moving. I'll need Red Cross verification, but I can get paperwork started. As soon as I have the Red Cross notification in my hands, we can process emergency leave orders. Let's get to the major, Major Moen."

Bob and Gunny Ortega doubled-timed the one hundred yards up a dirt hill. Inside, Ortega took charge. Bob, a silent spectator, listened to him explain everything. The major barked out orders. The office pogue yes-sir'ed the major and disappeared.

Once the paperwork was blessed by the major, Bob knew he'd be on his way home, but, and there's always a but, things quickly unraveled.

"Nothing to do but wait on the Red Cross," the major said. "But there's more, Sergeant."

Puzzled, his eyes red, filled with tears, Bob looked at the major. "Sir?" he said, his voice low.

"Your brother's remains were flown in yesterday."

"Flown in?"

"Here, Sergeant, here. His body was brought into the morgue yesterday. Most likely no one made the connection, what with the different last names."

Bob had been near the morgue yesterday, jockeying a forklift around. He'd seen trucks just 100 yards away, pulling up to the morgue. He'd glanced, didn't give them a second look. Why would he?

"Sir, since he is my brother, I want to escort him home."

"I understand, Sergeant. Let's see if we can make that happen—but there's something else."

"Sir?"

"Those remains, the bodies brought in yesterday, they're already on the way to Kuwait."

Color leached from Bob's face. He winced, just as surely as though he'd been physically struck. An ache filled him, heavy and suffocating. He left the major's office, squinted against the early morning sun, shuffled off to his CHU in a daze, waiting on the Red Cross while grief called up the long night ahead.

———

THIRTY HOURS LATER, *Red Cross, emergency leave approved*, Bob checked in with the airfield loadmaster. "I'll get you on the first available seat," the loadmaster said. "Don't disappear. Wait right here."

In a trance, Bob watched airplanes taxi to runways, followed them as they climbed into the Iraqi sky, carrying soldiers to Kuwait. He waited for an open seat, hoping, once he's on his way, to catch up to Mike.

Behind him, Bob heard a gravelly voice, the cadenced bark cultivated by all Marine senior NCOs. "See-ar-g-ent Koooogs!" Bob turned, saw the welcoming smile on First Sergeant Jonas Smith's face, the NCO he'd once reported to.

"What are you doing here, Marine?" Smith asked, his smile slipping away as Bob explained.

"Kugs, I'm sorry. Listen up, I know the NCO in charge of the mortuary. Let me see what I can find out."

Bob continued his wait. What began that day, while he waited for any bit of news from First Sergeant Smith, the feeling of Mike's presence, the chance for one last embrace, a final touch, the sound of Mike's voice, would become a part of Bob's everyday ache for his brother. But there was still more. The chase to catch up to Mike, Bob still at the starting line, quickly moved from a crawl to full sprint, a sprint that would become a marathon.

First Sergeant Smith returned. "Kugs, what I'm going to tell you, well, it's not what you're going to want to hear. Your brother's remains were not flown out yesterday. He was . . . he . . . he was flown out less than an hour ago. You must have seen the airplane he was on. I'll do what I can to have your brother held in Kuwait. With some luck, you'll catch up to him, fly home with him. I'll try." His eyes said he would do just that, wished that he could do more.

Emotions cascade. *Sadness. Frustration. Anger.*

By mid-afternoon, Mike dead now for more than 48 hours, Bob strapped himself into the jump seat of C-130 leaving for Kuwait. Several hours later, he shuffled down the cargo ramp at the rear of the airplane, milling about with other soldiers and marines walking toward the airport concourse.

"Do you know where the morgue is?" he asked a soldier walking next to him.

"Not sure, man," the soldier said, and hurried on his way.

Awake now for more than thirty hours, nerves frayed, emotionally spent, running on empty, Bob found the morgue.

"There's not a body here identified as Mike Doheny. You said he's, was, a civilian contractor?"

"Yes."

"The bodies of three civilian contractors were brought in but they've already been transferred to an airplane headed for Dover. You think the guy you're looking for is one of them?"

"He's my brother. Yeah, he's one of them. Where do I check in, try to get a flight to Dover?"

"Concourse, commercial airlines counter. You'll have to go to the armory and check in that M4, first."

Bob found the armory. Reluctantly surrendering his rifle—it's a Marine thing, two-hundred and fifty years of tradition inbred into every Marine. Make love to a woman but sleep with your rifle. Bob handed over his rifle, but not before removing a custom three-point sling, a gift from Mike.

Finally booked on a commercial flight to Dover, Bob shuffled onto the airplane, sidestepping until he found his row, *business class, more privacy.* He dropped into his seat, listened to the robotic drone of instructions, *remain seated for takeoff, fasten seat belts, tray tables and seat backs up.* He complied.

Tenting a blanket over his body, hiding his face, coaxed by the drone of the engines, he fell into a dreamless sleep. Thirteen hours later, waking when the airplane landed, grateful for the slide into a deep sleep that had suspended the ache in his heart, Bob went in search of Mike.

In Dover, at the morgue, another kicker. Each body must be positively identified before remains can be released.

"How long?"

"Could take as long as long as two weeks. Go home. Wait. The remains will be sent there."

What? I'm emptyhanded again, really? Go home. Wait. Check back. What the hell . . . this is not some piece of lost luggage. Go home and wait?

Bob, feeling like a hitchhiker thumbing another ride, this time home to Nebraska, boarded a third airplane in twenty-four hours. Home is a blur. Charli, *girlfriend, later wife, even later, ex-wife,* greets him at the airport. So do Marines from the reserve unit. A few friends. No one really knows what to do, say.

"Let's get something to eat," someone says.

"Chili's. Mike's favorite place," Bob said.

THE ALMOST TWO WEEKS EXPIRE. Bob, impatient, uncomfortable with the silence, *nothing coming out of Dover,* unwilling to continue the free fall into a bureaucratic bottomless pit, set off on his own course of action. *Josh Schulz.* Mike's roommate from 3-5 LIMA, Third Marine Battalion, Fifth

Marine   Regiment,   Darkhorse—*brothers*.   They'd   served
together since boot camp. Inseparable.

*Get in touch with him. I need a six. We can fly to Dover and get
Mike. No more waiting. I want my brother I want to bring him home
—now.*

Bob calls Josh. Emails. Doesn't go into detail. *Nothing.* One
day turns into three. Bob's emails, shorter, terse, fail to get a
response. Phone. Voice mail again. Frustration pushes him to
a breaking point. "GODDAMNIT CALL ME. MIKE'S
BEEN KILLED."

All caps, the email equivalent of shouting—still doesn't get
a response.

In Missoula, Montana, Josh, an Idaho Wildland firefighter,
rappeler, *off season*, settled in a duck blind, hoping to fill the
empty game bag hanging from his belt. The end of fire season
offered him, and men like him, a break until early spring.
Today would be the last day of this trip. He'd be home in the
morning.

When he does walk through his door, his answering machine
blinks like emergency vehicle warning lights. He hits playback.
The messages stun him. *Let me check the computer.* Familiar names,
Bob Kugler, Melissa Doheny, litter the inbox. He clicks on to Bob's
message, confirms what the answering machine has already told
him, makes a few calls, packs, includes his Dress Blues, and drives
the eighteen hours from Billings to Omaha. Stops twice for gas.

Bob booked the flights to Baltimore-Washington
International Airport (BWI), sixty miles away from Dover Air
Force Base, a long drive. Still needing more information on

Mike, *he has a contact number for SOC,* Bob calls. The voice on the other end, a man's, cold, laced with hostility, clearly annoyed at Bob's interruption, blows a long sigh of exasperation into the phone.

"There's remains here positively identified as Mike Doheny," he mouths. "Are you related?"

"He's my brother," Bob said.

"Do you mean stepbrother? The last names are different."

"Different last names don't mean anything," Bob says, his anger beginning to outdistance the voice on the other end of the phone. "You get it? He is my brother. I don't expect you to understand, just tell me what comes next."

The insinuation has never been lost upon Bob. He's heard it all his life, the oh, he's just your half-brother/stepbrother, the verbal asterisk people want to put next to their names. He feels a familiar anger building, knows if he lets it go unchecked, he'll explode. He stifles a heated retort. What's the point? This guy has already done the best he can to fit his head into a peculiar, but for him appropriate, anatomical position.

"Whatever," the voice says. "Dover will cart the body over to the airport. It'll be loaded onto an airplane leaving for Omaha in the morning. Is there anything else I can do for you?"

"No," Bob replies, swallowing his anger.

"Oh yeah," the voice says, needing to take a parting shot, "Just to let you know, he's not going to have a flag. That's the policy for civilian contractors."

Bob accepts the edict, decides not to take a flag with him.

LATE THAT NIGHT, Josh and Bob, in Marine Corps Dress Blues, step from the airplane, a long night in front of Mike's flight home tomorrow morning. At the arrival gate, a kindly woman listens.

"We're escorting my brother's body home," Bob said. "We fly out in the morning. I want to see . . . I want to, we want to see—"

"They hold the remains in bulk cargo," she said, gently finishing Bob's sentence. "They'll carry your brother out to the airplane in the morning, about an hour before takeoff. You might be able to see him when they load him. Just get down there early."

"Thank you, ma'am. My brother is a civilian. He was killed in Iraq. He served in the Marine Corps. I was told there cannot be a flag over his remains, some sort of policy, is that correct?"

"Oh, honey, once you get down to where they hold the remains, you can do whatever you want."

"Really?"

"Yes. I don't know who told you that, but they were wrong. If you have a flag, you may certainly cover your brother."

"Thank you, ma'am," Bob said, then turned to Josh. "Josh, we can cover Mike with a flag, man, but I don't have one. This sucks. I'm told no flag, so I don't bring one— dammit, it would have been the right thing to do. So now what?"

"Let's find a hotel, crash for the night. It's late."

———

"You awake?"

"Yep, can't sleep," Josh said.

"Me too. I haven't even closed my eyes. I can't get my head around Mike not honored with a flag. It's not right. We've got to find a flag."

"It's the middle of the night, man, where the hell are we going to find a flag?"

"I don't know, maybe we try the police department, fire department. They have flags, right? Maybe they have an extra. We're going to find a flag!"

Sorry, no, is all Bob hears when he explains. Josh fares no better. They spend over an hour on the phone. The idea becomes an obsession; nothing less than a flag will do—nothing. Then a suggestion. "Try the USO. Open 24/7, I'll bet they'll have a flag."

Bob hangs up. Explains.

"Let's give it a shot," Josh says. "You call."

"Yes, we have a flag. I'm looking at it right now. But it's pinned to the wall, up high."

"Oh," Bob says, deflated.

"Look, as far as I'm concerned, if you can get it down, it's yours. Come get it."

At the USO, Bob and Josh look at the flag twenty feet above their heads. Their eyes lock, exasperation spreads across their faces, dead-ended again. Bob, haunted by his decision not to bring a flag, looks up again, hopelessly.

"It's too high, Josh. It's too freaking high!"

"Trust me on this; someone is going to get that flag down for us. I promise you," Josh said, then disappeared, returning with someone officious. They look up together.

"I can get someone in maintenance see if they can get it down. We have a scissor lift. I'll call the manager, too. She might have another idea. Wait here."

"We can't," Bob says, looking at Josh. "Getting too close to morning, too close to departure. We've got to get back, check in for the flight. We probably have just enough time to get through security, check in, and wait for boarding."

BOB AND JOSH hurry to the concourse, empty-handed. The line for security screening already formed, Bob and Josh, wearing Dress Blues, fell into the queue. Nearing the body scanner, they tossed their overnight duffels onto the conveyor. Josh moved forward; leg ironed his way through. The alarm startled everyone.

"Step back, sir. Take off that belt buckle. Place it on the conveyor. Step forward."

Again, the alarm sounded.

"Sir, I'll have to ask you and the other Marine to step out of the line. Follow that officer. You'll have to take those uniforms off and go through a search."

Sanity intervenes. The power trip does not play well with everyone.

"What's happening here?" a man uniformed with a white shirt, high and tight, a neatly trimmed mustache, says.

"They keep setting off the alarm."

"Of course they do, look at the brass on their uniforms? You think these two guys are terrorists?"

"No, but—"

"But what?" White Shirt says, thwarting the power-hungry bag checker, then looking at Josh and Bob. "You two Marines go ahead."

Cleared through security, duffle bags reclaimed, boarding passes issued, they wait.

"Let's get down to the tarmac while they load the airplane. The lady said we could probably catch up with Mike before he is loaded up."

"I'm thinking the same thing," Josh said. "Still want a flag though."

"Yeah, me too. Let's go."

On the tarmac, Bob feels the vibration of his cell, hears the muted tone. "Hi, I'm looking for Sergeant Kugler?"

"I'm Bob Kugler."

"Sergeant, I'm the manager of the USO. I got a call about the flag. The guys were trying to get it down, but I had another one. It's yours. I'm here with it, but I can't get it to you. I can't get to the gates or the tarmac because I'm not a ticketed passenger. I asked if one of the TSA agents or someone from the airline could get it to you, but they won't do it."

Bob hangs up, turns to Josh. Explains.

Josh laughs. "Of course, they won't let her through. The whole goddam night has been, you can't do this, you can't do that. Screw it, man," Josh said, before disappearing. "I'm getting that flag. I told you now that we found one, that I was getting it. Keep them waiting until I get back."

Before Bob could reply, Josh disappeared.

While the airplane is boarding, Bob makes his way to the tarmac. Passengers are being ushered onto the airplane. Bob refuses to board.

"I've got to wait for my friend," he tells the airline official.

"We can't delay the boarding, sir. You'll need to move up the stairway."

"Not without my friend," Bob says, refusing to move forward. The impasse headed toward critical mass, the wrong decision leading to the start of an irreversible chain reaction, never gets that far. Bob hears, before he sees, a motorized baggage tug towing a line of baggage carts. The driver's orange jump suit catches the early morning sun. Josh riding shotgun, with a free hand waves at Bob. *Tucked beneath his other arm is a folded American flag!*

The baggage train rumbles to a stop. Josh jumps off the tug, runs toward Bob. He stands in front of him, tears streaming down his face. "Mike is on one of these carts," Josh tells Bob. Together they the begin checking the battle-scarred carts.

"This one," the driver of the tug says, pointing to a cart with an orange light flashing atop a white pole attached to the cart. "Take your time. They ain't taking off until we finish loading, if you get my drift."

Bob and Josh stand beside the cart. The driver pulls back the blue draped accordion slider, revealing Mike's remains.

Bob, after almost three weeks of chasing Mike from the other side of the world, has finally caught up with his brother.

What he sees shocks him. He recoils in disbelief.

The word **HEAD**, boldly stenciled on what must be the front of a dirty, grease-smudged, cheaply constructed paper box housing Mike's remains, stares at him like an angry drill sergeant. White cardboard stapled to an even cheaper frame of 1x3 furring strips make up the poor excuse for a coffin.

"Are you kidding me?" Bob said, his voice halting, almost unintelligible.

My God. My God, what if we hadn't intercepted Mike's remains? What if we waited in Nebraska, and this . . . whatever it's supposed to be, this tattered cardboard, dirty, NO FLAG, box had been the rest of the family's first look at Mike? Fifty dollars' worth of cardboard, staples, and wood. This? This is the best anyone could do for a son, a brother, a husband, a Marine—fifty bucks worth of stuff—fifty bucks . . . Nice. Real Nice.

"Josh, how did you get the flag?"

"You don't want to know."

"Okay, let's cover him. Stars go over the head, right?"

"I guess they do, yeah. Wouldn't be right anywhere else. You ready?"

"Yeah, let's do this."

They unfolded the flag, carefully began to blanket it over Mike.

"Flag's too big."

"This box is too small; a real coffin is longer."

"What'll we do?"

"Tuck it up in between the cardboard."

Pulling the flag to its full length, positioning it evenly, they let the overlapping ends of the flag cascade in piles at the head and foot of the coffin, down the sides, too. Together they lifted the end, surprised at the weight, lighter than expected, still— maybe heavy enough to be Mike's 160 pounds—maybe. With the flag secured at the foot, they moved to the head, lifted again, tucked, then secured the overlap firmly between slits along the sides. Baggage handlers stood off to the side, silently watching, heads bowed.

"I guess they got as much of Mike as they could," Bob said. "Feels like he's in there."

Bob and Josh stood at attention, held a salute as Mike's body was lifted from the cart and placed on a conveyor. They watched him slowly move into the belly of the airplane, alarmed when the flag snagged on the conveyor, holding their breath until it ripped free, a small tear.

Inside the airplane, finally seated, Bob and Josh listened to the captain. "Ladies and gentlemen," he said, his message silencing many of the passengers, "this is your captain. Marine Sergeants Kugler and Schultz are flying with us today. They are escorting the body of a Marine killed in Iraq."

While the airplane prepared for takeoff, a flight attendant escorted Bob and Josh into first class. The smell of leather, the plush comfort of a large seat big enough to unfold in, doting flight attendants, all of it overwhelmed Bob. Three drinks into the limit allowed, *neither Bob, nor Josh refused*, fatigue, held at a distance for the last two days, coursed through Bob. His face softened. His shoulders relaxed.

Am I really sitting in first class, escorting my brother's body home? I've been chasing him for almost three weeks, missed him by minutes three separate times. Now? Now he's resting down below and I'm here, treated like royalty. Is this real? Will I wake up, discover it's all just a bad dream? No. It's for real, alright. Mike is gone.

In Chicago, a layover while Mike is transferred to a connecting flight to Nebraska, *nothing direct*, Bob and Josh make their way to the cargo area, standing vigil. A solitary cart, painted deep blue, emblazoned with the emblems of every branch of the military, pushed to the side of the airplane, waits for Mike's flag-covered body. A uniformed handler stood beside the decorated cart, baseball cap in his hand.

"This is amazing. Where did this come from?" Josh asked.

"I had this done after my son was killed," the handler said. "After the way I saw my son housed in a banged up old cart, I didn't want anyone else to go through that, so I had this done."

Mike's remains peeked through the belly of the airplane into the light. The baggage handlers loaded him into the honor cart. Finally, *finally*, Mike rested in a warrior's chariot. Bob and Josh stood watch until Mike, carefully lifted from the cart, was gracefully slipped into the hold of a smaller airplane.

Josh turned and thanked the baggage handlers. Each one.

———

ON THE TARMAC IN OMAHA, the pilot asks passengers to remain seated until the remains of the fallen Marine have been unloaded from the airplane. Mike, impatient all his life, in no hurry now, would have told the pilot to let them go, he'd wait. For the first time in his life, he had nowhere to be. Bob and Josh leave ahead of the rest of the other passengers.

Outside, on the ground, Bob looks up. Melissa, Mike's wife stares down at him from the airport concourse.

PART FIVE

MELISSA DOHENEY

In early spring, a day after her semester ends, Melissa and Josh head northwest. Ten hours later, Nebraska in their taillights, they stop for the night. At a motel on the edge of the Wyoming boarder, Josh, before the motel clerk asks, says, "A room with two beds." He turned in time to see Melissa's soft smile of appreciation. Lights out, their goodnights collide. Tomorrow they'll hike into Glacier National Park along McDonald Creek in search of a secluded area where the creek pools quiet. It's there that they'll scatter Mike's ashes.

With the day still in front of them, they wake early. On the road Josh is quiet, has been for most to the trip. Melissa's comfortable with the silence. She stares at passing trees. Josh looks straight ahead. Montana, outsized and mostly empty, takes them into early afternoon. The park appears abandoned when they roll in, stretch, take turns in a weather-beaten jakes, then look for the trailhead.

"There," Josh said, pointing to a rift in the rough timber-lined barricade edging the parking area.

"I'll get Mike," Melissa said, returning with the urn, a pewter, bottle-necked amphora that held Mike's ashes.

Holding Mike to her chest, Melissa walked beside Josh.

Winter over, the ground had sucked up all the snow melt, greening everything in sight. Conifers, pine and spruce, their shaggy coats turned emerald green, lined the trail. Lady slippers and windflowers already poked through the littered forest floor. Willows thrived nearer streams.

The trail gently sloped, leading Melissa and Josh to the creek. No one in sight. Strange. Melissa is grateful for the solitude. They follow rivulets, streams, find the larger creek, wider than the shallow runnel guiding them. The creek flowing freely, bolder. They pick their way through boulders and brush, walk along the water's edge. The scents of new rain, the musky forest floor, last year's life decayed, feeding the new season's growth, thicken in a light afternoon wind.

Melissa is lost in her own grief, her own memories.

MELISSA, just a few days on the other side of her fifteenth birthday, took note of Mike Doheny. In a class of sixty-three students, a guy like Mike, broad chested, slim waisted, jaunty swagger, was hard to miss. His bad-boy reputation made some of the girls leery, others curious. One or two, smitten, clung to Mike in the school halls. Melissa, somewhere in between, smiled when he'd say hello, laughed a little when he'd flirt. They became friends, sometimes ran in the same crowd. Even pulled a few pranks together, like the Christmas they decided to swap out half the town's holiday displays, switching them from house to house. The night started out innocent enough, good kids with a silly plan. The semi-bad behavior gets them all in trouble. *Community Service.*

Three years later Melissa and Mike stand on the auditorium stage, diplomas in hand, uncertain futures in front of them. They're halves that fit together; they just don't know it yet.

MELISSA, first to enlist, ships off to Parris Island, Marine Corps boot camp. A reservist. She slips out of Mike's life. Feeling her absence, he writes, more often than Melissa expects. Their relationship, long distance, finds an easy rhythm. *Friends. Good friends.* Before Melissa returns to Broken Bow, boot camp and AIT completed, Mike enlists. They continue writing, visiting each time Mike returns to Broken Bow. The years between them overlap, inexplicably bringing them closer, despite the time that has passed and the distance that separates them.

Melissa pursues a college degree; Mike completes a four-year enlistment, signs on for four more. Love, impatient, refuses to take a back seat any longer. A decadelong attraction turns romantic. Months later on vacation in Vegas, Mike proposed. Melissa said yes. He slipped the ring on her finger.

By Monday, the fever hotter than any pepper sprout, they queued up in a line at "The Say I Do Drive Thru." At the take-out window, a clipboard is passed to Mike. He hands it to Melissa, pays the clerk. $140.00. Polaroid and T-shirts, no extra charge.

"Drive up to the next window, please."

They complete the paperwork, pass it to a self-ordained pastor. She scans it, just long enough to get the names right. Melissa stretches past Mike, looks through the window, making certain the pastor can hear her.

"I do," she said, Mike did too.

Vegas didn't notice Mike and Melissa, may not have "stooped and bowed," but Melissa and Mike "breezed into that city" just like Johnny and June. They left, wearing their T-shirts emblazoned with the words, "I got married at the Say I Do Drive Thru."

THE YOUNG COUPLE'S early lives in Broken Bow, not so different from each other, shapes them. Without saying it out loud, they make a silent pact to do better than others. Melissa, determined, closes in on a college degree, the first in her family. When Mike, a sergeant now, is transferred to Georgia, they buy a house. *Smart.*

Their intimacy blossoms. How long does it take to really know someone? For some couples that might take a lifetime, but Mike and Melissa own a shared history that hadn't left room for many secrets. Once they understood that they'd been on a collision course, admitting that they loved each other came naturally.

While in Georgia, Kings Bay Nuclear Submarine Base, Mike watches men he served with deploy to Iraq and Afghanistan. Unhappy with a rear echelon role, haunted, feeling like he'd abandoned men he trained with, men he'd prepared for battle, he looks to break out of his static tour. The Marine Corps makes it impossible for him to join the fight. He shares his disappointment with Melissa.

"I don't know what to do," he confides in her. "I'd have to enlist again. I would if I'd be guaranteed deployment." The only guarantee in the military, any branch, *follow orders.* The Marine Corps wants Mike where he is, pulling static security at Kings Bay.

Melissa and Mike discuss options, decide that Mike will step away from the Corps at the end of this enlistment. Melissa completes her time as a reservist. Mike flirts with the idea of joining Josh in Montana as a wildland firefighter. That career has the excitement Mike seeks, a real potential option, but Mike balks. Melissa still has college to finish. "Montana," he says, "can wait. Going now means living apart for almost two more years. I don't want to do that."

Somewhere in between all this they make a plan.

They spend time emptying the house, put it up for sale. Melissa transfers to school in Omaha. Mike settles things in

Georgia, but before he joins Melissa, the plan goes sideways. Lured by a sense of duty, first to the country, second to men he knew, he jumps at a chance to deploy to Iraq. *Civilian Contractor.* Something he knows he has to talk over with Melissa. Battling her own misgivings, a natural fear for Mike's safety, she agrees to leave the decision up to him. Loyal, she makes certain he understands, no matter what, she'll support him.

In a flash, Mike's gone. Melissa holds her breath, hopes that the decision does not turn into a careful-what-you-wish-for choice. *For either of them.*

Before the next semester begins, Melissa, already alone, buries her dad.

While Mike's deployed, Melissa learns to live with the reality that she could be blindsided by the six-o'clock news. Media, always quick to pounce on bad news, wouldn't wait to notify next-of-kin. A former Marine, she understood how notification, *KIA/WIA*, worked in the military, but this was different. She had no idea how it worked with civilian contractors, no one did. She feared hearing the news, held her breath when broadcasters stoically droned on, the detached tone that always seemed to begin with the phrase, *in other news,* the precursor to the latest casualty report from Iraq or Afghanistan, military or civilian.

Each day, for almost a year, worry consumed her. *He's doing everything the military is doing; he's in harm's way, I know it.* She'd wake in the middle of the night, unable to fall back to sleep. School, once a benign challenge, frustrates her. The empty side of the bed feels strange after lying next to Mike. Days, sometimes weeks, without word adds to her fears. *Bottle it up girl. You can't let him know how you feel. Anything going on with you takes a backseat. You don't, you can't become a distraction to Mike.*

Six months. Mike has earned vacation time, a generous ten-day respite. He learns from others that have gone before him that he and Melissa can spend the time together. He emails her. They decide to meet in Paris. Melissa scrambles, secures a passport. Packing for the trip, Melissa's first outside of the US, her excitement builds. *I'm going to Paris and Mike will be there waiting for me!*

Stepping from the battlefield onto the streets of the City of Love, the sense of the place, the romantic myth, rubs up against Mike's abrupt exit from Iraq. Edgy, sometimes to the point of distraction, his behavior worries Melissa. In mid-sentence he looks away, scans an open window, pulls back from crowded venues, jumps when a motorcycle speeds by.

He's not the same, I can feel it.

At the Louvre, Mike manages to snap a photo, capturing Romeo and Juliet. In Iraq, he shows the picture to a street artist, *there's more of them than you think*, pays him to paint a replica. It's good. Finished in time for Melissa's birthday. When the painting arrives, Melissa is surprised. Not a bad touch for the former kid from Broken Bow. Not long after Melissa's birthday, Mike redeploys. He's home for Christmas.

The next year is shaky for Melissa and Mike. Mike had come straight from the battlefields of Iraq, landing in Omaha, reuniting with Melissa in less time than it takes for the Earth to spin. Days turn into empty weeks. At night he lies next to Melissa but doesn't sleep, unable to turn off thoughts and images of Iraq. Mornings turn into a hasty silent breakfast, gulped coffee. If Melissa asks about the long night, he refuses to answer. They ride to work in silence. Cracks, the thinnest gossamer fissures, crawl along the surface of their relationship.

Almost a year passes. Mike takes a short-term deployment, *ninety days*, he's back in Iraq. When he returns, it's not for long. He decides to go back, alibies to Melissa that he should be there now that Bob has deployed. There's no logic to the decision. The truth, *Mike understood it*, he didn't fit in the civilian world anymore. Iraq had become a place more kind than home. In the weeks before he leaves, he returned to parts of himself, the Mike Melissa had fallen in love with.

On the morning he left, he held Melissa. "I didn't sleep last night," he said. "Leaving this time feels different. It doesn't make sense to go, I know, but I need to be there."

JOSH'S VOICE STARTLED HER. She tucked Mike closer to her chest. "Look, look up ahead. The water's quiet," Josh said, pointing to a shallow basin where the creek eddied. "What do you think?"

Melissa looked around. *No people. Good.* Sunlight, stingy on the tree-covered trail, reflected off the water. Melissa shielded her eyes, walked to the water's edge. Her feet sank in the spongy sand. A dragonfly chasing a damsel flitted just above the water's surface. A tall willow stood sentinel, leaning over the pool, her long leaves caught on the light breeze, silvered.

"This feels right, Josh," Melissa said. "It's quiet, as good a spot as any we'll find."

Josh nodded, Melissa uncradled Mike, looked at the urn. *How do I do this?* She gripped the top, pulled. *Nope.* She twisted. *Okay, got it, it's a screw type cover.*

Josh stood close, silent, ready to help if needed. Melissa placed the cover in the sand, stepped to the edge of pool, water licking the toes of her boots. She held Mike at arm's length, tilted the urn. Nothing. *So, what do I do now? Shake it? Tap the bottom. Mike, you are so stubborn.* She gently shook the urn, tipped it again. Still nothing. She held it sideways, tapped the bottom. Nothing. She tilted the urn, looked inside, handed it to Josh. He shook his longtime friend, urging him on. He budged, barely. Josh handed Mike back.

"Try again," he said.

Melissa took the urn, tipped it again. A sifting began to trickle out. Stopped.

She knelt in the sand, water wicking through her jeans. She pushed her finger into the center of the urn, stood and held Mike out over the water once more. Slowly a trail began to slip from the urn. A million motes, the tiniest bits of dust, glistened in the sunlight, then drifted to the surface of the pool, gathering in patches that spread over the water.

Melissa stood, silently watching. Mike slowly drifted on the calm surface of the pool, lazy circles, until the current found him, gathered him, pulling him to deeper waters, until he was gone.

PART SIX
BOB KUGLER

FROM THE TARMAC, BOB RAISED HIS ARM, A SAD WAVE OF HIS hand moved to a deliberate salute. Josh stood by his side, braced, eyes straight ahead. Gloved fingertips touched the black brim of Bob's cover. He stared at Melissa, held the salute. Melissa nodded. Bob slowly lowered his hand before she disappeared from the window, reappearing moments later on the tarmac.

A guard detail from the Marine Corps Reserve Unit out of Omaha formed up on the tarmac. Standing at attention, they waited to receive Mike. Bob, relieved of duty, no longer charged with escorting Mike, waited a few yards away. He stood at attention, jumped when he felt a hand on his shoulder.

"They've got it from here, Bob," Josh said.

Melissa walked to Bob, embraced him, held him for a moment, *wordless*, then stood by his side. She held herself together, former Marine Sergeant Melissa Doheny, at attention, the way she'd been taught, the way she remembered, waiting. In the dark. In the cold. Just a few days before Christmas. The cargo bay of the airplane opened. Mike's flag-draped remains poked through. The Marine detail stepped forward, carried Mike to a waiting hearse. Bob and Josh nodded toward each other, wordlessly grateful for the flag that camouflaged the insult holding Mike.

Inside Melissa's car, Bob rode shotgun. Josh and Melissa's mom sat together. Moments after they clear the airport, heading for open highway, *two hours to Broken Bow*, Bob's cell phone sounds off.

"Bob, this is Rob Passmore, I'm the Patriot Guard commander. Look man, I'm sorry we couldn't form the line. It's dipped below ten degrees, can't get the bikes out," he said. "But listen up, I've still got your six. I'm in my SUV. I'll escort you out of Omaha, until you're clear of town and on the highway, rolling."

In the morning, Bob and Josh visit the funeral home. Mike is at rest in a real casket. A new American flag blankets his remains. Bob asks about the original flag.

"It's here," the funeral director said. "It's pretty dirty, we thought it would be better to replace it."

"Thanks," Bob said. "I'll want to keep it, get it cleaned."

"Of course. I'll get it for you."

"Josh, I've got to call Melissa. Now that we have two flags, I want to give one to my mom and one to Melissa. They both should have one."

Bob explained to Melissa. "The guard unit will present you with the flag that covers Mike. We have two now, but I need to know which one you want. I'll give the other to my mother."

"Bob, if it's okay I'd like the flag that covered Mike on the way home."

"Done."

Bob dropped the flag off to a local dry cleaner, picked it the next day. At the funeral home he unfolded the flag. *Clean, but it's so wrinkled. It looks like crepe paper. I can't put this over Mike, not like this.*

Bob explains everything to the funeral director. "We have

a steamer. You could try it and see if it'll take the wrinkles out. It should work."

For the next several hours, in the back room of the funeral home, Bob worked on the flag. He draped it over a tall rack, slid the steamer over each paneled stripe, then the stars. Satisfied, he turned to Josh. Unwilling to let Mike go uncovered, Bob walked to one end of the casket, Josh to the other. They blanketed the USO flag over the mortuary flag covering Mike. Bob held the USO flag, Josh gripped the newer one and pulled, slipping the flag out from under the other. Mike remained honored.

Bob and Josh folded the flag that would be presented to Mike's mother. *Bob's mother.* A day later, at the ceremonial burial, the folded flag was gifted to Kathy Doheny. The Marine honor guard presented the USO flag to Melissa. Josh tore the sergeant's stripes from the sleeves of his Dress Blues, laid them on Mike's casket. Bob unpinned his service ribbons, placed them alongside the chevrons.

Before the ceremony ends, someone asks Bob why there wasn't an open casket. *Really? Do I really need to explain what happened to Mike, that he was blown up and incinerated? Are you really that damn stupid? Don't do it Bob, don't lose it here. Don't make it about you. This is Mike's time. Don't explain, just say no.*

"Yes," he said, when four-year-old Patricia, Mike's niece, turned to him, pointing to the casket.

"Is Uncle Mike in there?" she asked.

"Yeah, honey, he is," Bob said, leaning down to give her a hug.

PART SEVEN
WHAT FOLLOWS

BROKEN BOW, A TOWN THAT HAD MOSTLY IGNORED MIKE Doheny while he was alive, came out to honor him, claiming him as one of their own, a hero. A sometimes-troubled boy who grew into a good man. A man who watched over family. "The glue," Kathy Doheny often said, "that held the family together."

During a public ceremony, the town's Municipal Building filled to capacity. An overflow milled around outside. Inside the building, standing room only, well-wishers stood in the rear and to the sides. The Patriot Guard, in full regalia, formed a line in front of the building, ready if any Westboro Baptists dared to brave the single-digit Nebraska cold. *Cowards. They didn't.*

Kathy walked the line, shaking hands with each guard member.

Pipers blew life into tartan covered bags. *Amazing Grace* echoed loudly, shaking the auditorium walls. Some sang, over-powered by the blaring bagpipes. Bob, a decent enough tenor, couldn't find his voice.

Mike died with no chance to say "goodbye" or "I love

you," but he left behind a letter. The crowd quieted. Bob read. Mike had not forgotten anyone.

JOSH LINGERED behind for a few weeks after the ceremony, checking in on Melissa. When he knew she'd stand on her own, he went back to his life, a firefighter on the Salmon River Rappel Crew in Idaho. Eventually, Josh returned home to Montana, a life in the US Forest Service. Hours of solitary time in the Bitterroot Mountains National Forest. He sometimes still reaches out to Bob and Melissa, Mike the link in the almost two-decades-long chain still holding them together.

AMY MARRIED AND STARTED A FAMILY, eventually divorced, still lives in Broken Bow, not far from Kathy. John moved away, visits infrequently.

LONE SURVIVOR, Billy Joe Johnson, after fifty-plus surgeries, recovered as well as any seriously wounded warrior could. When he was well enough, he reached out to Melissa, reassuring her that Mike died instantly. "He wouldn't have suffered at all," he told her.

Melissa gave him one of Mike's dog tags.

MELISSA HAD LEARNED of Mike's death during the last week of the fall semester. She skipped all of her finals, called Bob, and left for home. Weeks later, on the first day of the new semester, she completed the finals, remedied course incompletes, went back to classes and lectures in a fog. The semester was harder to move through than thigh-high snow covering the Nebraska countryside.

Everyone—students, professors—knew about Mike. When she walked into class or a lab, the room would fall silent. They'd look at Melissa, confusion or pity in their eyes. She hated it, began looking for the empty seat on the rim of lecture halls far away from classmates. If sorrow overwhelmed her, *it did*, ambushing her just as sure as the attack that had killed her husband, before she'd let tears fall on the pages in front of her, she'd run out of the class or lecture hall.

Nothing's the same.

She'd walk to the passenger side of the car, absentminded, staring blankly, sigh and shrug, then walk to the driver's side, slip behind the wheel and weep. Nightmares began. She'd see Mike in a crowd, wake, know it was a dream, and cry. With grief as her only companion, she cried a lot.

Letters, forms, paperwork with strange requests, waited in her mailbox, one surprise ambush after another. *This is to acknowledge that all that was recovered of Mike Doheny is partial remains, sign below if you agree.* Robotically, she scratched her signature on the form, this one and dozens more, stuffed them into envelopes, licked a stamp—*they couldn't have a stamped return envelope?*—and mailed them back.

Cause of death: Homicide. *Homicide?* He was killed in action, an honor denied him. The insult added to her pain.

Two years later, she graduated, the first in her family to earn a college degree, becoming a Board-certified ambulatory pharmacist. The moment felt hollow. Mike's death erased the plans they'd made together. He was supposed to be there to celebrate with her, but the future no longer included him. She'd never have the child they'd wanted.

Slowly, deliberately, she began to distance herself from

family, especially Mike's, everyone except Bob. Being with them just reminded her of Mike, all that he would do for them. They'd lost him too, she understood, but sometimes it felt as if they blamed her. For some, pointing a finger at others eases their own pain. Loss, she knew better than most, is hard on everyone. Better for everyone that she put some distance between. No one's to blame.

She felt stuck. Years passed. Mike had been gone for more years than they'd been married, but moving forward felt impossible. They had a closeness that defied time and distance. In all the years that Melissa had known Mike, no matter how far apart they were, no matter how much time would pass before they were together, they always made it back to each other, picking up right where they left off. She loved him.

Eventually, urged on by friends, Melissa tried dating. Nobody made it to the second round.

Throughout the years, Billy checked in. They'd seen each other twice, once not long after Mike died, again a few months later. Billy stayed in touch. They'd talk. Sometimes about Mike, most times about nothing at all. A decade passed. Billy suggested they meet. Melissa agreed. Billy confessed that he had feelings for her, romantic feelings.

"How long have you felt that way?" Melissa asked.

"A long time, Melissa, years."

"Why didn't you tell me sooner?"

"Because I didn't want you to look at me and see Mike. I wanted to wait until you were ready."

"I see you, Billy," Melissa said.

They live together on twenty wooded acres in rural Tennessee.

Bob, just days after Mike's one-night-only, no-encore marquee appearance in Broken Bow, landed in Kuwait, retrieved his long gun, reattached the sling, *Mike's gift*, and found a seat on a C-130 bound for TQ. Walking to the airplane, he passed rows of up-armored Humvees and MRAPs. Dozens of the new, heavily armored trucks stretched in long lines, three deep—parked and idled, the same trucks he'd seen almost a month ago on his way home. The irony—contractors rolled out in lightly armored Ford trucks, a rolling house of cards with little chance of surviving an IED blast—was not lost upon him.

Back at TQ, *if he had compared notes with Melissa, their experiences the same,* everyone looked at him differently. Like Melissa, nothing felt the same to Bob. A blank check, drawn against the belief that he belonged here, had been cashed against insufficient funds. Being here didn't make sense anymore. The why of it, the all things Marine Corps without question, *that too,* suddenly there were too many unanswered questions.

He'd fantasized about his return, a Brad Pitt moment, the revenge seeker in *Legends of the Fall.* When given the opportunity to go outside the wire, *a voluntary, undefined mission,* he said no. He had new responsibility, *different.* Mike was gone. The things that Mike did for family would fall to him now. He knew, if something happened to him, Kathy would break under the weight of another lost son. The what-ifs of galloping off into harm's way were suddenly too great.

Redeployed, returned to the reserve center, he finished the remaining months on a final enlistment. Just like Mike, disillusioned with the military life, he walked away from the Corps. High and Tight, a landscaping business, was Bob's foray into the world of sole entrepreneur. Accompanied by Bella, his beautiful black Labrador, riding shotgun, her head hanging outside the truck window, the business flourished.

Bob, like Mike, is restless by nature, transient by heritage. Mowing lawns, mulching flowerbeds, it doesn't take long before the bloom is off. High and Tight is too pedestrian. Bob moves on. Without a plan, odd jobs rule his life. It's worse than any day pulling weeds.

Somewhere in the middle of it all, he married Charli, moved to California, flirted with some success as a standup comic, auditioned for a few bit parts on daytime soaps, didn't get the parts, *surprise*, divorced, *still friends*, and drifted through a few more jobs until Bella wasn't herself.

"Cancer, she doesn't have a lot of time," the vet said.

Together, they roamed the country. "Let's visit all fifty states, get to all the ones we can. You with me, girl?" Bella, oblivious to her own condition, happy riding shotgun, or sleeping on the ground next to Bob, lived out her remaining days safe by his side, or running ahead of him, warming the hearts of strangers they met along their journey, defied the odds for almost a year.

The journey is as much about Bob as it is about Bella. Memories, loitering through the years, take up too much space inside of him. In quiet moments beside Bella, he admits to himself what he's yet to say out loud. Losing Mike broke his spirit. Hurt and loneliness, uninvited guests, took hold of him the day Mike died. Asked to leave, they obey for a while, staying quiet, but always, always there.

Bob is forty now, but not when Mike's voice echoes inside his head. Then, then, he's the twenty-five-year-old younger brother locked in a time warp, listening to thirty-year-old Mike. Siblings by biology and circumstance, Bob and Mike were brothers by choice—inexplicable love. "Take care of things for me," Mike had written in the letter he'd left. If he'd had just a few more minutes, he would have added, "I'm okay, I'm okay, little brother."

ON HIS JOURNEY WITH BELLA, along the way, a stranger, a beautiful stranger, befriended Bob and Bella, *texts, many.* Bob and Kristen, the beautiful stranger, herself a dog lover, married. Kristen is the giver of life. Three-year-old Ivy Jeanne, beautiful, smart, tickles her new brother's feet. Micah giggles. There's an uncle that Ivy and Micah will never know.

Take care of things for me, Bob.

Mike and Melissa Doheny's drive-through wedding in Las Vegas.

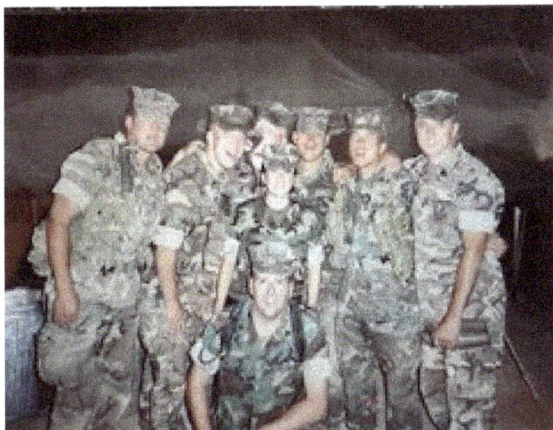

Melissa (center) was stationed at Twentynine Palms.

Mike with civilian contractor team; Billy Johnson, center. They took a team photo before every mission.

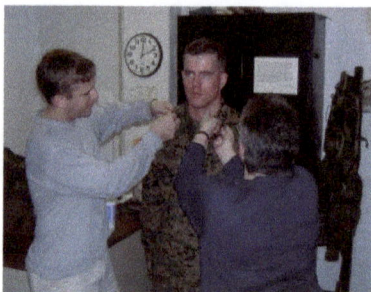

Mike and Mom pin sergeant chevrons on Bob's collar before his deployment to Iraq

Brothers, Bob Kugler and Mike Doheny

Mike with best friend Josh Schultz. They served together in the Marine Corps. Later, Josh would help Melissa spread Mike's ashes.

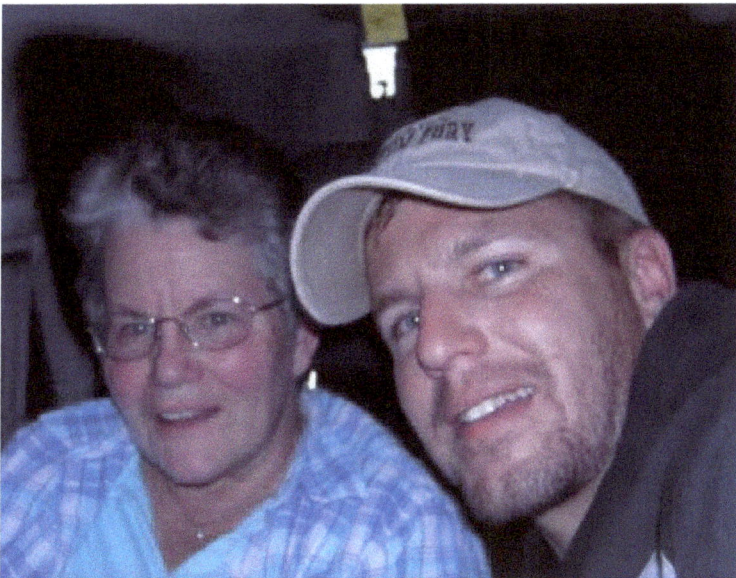

Mike Doheny with his mother, Kathy Kugler. Mike Doheny, April 18, 1977—Dec 9, 2007

BOOK THREE

PART ONE

BREAKING NEWS

AUGUST 26, 2021

In Kabul, Afghanistan, late summer heat seared the runways, tarmac, and taxiways of Hamid Karzai International Airport. Smoke rose from an explosion outside of the airport's Abbey Gate where thousands of people trying to flee a Taliban takeover waited. Eleven American Marines, an American soldier, and an American Navy corpsman lay dead. The two-decades-old war was ending. America was leaving.

Six days earlier the photo of a young woman Marine splashed across news outlets around the world. Sergeant Nicole Gee, part of the American evacuation team in country since mid-August, cradled a baby in her arms. The caption: "I Love My Job." Her job, the task that fell to a few of America's women Marines, members of the Female Engagement Teams (FETs), was to search Afghan women trying to flee their country. The FETs rescued children, some just infants, separated from their mothers— given up after the women, men too, hoped that their children would be saved by America. The FETs carried babies to safety, cared for them while security vetted the women desperate to pass through checkpoints and on to the airport, maybe their only chance to leave Afghanistan and start life over in another country.

In Lincoln, California, Misty Herrera Fuoco, Nicole's sister, caught news of the blast. Hundreds injured, almost one hundred killed. Thirteen American military among the dead. Friends, family texted, called, asked if she'd seen the news. *Is Nicole okay?*

Weeks earlier, Nicole had sent a text to Misty, "I've got orders to deploy to Afghanistan."

Misty, older than Nicole, balanced three-month-old baby Hayden on her knee and typed a reply, "Okay. Be safe. I love you."

"Thanks," Nicole typed, "there's a lot of us going. We've got numbers. We've been training for this. We're ready, so don't worry about everything you're seeing on the news. We're more organized than everyone thinks. I'll be okay."

The two sisters continued to send emails and texts almost every day. They connected on the night of August 25th, the day before the attack, traded messages about the picture of Nicole and the Afghan baby. Other stuff, too. Sister stuff. Small talk, if that's what you can label a text.

"I've had a bunch of people message me and ask about that pic. They want to know is that really your sister? That pic, it's literally everywhere across the globe," Misty wrote in her text.

"Aw dude, that pic is going down in history," Nicole messaged back.

They shared what looked like a scam request, soldiers got them all the time, one of many since Nicole's picture went viral. *People posing as evacuees, usually asking for money.*

"Hopefully nobody falls for the scam and does something dumb," Misty replied.

"Yeah, scammers are relentless."

"I know."

"PS. Your husband and his brother, Mikey, are flying into California tonight. Jarod has some extra leave. He's staying with Christy at the Thunder Valley Casino Hotel. I'll see them tomorrow."

That was it. That was the last time the two sisters connected.

THE NEXT MORNING, Misty was left to wonder if her sister was among the dead or wounded; so was the rest of the family, and Nicole's husband, Marine Sergeant Jarod Gee.

Misty called him.

"What do we do now?" Misty asked, her voice trembling, lip quivering.

"I know that if something's happened to Nicole, I'd probably already have been notified," Jarod said. "I'll come to the house; we just have to wait."

What-ifs and yeah-buts fill the hours. Everyone constantly checks the news. Misty is bombarded with texts from friends. Jarod shows up. His mother too. The text chain grows throughout the day. Questions. Everyone has questions. Everyone is guessing. Everyone wants to reassure the other that Nicole is okay.

She's just one of 2,000 marines and soldiers, navy, too.

Can't be her, we'd know by now if it was.

She's okay, it's Nicole, nothing ever happens to her. You'll see.

The day passed into early evening—night. No word. Misty has two children, one just three months old, needed to take care of them. Jarod said his goodbyes, returning to the hotel with his mother Christy, and brother. Everyone, friends, family, Jarod, Misty, wanted to believe that silence was good news, a hope-filled guessing game. *Optimism. Wishful thinking. Denial.* She must be okay. No word all day. That's got to mean she's okay. We'd know by now if she's hurt, worse, otherwise . . .

But there is an otherwise. *On leave, Jarod's on leave.* The

Marine Corps can't find him, at least not right away. Sometime in the pre-dawn hours of August 27th, the Marine Corps caught up with him.

A WEEK EARLIER, Misty and her husband Gabriel had closed on a new-to-them house. Determined to put their own stamp on the place, not wanting to move in until most of the work was done, they'd painted every room. A hectic, busy week made the house move-in ready. Now, with a long night ahead of her, Misty sat among dozens of unpacked boxes scattered around the freshly painted living room, in the halls and bedrooms. Three-month old Hayden slept, at least for now. His brother Lorenzo, almost three, already down for the night, slept nearby. Misty could hear the steady breaths of her sons, light whispers in the dark.

Exhausted, she closed her eyes, tried to sleep. No use, her eyelids fluttered, blinked open. She stared into the darkness, remembered the day, wanted to sleep, wished that she could. Anxious uncertainty filled her head. She tried, but couldn't force herself to trust the voices she'd heard all day. *We'd know already. She's just one of 2,000 soldiers, can't be her, she's okay, okay . . . okay.*

She clung to the words as her eyes finally closed, a dream-filled sleep.

"WHAT ARE YOU GOING TO BE?" Nicole asked, her ten-year-old eyes bright with curiosity.

"I don't know. Is it time to decide on a costume already?" Misty said.

"Time! It's only two weeks until Halloween, just two weeks. We've got to be ready!"

Remnants of old costumes, ghosts of Halloween past, the two sisters trick-or-treating together since Nicole turned five, hid in a closet. They rummaged through the pile, pulling out an outfit that resembled a blueberry, questionable to everyone but Nicole who'd worn the disguise a few years earlier. Pirates' garb and witches' toggery, more identifiable, but worn last Halloween, wouldn't do, at least not without exhausting other options.

Old store-bought masks, the plastic faces lined with cracks, didn't make the cut. A check-in with cousins, compare notes, swap out old costumes, usually produced enough items to piece together something new. Not this year. Nicole, relentless, determined to have her costume ready, mixed, matched, and married enough leftover pieces and cobbled together something resembling a ballerina or the finery of Oz's good witch. Misty, happy that Nicole hadn't decided on a flying monkey, settled on the old witch's ensemble. Halloween fell on a Friday. Extended curfew, later bedtimes. Fun!

Halloween day, early morning rain gave way to a late-day mix of sun and clouds. Weather wouldn't have mattered to Nicole; she'd have had a plan, some scheme that would have kept them dry, especially the loot bags. Twilight, the last soft glow from the sun dipping below the horizon, its message clear, time to hit the street, meet cousins, canvas the neighborhood, knock on doors, fill their bags. An hour later, shortly after dusk, the group having plundered the local neighbors' cache, Misty, Nicole and cousins piled into mom's car. Chauffeured to the outskirts of their own neighborhood, they continued the benign pilfer until mom signaled time to go.

Later, cousins back at their homes, a few sleeping over, Misty and Nicole emptied the night's haul onto the kitchen table. Dozens of candies, Butterfingers, bite size, Almond Joy, Twix, littered the table top. An apple, bruised, took up residence in the middle of Misty's pile.

"Don't mix yours with mine," Nicole said, casting a warning glance at Misty, who scooped her heap into a large bowl. Easy access.

Nicole began counting her stash, separating and sorting by brand and size. Satisfied, she gathered her stockpile, carting everything off to the bedroom she shared with Misty. There, on her dresser top, she reorganized *everything into precise rows, a mock military formation of Hershey's, Mr. Goodbars, Nestle's Crunch, Junior Mints, all to be strategically consumed over the next few weeks. Misty went through her yield by early Monday, certain that Nicole would share.*

The apple—trash.

The costumes folded, placed into plastic bags, were probably packed away in one of the boxes scattered about the new house.

———————

HAYDEN'S CRY pulled Misty awake. She changed him, fed him, rocked him, soothed him back to sleep, morning light still a few hours away. Misty closed her eyes, dozed off, dreamt of Nicole with the Afghan baby in her arms. Not surprised. Nicole loved children, especially the little ones. The few times she'd been home, she'd held Lorenzo, couldn't stop holding him, couldn't put him down. And oh—her mock protest when Misty told her she was going to have another nephew. "My due date is April 30th," Misty had said. "Wouldn't it be something if Hayden's born on May 1st, your birthday?"

"No way!" Nicole had said. "That's my birthday. He can have any other day, but not that one, that one is mine."

"Oh, I thought you'd like it, if you two shared birthdays."

"Nope, that's my day. You just make sure you keep him in there until after my birthday."

"Ha, like he's going to listen."

"You better keep him in there."

"Okay, I'll try until after your birthday."

———————

A KNOCK ROUSED MISTY. She lay Hayden in his cradle, opened the door. The world was about to throw all its cruelty at her. Jarod, his face swollen, his eyes red, stood in front of her. *Denial. One last thought, maybe he's been up all night at the casino. That could be why he looks so bad—could be . . . let it be . . .*

Misty's right—almost. Jarod has been up most of the night, but not at the slots or blackjack tables. Sometime in the first few hours after midnight, the Marine Corps caught up with him. *Nicole is one of the thirteen.* Jarod started to speak, choked back a sob, bowed his head, nodding side to side. Misty's gaze dropped to Jarod's hands. His fingers tangled together. The skin of his knuckles stretched thin. She panned to Jarod's chest, up to his face. He raised his chin. Misty saw the pain in his eyes. He waited, knew that Misty understood what he's about to tell her. *So hard.* He cleared his throat, began to speak again.

"Nicole was killed," he said, his voice bloated with grief.

The small pieces of hope Misty had clung to disappeared on the downbeat of each word. She tried to speak, to answer Jarod, but her voice failed, her throat too constricted.

"No," she finally managed, refusing to give in, to believe it. "I don't believe it. She can't be, not Nicole."

Jarod wrapped his arms around Misty, held her. More family gathered, less than a handful for now. They sat, circled on the floor of the new house, furniture not yet fully arranged. They embraced, cried, tried to buffer one another from the pain. Told each other stories about Nicole. Lorenzo crawled onto Misty's lap, pressing himself against her. Her tears fell uncontrollably. Lorenzo looked up into her face.

"Don't cry, mommy," he said, reaching up with his tiny fingers, wiping tears from Misty's cheek. "It's okay, mommy, don't be sad, don't cry."

"I know honey. I'll try, it's just hard. Mommy is in a sad place right now," Misty said. Lorenzo, not yet three, wiped more tears from his mother's face.

PART TWO

KELSEE AND NICOLE

AUGUST 25, 2021

At the Entry Control Point (ECP), the day was fading. Blistering heat, stubborn, begrudgingly surrendered to an early evening breeze. A night rhythm had begun. The crowd surrounding Hamid Karzai International Airport grew increasingly unsettled. They'd arrived with nothing, each accumulated life left behind in the haste to escape. Facing another long night, they sought what little comfort they could find. Instead they joined a frantic mass of humanity hoping for a miracle—escape. The breeze, warm, offered no relief. Fires, flashlights, lamps, floodlights, glared at the sky—light still ample. Thousands of voices filled the night.

Half of Afghanistan, at least it looked that way, had gathered outside the airport since the Taliban began its takeover of the county, soon after the American withdrawal had begun. As the number grew, swelling to thousands, refugees caught in a roiling sea of bodies crowded each other, the forced intimacy more than many could endure.

Kelsee wondered if the chaos of the day would somehow quiet with the onset of nightfall. Her answer—not even a brief interlude. Night brought the same nightmare of the day—worse. The melee surrounding the airport had grown more desperate with each passing hour. Kelsee, Nicole, and Molly, three friends assigned to FETs, were tired. They'd shuffled to and from the front, the area near the gates, several times throughout the day. Twice, maybe more, they'd joined the evacuation teams at several of the lesser-known gates. Their orders—stay at the ECP, stay behind the fencing—ignored. They'd worked their own details, should have been relieved, but they were asked to help another team—short-handed. Ten busloads of refugees, appearing out of nowhere, needed searching. Their day had been a continuous loop, bouncing from one team to another with little or no downtime.

Near East or North Gate, hard to know in all the confusion, Kelsee closed her eyes, inhaled, released a long sigh of exhaustion, sought a moment to collect herself. She heard shouts from women trying to get into the airport. Her eyes blinked open. She looked at the crowd in front of her.

The scene had been the same for days—women with children, desperate to escape, trying to find a way through any of the gates that would lead them into the protection of the Americans. But there are consolations that even a mother's love is powerless to give. No matter how desperate the women were, Kelsee, even with the knowledge of what might happen, had to turn them away—a hard order to follow.

Kelsee looked up, stars above her head. The FET she was part of, Nicole too, worked throughout the night—past dawn. Sunlight flecked the sky, chased away the last night cloud, and still they continued to search the women lined up in front of them.

———

TWO YEARS EARLIER, almost to the day, Kelsee had stood in the dark. The South Carolina August night, still hot and humid, left her sweating. Dozens of men and women, few, if any, older than twenty, piled out of a bus, circled in a crowd, waiting, wondering what would come next. They didn't wait long. Shouts from three Marine Corps drill instructors pierced the night. "Get your feet onto those yellow foot prints, shut your pie holes, look straight ahead, and stand at attention."

With just enough light to reveal yellow foot prints painted

onto the asphalt, Kelsee and the mix of men and women hurried to comply. In minutes the men were rushed off to the shearing room, heads shaved faster than a speeding bullet. The women recruits, sixty of them, now members of Platoon 4042, 4th Recruit Battalion, Oscar Company, had become part of an almost 250-year-old tradition, the first few seconds of Marine Corps boot camp, victims to the exploding shouts of Marine Corps drill instructors. Mock mayhem, orders barked out in staccato bursts, created a forced chaos that made the women comply without hesitation.

KELSEE HAD MADE the decision to join the Marine Corps just a month after her seventeenth birthday, soon after the beginning of her senior year of high school. Her dad served in the Marine Corps, had been reactivated for the first Gulf War, Desert Storm. By the time the Marine Corps processed his re-entry, the war was already winding down. He didn't deploy. *Lucky.*

When Kelsee told her parents she wanted to enlist, she gave them the few reasons that made sense: *she'd been curious about careers in the FBI, maybe even the CIA, she knew military experience and a college degree would help.*

"I can accomplish both in the Marine Corps," she told her parents. "It will give me a leg up once I'm ready to try to get into one of those agencies—after I finish my enlistment. And, I can go to college while I'm in the Corps."

Still, her parents had reservations. She could find herself in harm's way. *Iraq. Afghanistan. Syria.* A good chance she'd find herself deployed.

"Maybe Marine Corps Reserve," she offered, surprised when the suggestion seemed to anger her father.

"If you're going to join the Marine Corps," he said, "then

be a Marine, go active duty, none of this Reserve nonsense. Go active or don't go at all."

Kelsee celebrated her eighteenth birthday at Parris Island. In November, her mother and father, other family too, her brother Gage and younger sister Kaci, all proud, drove the ten hours from Indiana to Parris Island. Marine Private First Class, Kelsee Lainhart, marched across the parade ground, eyes right as Platoon 4042 passed in front of the reviewing stand and her family.

Wanting a military occupation that would train her for a future outside the Corps, Kelsee had signed her enlistment contract with the agreement that she'd become a PMOS 0231, a Marine Corps Intelligence Specialist. Six months after boot camp and intelligence school, Kelsee found herself attached to the Second Marine Division, 2nd Reconnaissance Battalion, Alpha Co., at Camp Lejeune.

By summer 2020, the 2nd began training for deployment. Kelsee, already a lance corporal, was growing into her job, a military role more challenging than she'd initially expected. She worked hard, learning her trade, but not without a few struggles along the way. The understanding that lives depended upon good intel was not lost on her. She learned how to gather information—terrain assessments, area demographics, language, customs, culture, the likelihood of hostile activity or risk, weather—all the intelligence Marine Expeditionary Units (MEUs) need, if and when they might be called on to respond to a situation with boots on the ground—anywhere in the world and at a minute's notice.

By February of 2021, Alpha Co., after months of training, was ready to deploy. Kelsee too. She'd taken a circuitous route, joining the deployment group when another Marine dropped out. Kelsee and another lance corporal, both with the right rank and skill set, were singled out for a potential replacement. Kelsee. the more vocal of the two, the more decisive, quickly sounded off.

"I don't want to pass up the opportunity to deploy," she said, loud and clear.

The other Marine, not as gung-ho, hemmed a bit, making the decision easy. Kelsee secured the orders, joined the Marines already training for deployment. In March she boarded the USS *Iwo Jima*. On board, settled into quarters, she relaxed. She wore a 2nd Recon hoodie.

"Hey," Sergeant Nicole Gee said, surprise all over her face, "Is your boyfriend Recon?"

"Huh? Oh, the sweatshirt, yeah—I mean, no. No boyfriend and I'm not Recon. Just attached, wearing the hoodie."

"Oh, my husband's 2nd Recon," Nicole said. "I'm Sergeant Gee—Nicole."

"Wait, what. Gee? I must know your husband, Sergeant Jarod Gee. He was barracks manager at 2nd Recon, Lejeune."

"Yep, that's him."

The two young women struck up a conversation, becoming friends. Nicole knew all the Recon Marines because of Jarod. Kelsee, attached to the 2nd, knows them all too. Another Marine, Molly Lewis, settled in with Nicole and Kelsee. All three women, each from different units, now deployed on the *Iwo Jima*, developed a friendship. They're part of the Marine Expeditionary Unit. The bond between them strengthened while all three served together on ship. They regularly played cards, *Egyptian Rat Screw*, against the men, usually besting them.

———

By SUMMER, the fellowship briefly splintered. Kelsie, first to leave, landed in Kuwait, the paradigmatic jump-off point into

Iraq and Afghanistan for American military. Nicole and Molly passed through Kuwait, missed Kelsee, and made their way to Afghanistan by mid-August. Kelsee joined them just a few days later. Nicole and Molly had trained up for FET, Female Evacuation Teams.

INSIDE THE AMERICAN military compound on Hamid Karzai International Airport, Kelsee's integration into the intel unit stalled. A few days of do nothing, keep-busy assignments, all she was tasked with, left her restless. More than willing to escape the tedium of do-nothing, bullshit light duty assignments, radio watch, guard duty, admin, wanting to feel useful, she wondered about joining a FET. She had balked when asked, then quickly pivoted.

"I don't have the training, sir," Kelsee replied, looking at the officer who'd approached her with the offer to join. "Don't you have to have special training, sir?"

"There's no time for that. OJT, Marine. You'll learn on the fly. You in, Marine?"

"Yes sir. It'll be a better use of my time, working on a FET team."

"Damn right, it will! That's the spirit, Marine."

Kelsee joined the same team that Nicole had become part of. Molly, part of another FET, still spent down time with her two friends. Kelsee began working FET shifts at ECPs with Nicole and other young women, all of them experiencing life beyond their years. Thrown into the mix, Kelsee did indeed learn on the fly. *Good instincts.* Nicole and the other FET team members, specifically trained in FET tactics, were easy to model. Kelsee's days filled, she searched women, those allowed as far as the ECPs. The FET, normally limited to the ECP areas, sometimes worked outside the wire. Helping at airport gates exposed the FET to risks they'd supposedly been prohibited from taking. But, when unit strength dwindled at the gates, or Afghan women needed to be searched, command looked the other way. *Situational bending of the rules—orders.*

At the gates, the task for the FETs sometimes required a physical search or coaxing women away, *women without any documentation.* When women, any refugee, made it as far as the ECP, Kelsee, Nicole, and other team members searched the women and children. A complete search, rifling through heavy, long flowing gowns, head scarfs, the worst, a woman wearing a burka, took time and patience—*and—something more.*

Searching, patting down, running a hand over clothing required an intimacy that brought the women Marines face to face with the refugee women. Kelsee discovered that without privacy, the women simply urinated in their clothing—*worse!* Whatever they wore, burka, long gowns, all their clothing, stiff with sweat, urine, and feces, smelled worse than anything Kelsee could have imagined. The stench made her gag, filling her mouth with a taste so violently bitter that she fought to keep down what little food she managed to eat. Her eyes, irritated as if she were caught inside a smoke-filled building, watered uncontrollably.

Women arrived at the ECPs carrying unconscious children. The women, barely conscious themselves, collapsed when they reached the ECPs. No one knew how many days they'd have gone without food or water. Not long after Kelsee joined the FET, during one of her shifts at an ECP, a woman carrying a young child, a toddler, staggered toward her. The woman's legs buckled, she collapsed into a seated position, unconscious, the toddler still in her arms.

"Oh my God," Kelsee said, turning to the Marine closest to her, "I think she's dead."

"Try to revive her!"

Kelsee yelled directly into the woman's ear. Nothing. She shook her. Still nothing. She took the child, sat her next to her mother. Kelsee performed a sternal rub, a painful stimulus, a last resort technique, hoping to revive the woman while the child screamed.

"Corpsman!" Kelsee yelled, hoping a corpsman would respond. He did. He began a more vigorous sternum rub, screamed into the unconscious woman's ear, fought to revive her. Kelsee stood aside. The corpsman refused to give up, continued massaging and yelling. The child, eyes wide, frightened, inconsolable, reached for her mother. Kelsee tried to calm her.

The corpsman succeeded in reviving the woman.

Consoling children became a routine task for the women Marines on all the FETs. FET members, their male counterparts too, would take a child, usually a four- or five-year-old, and try to comfort as best they could. Kelsee and Nicole, other Marines too, gave food and water to the refugees, especially the children. Everyone recognized that the older children understood the pain their mothers were in. Everyone could see the sadness, the fear, in the children's eyes.

In English, American English, Kelsee would talk to the children.

"Your mother will be okay," she'd whisper, offering water, maybe the first drink a child may have had in days. She shared snacks from some of her MREs, offered gum and treats to many of the children. Careful to control her own emotions, Kelsee kept her voice soft, deliberate. Words, unintelligible to the child, didn't matter. Kindness is the same in any language.

Sometimes, if Kelsee was lucky, a child spoke English.

———

DAYS PASSED QUICKLY for those trying to escape. With the complete withdrawal nearing, the panicked crowd surged around the airport, threatening to wash over the guarded perimeter. Gates closed, at least the larger ones like the North and East Gates. A few smaller gates may have had some access. The crowd, men, women, and children, resorted to wading through a sewage canal moating the airport. They lowered themselves into the cesspool. Waist deep, they waded through the viscous slurry, holding infants above their heads. Older children clung to their mothers' and fathers' backs. For almost ten days the turmoil, a twenty-four-seven continuous loop since the FETs arrived, was like a bad dream the FET team members couldn't wake from.

AUGUST 26, 2021

Like the lyrics of Willie Nelson's *September Song*, the days had dwindled down to a precious few. East and North gates closed for good. Speculation surrounded the shut-downs. The Taliban, originally cooperative, had suddenly turned threatening, maybe that was the reason, or maybe the Marines were stretched beyond capacity; maybe it didn't matter why. Abbey gate remained open, becoming the single main point of entry. Terror replaced panic. The crowd, increasingly unmanageable, crossed the sewage canal in earnest, scrambling up an embankment that led to a three-foot-high retaining wall. Marines on the other side, their backs to the fencing just a few yards behind them, there to prevent a breach, turned people away—physically. The mass gathering, the confusion, Marines preoccupied with the crowd—*a suicide bomber's dream come true.*

Early that morning, Kelsee and Nicole, after working non-stop over the past twenty-four hours, slipped off their gear, wolfed down tasteless MREs, then collapsed onto their bunks. They fell asleep immediately, the oblivion of the exhausted soldier shutting out thoughts of the past twenty-four hours, the past ten days. Just a few hours later they geared up, donned full battle rattle, and reported for duty.

At an ECP, they relieved another FET, the team Molly was

attached to. Molly's team leader met them, told the women they'd most likely be asked to head out to Abbey Gate.

"I pretty much expected that," Nicole said.

"You guys do not go," she said. "Understand? When you're asked, say no. Don't go. It's not your job, stay at the ECP. Your job is to search women and children here at the ECP, inside the wire, not to turn women away at the gate. You search the ones that make it this far. I'm telling you, don't go!"

Kelsee, intelligence specialist, trained to gather information, sees the future. It's not a question of if, just when, they'll be attacked. They're targets—easy targets. Kelsee knows heading to Abbey gate is not a good idea. She understands the threat better than any of the FET team members. Before landing in Afghanistan, she'd been tasked with research. She'd learned through that research that the threat of an IED or suicide bomber had a real high, *potentially imminent*, probability. She voiced her support for staying at the ECP.

"It's the 26th already. We are supposed to be out soon. Just a few more days. Intel suggests the likelihood of attack will increase as the days draw down," Kelsee said. The other women, less knowledgeable, perhaps a bit too "Gung Ho," wanted to be as close to the action, the so-called front, as they could get. *I don't like it. I don't like this at all, someone is going to get hurt.*

But Marines at Abbey, short-handed and inundated with Afghan women refugees, kept hoping for a FET to join them. With just men at the gate, roughing a woman back down from the wall, *they could, and sometimes did*, was bad optics.

I don't like any of this. I've spent months training with these guys before we got here, men and women too. They're more than just Marines I serve with, they're friends. I don't want to see any of them get hurt— goddammit, this is not smart.

When a call comes from the gate, specific now, "Can a FET team be sent to the gate?" an officer at the ECP looks to see if there is a team available and if they'll go. They don't have to. Nicole, a chine of optimism against the bedlam, the insanity, always optimistic, always willing, let the officer know she'd respond.

"With permission, I'll go sir," she said.

He signed off.

With the officer's blessing, Nicole turned to Kelsee, "I'm going. You want to head out with me?" she asked.

Ignoring her own skepticism, too conditioned by training to refuse, drawn into her own catastrophe, the *no* in her throat became a *yes* that escaped her lips. "Sure, I'll go," Kelsee said.

The two of them left the ECP and hurried to Abbey Gate. A FET was usually comprised of at least eight, but only Nicole and Kelsee moved out.

At the gate, the job quickly escalated. Afghan men sloshed through the sewage canal and scrambled up the short incline to the retaining wall. They waved papers, but they were not vetted or approved to move to the ECP. They were met with stiff, no bullshit, get your ass back down orders from the male Marines. If they didn't quickly comply, they were met with force, physically collared and turned away.

Nicole and Kelsee wait at the wall. Women splash through the canal. Fear emboldens them. They climb out, reaching the wall, too many for the Marines to turn away without force. But American men aren't supposed to touch the Afghan women, *can't have that image splashed across news feeds around the world.*

There's no place for the men or women to go, other than back across the sewage canal. They're incredulous. The look of disbelief twists their faces into crying theater masks. Tragedy captures center stage. They'd braved the traverse, certain it was a one-time thing. *How could anyone force them to return through the hell they'd just waded through? Forced away, the tomorrow they'd hoped for disappeared.*

"Sister! Sister!" women shouted at Kelsee and Nicole, their voices shrill.

"Help me. Help me. I have papers. Take my daughter. Take my son. Please!"

They smiled at her.

They pleaded with her.

They shouted at her.

They tried to force their way past her.

Thwarted, the Afghan women waited on the other side of the moat. They'll try again, but for now Nicole and Kelsee are ordered back to the ECP. An hour later, this time there's no pretense, they're back at Abbey Gate. The Afghan women, regrouped, have surged across the canal. They shout, cry, beg, threaten, offer money. Nicole and Kelsee deal with the onrush again and again, stand down, return to the ECP once women have been turned away. But the women keep coming. The call and response, several encores, matinee performances, moved toward early evening. Nicole and Kelsee were back on stage.

The Marines at the wall, men, hectored by the crowd, grew heated. Tempers flared. Marines began to match the crowd's unruly escalation. Nicole and Kelsee, at the wall, positioned themselves close to one another, hoping to blunt the flow of women and children. Kelsee encounters a woman with two children, boys, one a toddler, the other a preschooler. The woman's clothes drip with sewage. She's climbed to the wall, won't listen when Kelsee orders her back down. She shouts. Unintelligible. Kelsee tries again, reasoning with hand gestures, quieting her own voice. The woman is immovable. The preschooler climbs onto the wall.

"Get her and those kids back down!" shouts a Marine, losing his temper, waving his rifle. "I don't give a flying fuck if she's a woman. You make her go back down or I'll throw her into that fucking cesspool myself!"

"No, you won't. You're not fucking throwing anyone back down that embankment," Nicole and Kelsee shouted back.

Standoff.

Nicole and Kelsee argue with the Marine. "I've got it,"

Kelsee shouts back at him. Nicole nods in support. The Marine backs off. Kelsee does indeed have it. She manages to move the woman back down to the edge of the canal. The woman starts across, turns, standing in the human waste. She has the toddler with her. She points to the wall. The older boy squats on top of the wall, fingers digging into the cement, clinging, clawing, fighting Kelsee as she tries to free him and reunite him with his mother.

Kelsee is stretched out on top of the wall, prone, her rifle slung over her back, one leg stretching to touch the ground on the safe side of the wall, the other bent-kneed against the concrete. She reaches for the boy. *A balancing act.* He fights. Struggles. Does everything to keep himself leeched to the wall. Kelsee readjusted—repositioned herself, tried to get better leverage, got her hands on the boy. Nicole, just a few feet away, preoccupied with another woman.

A sea of people. Thick. Loud. Teeming. One man's hatred ripples through the crowd, he's intent on killing

There was no moment when understanding turned to fear. The blast was too quick. There was no time to break loose and save herself; Kelsee wouldn't have even if she could have. There was the boy. The illusion of safety, the wall that she should have been behind—how would she get the child—her Kevlar, body armor, it was all just that, an illusion. Nothing protects a human standing in the way of a supersonic blast driving thousands of steel ball bearings toward anything in its path.

The world turned upside down in a millisecond. Smoke, dust, falling chunks of earth and concrete are everywhere. Kelsee, deafened by the blast, could see her hands, hands that a second earlier held onto a little boy, hands that are bloody, littered with torn chunks of flesh—hers—the boy's?

She's a rag doll littering the wall. Tattered and torn. Shrapnel has blown a hole in her arm. The blast that smashed into her lungs forced a grunt through her blistered lips, a sound she knew came from her, but so foreign she does not recognize her own groan of pain. Ball bearings riddle her body. One darts through her flesh, finds a path, the narrowest of lines, nicking her spine. T-1 and T-2. One more lodged in her skull, taking up permanent residence. Blast force stuns her entire body, her spine protects itself, shuts down travel.

"Jesus, I'm floating. I'm weightless."

She can see Nicole. She lies just a few feet away. On her back. There's a thin line across Nicole's forehead, a split in her flesh, the wet of blood rising before the true wound would reveal itself. "Oh, that doesn't look too bad. She's probably knocked out—yeah, she just looks unconscious."

BODIES ARE PILED UP EVERYWHERE.

Kelsee made eye contact with another Marine. "Help me!" she shouted, waiting, hoping. The Marine heard her. He rushed to her, pulled her off the wall. Paralyzed, unable to grab hold of him, she fell. She couldn't feel where her body began—ended. Unable to lift her head, and look for herself, she yelled at the Marine.

"Are my legs there?"

"Yes!"

"Don't fucking lie to me. I can't feel my legs. Goddamn you, don't fucking lie to me. Don't you dare!"

"Your legs are there. I'm telling you the truth. Your legs are there."

"Okay," Kelsee said, relieved, believing.

"Your legs are there. I wouldn't lie about that," he said again, pulling off her rifle and dragging her away from the wall. Marine Sergeant Wyatt Wilson rushed to help. Seriously injured, his own body ripped open by the blast, Wilson slid an arm under Kelsee's knees. He grabbed her flak with his other hand, helped carry her until he collapsed. Later, in the CSH, he'd fight for his own life; doctors manually massaged his heart until it beat again.

Without help, the lone Marine carrying Kelsee dropped

her. Others rushed to help. Kelsee tried to look for Nicole again, believed she was okay. She couldn't raise her head. She'd never see Nicole again. The Marines pulled her through a hole in the fencing, pulled off most of her gear. A shout. *She'll bleed out!* Someone wrapped a tourniquet around her arm. She's lifted into a medevac truck.

"Go with her," someone who looked, sounded, like he was in charge said. "Go with her and stay with her until she gets to the hospital."

A familiar face, a friend, Chris, appeared out of nowhere, next to her, looking for more injuries. Kelsee, barely able to move her head, could see other uniformed Marines, their lifeless bodies stacked near her.

They're dead, gotta be. They're not moving. No one is helping them. Look away, look away.

Chris, by her side, fighting to keep his balance, *the driver speeding, the truck swaying,* stayed with her. Kelsee was bleeding from multiple wounds; steel bearings, shrapnel, dirt, pebbles mottle the entire right side of her body. A ball bearing lodged itself in her skull, would remain there, *removal risky, probably do more harm than good.*

Before she's carried into the CSH, Chris breathed a sigh of relief. He disappears, ordered to go back and help others. "Don't worry," Kelsee said, anesthetized by shock, not feeling much pain yet—unable to see the full extent of her own injuries. "I'm fine, really."

Chris knows the truth; it's right in front of him. Kelsee is bleeding from dozens of wounds.

Doctors and medics are overwhelmed, never expecting a mass casualty event. Shouts from doctors, cries of the wounded, rants from Marines bringing in the wounded, a madhouse clamor, echoed inside the CSH. Marine Staff Sergeant Joe Bennaugh, team leader from another evacuation team, a friend, knelt next to Kelsee, still strapped to the evacuation stretcher.

"This is so fucked," he mumbled, choking back sobs. *"It's so fucked, so fucked, so—"*

"Did Nicole make it?" Kelsee asked, interrupting him, her own image of Nicole, seemingly unconscious, still stuck in her mind. *She must be here somewhere too, getting looked at. The cut on her forehead didn't look bad, she's got to be here.*

"No," Bennaugh said, quickly changing his reply. "I don't know. I don't know," he repeated, his answer satisfying Kelsee, at least for the moment.

Shock began to retreat; its replacement—pain—eager to take over, took hold of Kelsee. The tourniquet, its tight clamp closing off blood flow, sent numbing pain through her arm, a pins and needles fire racing down to her fingertips that felt as if it was devouring her.

"Get it off!" Kelsee shouted. "Take it off. *Please!*"

Medics obliged. Relief flooded down her arm. Blood did too. Quick to act, *anticipating*, the medics packed her wound, staunched the bleeding. On three, they moved her off the stretcher and onto a gurney. Wheeled into a room functioning as an ICU, doctors pushed an intravenous needle into a vein. *Pain meds and fluids—relief.*

Team members, Marines that Kelsee knew, drifted in and out of the CSH, checking on her. Kelsee could hear the commotion in other parts of the CSH. Med teams triaged the flow of wounded. Kelsee asked about Nicole. Some of the Marines simply looked away, did not answer, others offered their "I don't knows." Kelsee still believed that Nicole was okay.

Doctors continued to stabilize her. Her wounds were serious, life threatening. *Spinal shock, heart rate fluctuating, blood pressure dropping, vitals rampaging. Doctors fighting to stabilize her.* She's quickly scheduled for evacuation to Landstuhl Regional Medical Center, the United States' military hospital in Europe.

Sergeant Lewis, *Molly*, member of the *Egyptian Rat Screw*

all-female card playing triad, friend to Kelsee and Nicole, escorted Kelsee to Germany, then back to the States. She contacted Kelsee's parents, assured them, *she's going to be okay, really*, that Kelsee was stable.

Days after the attack, in the ICU at Walter Reed, Bethesda, Kelsee woke from a medically induced coma. Surgery on her arm, *while she'd been asleep*, had gone well. Shrapnel, as much as could be, was removed. Conscious now, the stamina of youth on her side, alert, questioning everyone about her own injuries and still wondering about Nicole. Whenever she asked, the answer is the same *I don't know* she's been hearing since the attack.

Checking Instagram on a gifted iPad, angry at the world, *no one will tell me anything, what's the big secret—goddammit, somebody tell me what happened to Nicole! Just like her to be fine and I'm the one in a hospital bed—anyone is going to step in it—get away clean, it's gotta be Nicole. How the hell can she be fine and I'm the one so messed up? Dammit this pisses me off. We were only a few feet apart—what the hell are all these messages? What's going on!*

Kelsee taps and scrolls—cryptic messages, Hayden's variations on a theme. But everyone seems to dance around the issue. Messages that say I'm sorry, still leave Kelsee wondering. Was Nicole wounded too? Is she, maybe, here at Walter Reed? Or is she dead? *What is everyone sorry about? What? What's happened to Nicole? What? What!*

Kelsee's mother, back in the room, watches her daughter's one good hand flit across the iPad screen. Messages blink like a flashing strobe. Kelsee scrolls, reads, each message more confusing than the last. Her face florid, anguish beginning to rise, Kelsee is frantic to find one definitive message, one that will finally answer the question that has eaten away at her since she last saw Nicole—*is my friend dead, was she killed?*

"What are you doing?" Kelsee's mother asks, looking at her daughter—visibly upset.

Kelsee, intent on the messages, looking for the truth, doesn't answer.

"Kelsee, answer me, what are you doing?" her mom asks again.

"Will you leave me alone!" Kelsee shouts back at her. "I'm trying to see if my fucking friend is dead or not."

Images of Nicole fill the screen of the iPad. Pictures of Nicole holding a baby. Headlines, "Among the Thirteen American Military Personnel Killed, Sergeant Nicole Gee."

Kelsee watched Marines unload Nicole's casket from an airplane at Dover. She watched on social media. And just like that, Kelsee learned, confirmed for herself, what everyone had known for days. Nicole is dead.

Resentment turned to guilt. Tears flowed. *I thought you were okay, Nicole. I'm sorry for even thinking, for thinking that you were . . . for being mad that I'm the one so fucked up, thinking you skated, that you were fine and I'm not. I'm sorry. I'm alive and you're dead, and I was mad. I'm sorry.*

Kelsee has outlived a friend, a sister in arms. Questions. What is survival supposed to feel like? Relief? Shame? Regret? Mercy? Is a soldier supposed to feel shame because she outlived another's sacrifice? The answer—almost certainly not. Living is a selfish instinct. Death doesn't select, pick, or choose. On the battlefield, death is random, indiscriminate. There's no "you're next in queue," no reason why some live when others die. What's left for the millions of battlefield survivors, Kelsee too, is the complex tangle of survivor's guilt.

In the days that follow, Kelsee, still at Walter Reed, Bethesda, recovers. Youth and physical conditioning are on her side, her strength and vigor quickly return. Some of the steel ball bearings will remain forever lodged in her body. Nerves in her spine, pathways to her legs, shut down by the blast trauma, a natural response to protect the spine—to protect life, remain closed. Kelsee cannot use her legs.

Jarod, Nicole's husband, steps away from his own grieving, and takes time to visit with Kelsee while she's still recovering at Walter Reed. They talk about Nicole. Jarod is wearing an honor bracelet for his wife.

"Do you have one, did you get one yet?" he asked.

"No, I didn't. I wish . . ."

Jarod removed the Bracelet of Honor, silver and black, engraved,

NICOLE LEANN GEE

19980501-20210826

TIL VALHALLA

HE MOTIONED to Kelsee to hold out her arm, then slipped the bracelet into her hand.

By the end of September, Nicole, home at last, ready for her final duty station, Arlington National Cemetery, was laid to rest. Kelsee is anxious to be there, but plans change. A coveted bed opens, *take it or lose it, don't know when there will be another*, at Shirley Ryan Ability Lab, a place that will give Kelsee a fighting chance to regain the use of her legs. There's no chance to say goodbye to Nicole.

NICOLE'S BATTLE ended at Abbey Gate. Kelsee's had just begun. Most of the ball bearings that riddled her body that day and nicked her spine have been removed. Some remain. One is lodged in her skull. Pummeled by a supersonic blast, a force that should have crushed her lungs, *it didn't*, bludgeoned her body so savagely that nerves and tissue along her spine still refuse to reopen pathways to her legs. Rehab and physical therapy five days a week at the Shirley Ryan Ability Lab, formerly the Rehabilitation Institute of Chicago, doesn't promise that Kelsee will walk again, but it's the best hope that if there is a chance, they'll make it happen.

In between the physical therapy workouts, there's a first semester of college wrapping up. Kelsee and Oli, her service dog, travel home to Indiana on weekends, the trip five hours one way with a pit stop. By Sunday night they're back at Ryan. Monday morning, when her eyes flutter open, there's a hope-filled wish for just one more miracle.

PART THREE

THE MORNING AFTER

AUGUST 27

Mid-morning found Misty, still trying to wrap her head around the news of Nicole's death, with plenty to do. Calls. Who needs to know first? Everyone will have questions. Misty doesn't know much, neither does Jarod, just that Nicole has been killed. She called her dad before anyone else. She thought, *Thank God mom is not alive, this would crush her.*

Mom and dad, funny how they were good at being friends, just not good at being married. Misty knew, even at twelve, Nicole did too, that a divorce was coming.

She called her dad.

"Hey Honey," Misty's father, said, recognizing Misty's cell phone number.

"Daddy, sit down, I have something to tell you," Misty said, her voice almost pleading.

"Baby, I'm busy, I'm working." he said, his focus on the controlled chaos of the job site he managed.

"Daddy, Nicole was killed."

"What? I don't understand. Look, I gotta go, I have a full crew here," he said, and ended the call before Misty could be certain he understood.

Before she had time to call him back, make certain he understood what it was that she had told him, her cell phone sounded off. "Daddy?"

"Yes, baby, it's me. I can talk now. I don't understand. Tell me what's going on, what's happened to Nicole?"

"She was killed, daddy," Misty said, forced to say the words out loud for a second time. "Nicole was killed, daddy, yesterday in Afghanistan."

"Where are you?"

"Home, at the new house."

"I'm on my way."

Misty touch-screened her brother's contact, waited, got his voice mail. She called her husband. He left work, hurried home. Misty's aunt called her.

"My daughter called," she said. "Is it true, has Nicole been killed?"

"Yes," Misty said. "I was about to call you."

"I don't want to hear this. I can't handle this kind of news. Stop talking. I can't do this. I don't want to hear it," she said and hung up, her tone a little frosty.

The aunt's unexpected reaction unnerved Misty. *I can't do this. I can't do this, who can!*

Annoyed, Misty pushed her cellphone away. *I'm done making these calls. This is crazy, too much for everyone to deal with, too many emotions . . . I'm done being the bearer of bad news, done breaking everyone's heart. I'm done.*

Grandmother stepped in. "I'll do this, Misty," she said, taking over, calling the rest of the family.

PART FOUR
NICOLE AND JAROD

LATE DAY, AUGUST 27, 2021

Jarod stayed with Misty for most of the day, returning to the hotel just after nightfall, physically and emotionally spent. Silence filled his room. The news that he'd craved, the news that he been forced to wait for, had been delivered. In the quiet, a tightness gripped his chest. Tears blurred his already bloodshot eyes. The life he and Nicole had planned after the Marine Corps, a new house, a place they'd turn into a home, a sense of permanence after nomadic military careers, children, they both wanted children, that life now impossible, that life shattered. They'd met in high school, hometown kids. Nicole's first kiss. The teenage infatuation fizzled, reigniting a few years later, after high school was behind them.

AUGUST 2016

For Jarod, marrying Nicole wasn't a question of if, just when. Nicole felt the same. She waited, a lover's limbo. Sooner or later, Jarod would ask.

Maybe it was Memphis. Maybe it was southern summer nights.

Maybe it was you. Maybe it was me. Or maybe it was the morning Nicole tied his wrists together and pushed him into a swimming pool. *Nothing says love like your girlfriend pushing you into the deep end with your hands bound together. Wait, what? Hold on, there's an explanation.* Jarod, ready to enlist in the Marine Corps, wanted a coveted billet in Marine Recon, but Jarod didn't know how to swim, a ticket to admission into Recon. Nicole, already a strong swimmer, working out almost daily at the Northern California Swimstitute, was eager to oblige. She taught Jarod the basics, ran him through some of the same things the Marine Corps would require, and when she thought he was ready, she tied him up and pushed him into the pool.

Whatever it was, Jarod, with a clock ticking, *he'd already enlisted in the Marine Corps*, decided to propose. With Misty as his accomplice, he went, where else but to Jared's. Misty had window shopped with Nicole. She easily steered Jarod toward Nicole's picks.

The rest of the plan, steal Nicole away to Jarod's family's vacation retreat in Oregon, a private oceanside getaway where he'd propose. Everyone knew—Jarod's mom, brother, grandparents, too. If Nicole suspected, *she probably didn't*, she said nothing.

Until the moment they were ready to leave for Oregon, Misty had held onto the ring, hiding it from Nicole. The plan, secret the ring into Jarod's backpack just before they were ready to leave for Oregon. If hiding the ring from Nicole had been tough, slipping it into Jarod's backpack proved risky.

With bags in the trunk, Nicole fiddling with something on the front seat, Misty, like Marine Recon on a mission, silently moved to the back of the car. She fumbled through the bags, found Jarod's backpack, ready to slip the ring inside. Nicole, always thorough, ready to count packs, *got to make sure we have everything*, walked to the trunk for a final inspection, surprising Misty.

"What are you doing?" Nicole asked.

"Huh? Oh, nothing, just moving things around, making sure everything fits, everything's here," Misty said, certain she'd been caught in the act.

A day later, before the sun burned off the morning mist, while ocean swells gently pulled at the shore, Jarod knelt in the sand, held out the ring, and offered himself to Nicole.

———

"WHAT'S OUR BUDGET FOR A WEDDING?" Nicole asked, fidgeting with the ring that Jarod had slipped on her finger.

"About zero dollars," Jarod said.

"So, let's just elope, let's just do it!"

Days later, back home in California, Nicole called Misty, "Hey, we're going to get married tomorrow, do you want to come?"

"Well yeah! Of course, I do."

———

BY DECEMBER, Jarod left for Marine Corps boot camp. Intrigued by the Marine Corps mystique, wanting to be with her new husband, Nicole left for Marine Corps boot camp months later. For almost three years, husband and wife served together, until Nicole deployed. Jarod, plagued by a chronic injury, remained at Camp Lejeune, where the couple wisely purchased a house, reasoning that with two incomes they could afford a mortgage, build some equity, *all just part of the plan.*

By August 2021, Nicole and Jarod had just months left on their enlistments.

———

BACK AT THE HOTEL, Jarod lay on the bed, unable to sleep; hours slowly dragged through the night. Startled by a loud rap on the door, he bolted upright. The Marine Corps CACO had come to collect him, to bring him to Dover where he would wait for Nicole.

PART FIVE

MISTY

Misty saw Nicole's body for the first time in a chapel inside Mt. Vernon Memorial Park, a quiet place. When the funeral director asked, *Nicole looked presentable to her,* if a viewing would be okay, everyone agreed. The possibility of an open casket, a last chance to see Nicole, surprised Misty, others too.

Jarod, Mallory (a Marine sergeant who was good friends to Nicole and Jarod), other friends, most of the family, everyone in queue behind Misty, gave her a private moment, more time than she needed, more time than she wanted. She stepped up to the open casket. What Kelsee had seen, blood on Nicole's forehead, had been a steel bearing that pierced Nicole's head just above her eyebrow. Another pierced her throat. More would have riddled her body, torn at her flesh. *Misty knew that much.* But she didn't know, didn't want to know, the full extent of Nicole's wounds, not after some of the things she been told or heard. *If there are body parts, remains that later are identified, those remains can be placed in a saltwater casket and buried at sea.*

Misty stared down at her sister.

Look at you. You look like my sister, but you can't be. Your face, how smooth, where are those tiny little wrinkles, the lines around your eyes, the crinkles at the corners of your lips? Your cheeks, the color is all wrong, waxy. There's no smile. You always wore a smile, even when you were sleeping. Your gloves, are your hands inside? Your arms too? Is it you or something else filling the sleeves? You were so full of life. How can this be you?

Misty slowly moved away, took a place on a polished chapel pew. Others, so many people, filed by Nicole, saying goodbyes, some lingering, others moving on after a quick touch on Nicole's shoulder, her gloved hands—her heart.

Stifled cries, a soft cacophony of grief filled the chapel. Mallory stood. The chapel quieted. Mallory lifted her voice, sang *Amazing Grace*, beautiful, sad. Everyone cried openly. Grief overwhelming even the most stoic among them.

"What are we all doing?" Misty's uncle said, standing and admonishing everyone. "Nicole wouldn't want us sitting here, crying like this!"

"Yeah, she'd probably want us all to do pushups," Misty's aunt said.

Cries turned to smiles. Everyone began to laugh openly, collectively stood. The center aisle filled. Someone did pushups on a pew. A few dropped to the floor, modified pushups, *hardcore too*. A voice called out a number, "Twenty-two. Count them off. Stop there." Most family members understood, *part of a month-long challenge, twenty-two a day for a month*, a reminder of the number of daily military suicides, a call for action.

EARLY THE FOLLOWING MORNING, Nicole was moved from Mt. Vernon to Lambert Funeral Chapel in Roseville. At the entrance, a silent, somber member of the funeral staff, well-practiced at the art of sympathy, stood by the entrance, head bowed like a penitent. He nodded as each family member filed inside, his head bobbing like a bottleneck doll in the back window of a car. Misty understood, she'd been readied for this, a more private family viewing. No well-wishers, no curious public outside.

Misty paused by Nicole's casket. She looked at her sister, a final time, a glance, no more, then moved away. Family filed by, *a final look, a last touch.* Tomorrow Roseville, claiming Nicole as one of their own, *she was hometown*, would have their chance to salute and honor Nicole.

———

INSIDE THE BAYSIDE Church auditorium a quintessential bagpiper, resplendent in Scottish Highlander regalia, his cheeks puffed as he filled the bag with air, piped the family to their seats. His sound, soft, whimsical, *unusual*, offered a melody some may have recognized. If they did, the significance held special meaning. To others, unaware of the piper's choice, *Skye Boat Song*, the meaning would be lost. Perhaps someone in the know, lost in a crowd of twelve-hundred, mouthed the opening lyric . . . *"Sing me a song of a lass that is gone."*

The piper marched off, disappearing beyond the outer edge of the crowd, the echo of the song, a fading decrescendo. A young pastor, trim, confident, walked to the podium, *center stage*. He slowly raised his hand. Murmuring and chatter dwindled. Silence fell. A few relieved sighs stippled the quiet. The pastor dutifully waited. He looked out over the crowd, said nothing, paused. Hushed, the crowd looked on expectantly. *He had them.* Now he could begin.

He offered a few opening remarks, an invocation, his voice, clear, soothing. Family members, cousins, aunts, spoke, remembering Nicole with their own stories. Mallory, *Marine Dress Blues*, fighting through tears, Jarod standing next to her, pushed back her emotions, offered her love for Nicole, chronicled some of her final days, wrapped her voice around her lost friend, and closed with the pledge every Marine offers to one another. "Semper Fidelis," she whispered into the microphone.

Nicole's father offered a few words of his own. "A soldier dies twice: once wherever he, *universal pronoun*, takes his last breath; and he dies again when he's forgotten. I ask you not to forget Nicole," he said, then turned to a friend. She read the remainder of his remarks. They left the stage together, but not before he asked again, "Please, remember Nicole."

Misty stood, *front row*, walked the short distance, her long blond hair, just like Nicole's, flowing. She moved with purpose, sure of herself, *Nicole wouldn't have stood for less*, then climbed the few steps to the stage. She slipped behind the podium. She looked down. In front of the stage, flanked by Marine sergeants, Nicole's flag-draped casket rested on a wheeled platform.

She looked up, out over the crowd, *so many, so many had come.*

"My name is Misty Herrera-Fuoco, I'm Nicole's sister," she said, her voice strong. She talked about Nicole, *my sister, my best friend*, read a poem penned by a Marine who'd served with Nicole. She kept her remarks brief. One story she might have told, she chose not to, was the day she met Nicole for the first time.

Mom gave birth in a large birthing room at the hospital. Misty, two-and-a-half, and her dad waited, watching television, Barney, Misty's favorite, while mom, nurses, doctors were doing all the hard work. Nicole greeted the world with a little squawk, then with nothing more to say, she stopped breathing. Hospital staff did everything, cleared Nicole's throat, put her on a breathing machine. Nothing! Misty began to sing along with Barney, the show ending. "I love you, you love me, we're a happy family," she sang. Maybe her voice annoyed Nicole. She began to cry, loud.

Misty closed her remarks with a quote. "We the willing, led by the unknowing, are doing the impossible for the ungrateful. We have done so much, with so little, for so long, we are now qualified to do anything, with nothing."

A few, maybe more than a few, puzzled over Misty's final words. Kelsee, watching the live stream, Mallory, sitting next to Jarod, understood. *Kelsee and Molly, alongside Nicole and dozens of other Marines, had lived through the final days of chaos, the final days of America's end to active war in Afghanistan. They'd been willing to help those who could not help themselves, leading unknowing Afghan women and children, men too, to safety.*

———

IN ARLINGTON, *late September,* summer, not ready to move aside for autumn, hesitated. An errant leaf, *autumn moon gold*, a soloist auditioning for fall, floated to the ground. Grass, still green, had defeated August's punishing heat.

On this sun-bathed morning, after a ten-day hurry up and wait, *she would have laughed*, Nicole arrived at the National Cemetery. Jarod and Rick, their benign disagreement settled, Rick wanted his daughter buried at home, Jarod believed she belonged with the almost half million heroes. Rick understood, agreed.

Misty, Mallory, Jarod, almost the entire cast from the Roseville Memorial, reassembled. Six Marine pallbearers lifted Nicole, slid her from a hearse, its black mirror finish reflecting the images of gathered onlookers. Shuffle stepping, the Marines surrendered Nicole to a waiting Army Old Guard caisson. The horses tugged against polished leather harness, the caisson rolled forward, juddering its way to the grave site.

Nicole's tour of duty complete.

PART SIX

LIFE WITHOUT MY SISTER

Misty returned home. Life ahead, the days, weeks, months that will turn into a year, two, a lifetime, wait for her beyond the unimaginable, *life without Nicole.* The crowd that had surrounded her, *no one would puzzle over Misty's grief,* friends, family, Mallory, Jarod, Dad, scattered, slipping back into their everyday private lives. *Work. Mortgages. Husbands. Wives. Children.* Everyday life clawed at Misty too, slammed into her. She'd only just begun a new career, real estate, *her new employer, take all the time you need,* two children, one a newborn, a just-moved-into home, and a husband.

In her car, *groceries, work, an errand,* grief pressed down on her chest. It tightened like a blood pressure cuff, wrapping itself around her, squeezing until her breathing came in short staccato gasps. A flush of sadness rushed through her body. Weak, dizzy, anxious, stricken with grief, unable to breathe, she felt herself fading into oblivion. She fought, gulped in air, breathed. "My God, what was that?"

The attack, the first, not the last, faded. For a time, *too risky,* she stopped driving alone. She learned to cope, recognized the warning signs. In the car, the moment she feels the slow rise, the flush of sorrow, red blotches of heat welting her neck, she distracts the grief, blasting the radio until the car shakes, chasing the grief away. Other drivers, *hearing the booming radio, feeling the vibrations*, look, saw Misty, her head shaking, hair flying, quickly look away, stare straight ahead, hoping for a flash to green, a screech of rubber when the light changes.

ALMOST A YEAR LATER, on a sun-filled morning, the Saturday before Memorial Day, in the white marble forest of Arlington, Misty laid a blanket down in front of Nicole's headstone. She slipped off white sandals, felt the soft caress of thick grass, clear coated with last night's dew, against her bare skin. She tucked one leg close to her body, made a seat for Lorenzo leaning into her chest, nibbling on treats he plucked from a bag of snacks. One-year-old Hayden, on all fours, crawled over Misty's legs, searching for a toy hidden in the folds of the blanket. With her two sons preoccupied, Misty looked at Nicole's headstone.

Visitors, Marines Nicole had served with, a cousin who lived nearby, surrounded Nicole's headstone, black letters contrasting against the white marble, with a perimeter of flowers. The cousin, *Waldorf, Maryland*, visited often, leaving behind a can of White Monster, Nicole's favorite. Someone leaned a bottle of Glenfiddich against the base of the stone, *Nicole would have wanted to toast the fallen heroes*. A picture left behind, *anonymous*, Nicole and two other Marines on liberty in Greece, in civvies, tourists just months before Afghanistan.

Misty knelt, leaned forward, adjusted the photo, propped it up, straightened the bottle of Glenfiddich, tidied the flowers, up-righted the can of White Monster. In the warm sun, Lorenzo and Hayden still content, she sat back on her heels. Strands of memory unspooled from the threaded bobbin of her life with Nicole.

"Mom," Misty said, not long after graduating high school, "I want to get a place of my own." Without protest, *okay, if that's what you want*, Misty housed herself in an apartment, made it comfortable on her own dime. Once settled, *an uncanny knack for knowing who needed a place to stay*, Misty took in friends like strays. Just weeks later, Nicole, *sixteen, high school*, moved in. Misty could easily have become less a sister, more a mother —*she didn't*.

Just a few short years later, Nicole moved out, *Marine Corps boot camp*. Misty continued to keep the house full, friends, a husband now, but the piece that had fitted perfectly into the sisters' private puzzle, *Nicole*, was missing.

They could talk for hours—about everything—nothing. "I think I want to join the Marine Corps," Nicole confided, her voice laced with a what-do-you-think tone.

"You," Misty said, *reminding, reassuring*, "can do anything. Are you sure this is it what you want?"

"I think so, yeah," Nicole said, rattling off, cataloguing the pros and cons. "I mean I know you sign your life away. I know the pay's not great. I make more money now, but I can finish school even while I'm on active duty, on the Marine Corps' dime. VA loans for a house *later*, that's a plus. Jarod and I have talked it out, talked with the recruiter too. After boot, we'll be stationed together, *off base housing*, the recruiter seemed pretty certain."

"I guess if it's what you want, it all makes sense," Misty said. "You know I'll support you, no matter what you decide."

Nicole reported to Parris Island, the Marine Corps's iconic boot camp in South Carolina, but not before completing her semester courses, giving a two months' notice at work. Always a gym rat, she doubled her workouts, readied herself for the physical demands of boot camp. She aced boot.

MISTY CONTINUED to keep the house full. She'd never lived alone, had a husband now, and friends that needed help, a place to stay—but she didn't have Nicole. Until now, they'd never been apart. For the next three years they texted almost daily, facetimed too, talked frequently, sometimes for hours, *sharing everything*, jabbering about husbands. They knew each other's secrets. Nothing was off limits, *sisters, best friends, kindred spirits.*

Nicole came home to meet Lorenzo. She came home again, *mom passed*, just three months later. Another year passed. Misty called Jarod.

"I want to see Nicole, you too, surprise her. I've got some vacation time."

Co-conspirators, *covert operation, just like the hidden ring*, Misty and Jarod planned the mission. Saddled up, Misty led her squad. Her husband, Gabriel, her brother, even Lorenzo, fell in, mission priority clear—keep the secret, maintain the element of surprise. They arrived under the cover of darkness, 2200 hours, assembled outside the house, *Jarod and Nicole's*. Misty led a frontal assault, knocked and pushed her way inside, blindsiding Nicole.

"Hey, I brought your favorite nephew to see you," Misty said. Nicole smiled wide enough to eat a banana sideways.

They stayed for five days. No one knew, *couldn't have*, that this would be the last time Misty would see Nicole alive.

THREE MONTHS after Nicole's death, *Thanksgiving*, cousins, friends, Jarod too, he drove up from North Carolina, came together in Maryland. Misty, plagued with COVID, missed the gathering. By Christmas, Misty pulled family together in her new home, *big enough*. The first get together since burying

Nicole, cousins, aunts, uncles, Misty's brother, people scattered all around the country came, Jarod too. The memory of Nicole pulled them together.

A good meal. More memories. Some tears. Laughter too. Mostly quiet moments holding each other's hearts.

Christmas came and went. Family scattered again. Lorenzo turned three. A few months later, May, Hayden' first birthday, just days after Nicole's, a time Nicole would have loved more than anything.

There's no sell-by date on grief; life goes on. Misty dove headlong into her new career, her babies, her husband, a new house, the aftermath of Nicole's passing. But she still has conversations with Nicole, one-sided now, sometimes even talking out loud.

YOU'RE STILL CLOSE, different, but I can feel you. I miss you. I want to tell you things. Hayden's walking, talks pretty good too. Lorenzo stood in for you at the wedding, the one where you were supposed to be bridesmaid. He wore a little tuxedo. He was ring bearer, very serious. I heard a new song on the radio. You'd love it, I know you would. I miss driving together, we sang songs in the car at the top of our lungs, people must have thought we were crazy. There're so many good things in my life . . . just not you, and I miss you.

I read the letter, the one you sent, the handwritten one about the picture of you and the baby, so calm. You remember what you wrote? I have it here. You wrote, "I just blew softly on the baby's face."

Nicole Gee, sister Misty, and cousins on Halloween

Nicole Gee and her sister Misty

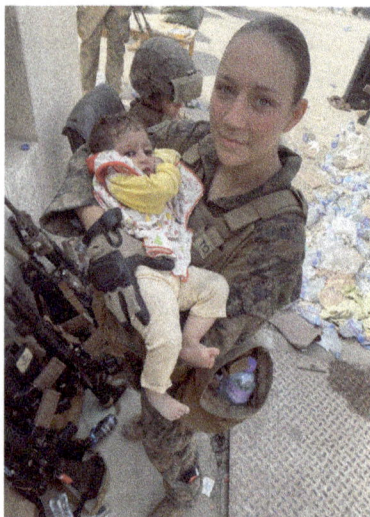

Nicole comforting Afghan child just days before she was killed

Misty helping Nicole dress for her wedding

Nicole and Jarod

Nicole Gee and Kelsee Lainhart (center) with Marine Recon team on the morning of August 26th

Afghan refugees outside Hamid Karzai Airport during the final days of the American withdrawal from Afghanistan

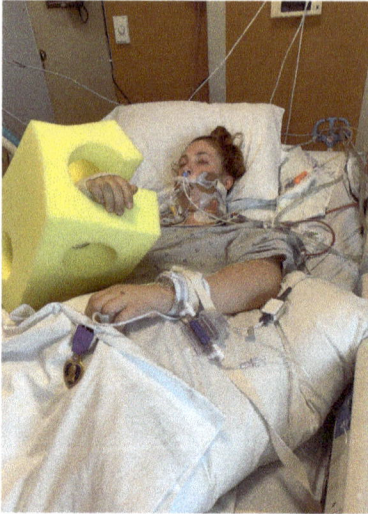

Corporal Kelsee Lainhart recovering from wounds suffered during the suicide bomber's attack on August 26th

Sergeant Nicole Gee, May 1, 1998—August 26, 2021

BOOK FOUR:
VOLUME ONE

PART ONE

ANDREW

THOSE WHO KNEW HIM AS A FRIEND, A SOLDIER, NOT THOSE closest to him, called him PK. To his mother, Helen, to the others who loved him most, he was Andrew. When he left that last time, in the fall of 2012, to do good in another part of the world, Helen convinced herself that nothing terrible would happen to him. Andrew would return. He always had. But stories about war hardly ever end with boys as old men.

2002—GIANTS Stadium.

The West Point Military Academy cadets marched onto the field. Navy would follow, take their turn, take the field too, once Army settled into the stands, *one hundred twelve years of tradition.* The game, Army, the Black Knights, against Navy, the Midshipmen, played on the sixty-first anniversary of the attack on Pearl Harbor, quickly turned into a rout. Navy sailed past Army, leaving the cadets in their wake, the final score 58-12.

Helen and Bob, *second husband*, met Andrew before the game, before he fell into formation and marched onto the field. The sight of him, handsome, dashing, in an Academy winter long coat, an unfettered cape rakishly tenting his shoulders, rows of polished brass buttons, the coat worn over the winter grey uniform, stirred something unexpected in Helen.

The invisible thread that had tethered the boy to his mother, frayed against the stretch of years, pulled apart. Helen could almost feel the last strand break away. The boy disappeared. In his place a young man in wool wrapped his arms around her. Helen hugged him, pressed her cheek against his chest, felt the wool against her skin, their breaths, a plume of steam against the cold December day, haloed around them.

"Need to go, Mom," Andrew said. "I've got to fall in." Helen let go, stepped back, watched him disappear, hurrying to join the hundreds of other cadets. In that moment, she understood. The realization, a flash, bam, alakazam instant, all that they'd accomplished together, hit her right between the eyes.

THE MAN she'd married before Bob, Henry Keel—business man, homeowner, same religion, important to Helen, *Catholic*, already the father of a three-year-old little girl, *he must be okay with children*—checked off all the boxes. But Helen later learned that the things that made sense, those checked-off boxes, were erased by Henry Keel's drinking. It didn't take long, but Helen understood—this thing they were doing, it wasn't going to work.

Henry, fun-loving, *more fun than loving*, confirmed what Helen already knew, the marriage, only weeks old, was already on life support. Henry hadn't wanted more children, *maybe he should have thought about that before*, made it clear to Helen, pregnant just a month after their *I dos*, that she could stay until the baby was born, then—*well then*—she should leave, take the baby with her. He pulled the plug.

She would have left anyway, *of her own volition*, didn't need his urging, didn't want him anymore. Six weeks after Andrew was born, *almost a decade before the Family Medical Leave Act,* Helen found a place of her own in Coral Gables, went back to work, enrolled in night school, and took care of her infant son. Graduate Helen Pedersen, BA in Nursing, Cum Laude, delivered the commencement speech with baby Andrew on her hip. In time, she left Florida and moved north, closer to family and friends, Andrew, three years old, by her side. Mother and son found their own rhythm—alone—together. Henry didn't protest, not yet; later, *when it was all about power, control, and money,* he did.

Andrew turned four at Dartmouth, five at Yale. Helen worked at both university hospitals. In his five years he'd seen seven different bedrooms. Unfazed. "Born happy," Helen said, when anyone asked how Andrew was doing. "As long as he has me, as long as we have each other, we're fine."

In Connecticut, surrounded by Helen's family and friends, Andrew flourished. Helen found a place near Andrew's young cousin. *Quiet street. Cul-de-sac.* Andrew watched the older boy, studied him deftly looping inside the circle on his bicycle. No one said no when Andrew, anxious to try his hand, convinced the older boy to let him give it a try. *No training wheels!*

He straddled the crossbar, *boy's bike,* toes grazing the pavement, not able to reach the lowest pedal if he tried to plant himself on the seat. He adjusted. Standing, he pushed off, wobbly—smiling, pedaling cautiously at first, then stronger, with intent, propelling himself, moving forward with greater force. Shaky, he circled the cul-de-sac. Within a week, he became practiced. By summer's end, before his first day of kindergarten, he rode well.

He managed, too, to have his appendix removed that summer.

CONNECTICUT WORKED for mother and son. Helen found a good position at Yale New Haven Hospital, worked hard, made herself indispensable, began building a life for herself and her son. Hardworking, loving, this is what Andrew saw, what he understood, *what he modeled.* He became inquisitive, happy, trusting. Already physically ahead of others his age, he grew into a little athlete. Before he turned six, *needed to be seven, that was the mandate,* he finagled early entry into Tiger Cubs, first step in the hierarchy of the Boy Scouts of America.

He burst into school life, surprising teachers with his energy, more curious than most, needing to know the why of things, unsatisfied until he had answers. Bored easily with the everyday *baby stuff,* he could overwhelm his kindergarten teacher. She'd just never seen someone with his, *how might she have put it,* with his enthusiasm!

To rein him in, the teacher bribed Andrew, developed a coupon program. He could earn up to two points a day; ten points earned a coupon. *Redeemable? Helen wasn't certain.* But the coupon program, well known to most kindergarten teachers, could earn a pick from a prize box, or lunch with the teacher, or best yet, the student could even wear slippers or a funny hat to class.

Andrew moved through the public school system, distinguishing himself and positioning himself for life in an environment that would take the full measure of who he was becoming. To the outside world, friends, later soldiers too, middle school was where Andrew became PK. "I'm tired of calling you Pedersen-Keel," Coach yelled out, "From now on you're PK. I can't be singing half the alphabet to get your attention." The soubriquet stuck.

High school, Avon Old Farms, a private school for boys, opened the door to Andrew's future. He bolted through, becoming an athlete-scholar. Using his average height, speed, and strength, the special teams football player realized his passion, playing high school football. Already an able word-smith, he became editor of the school newspaper. The school matched Andrew's ambitions, cultivated them.

Andrew could have been just Keel, that name belonged to his father, but not to Helen, *she didn't want it.* But wanting her son to always have a last name matching her own, Helen kept the Pedersen for both of them. When Helen married Bob, *ahead of her time,* she did the hyphen thing, becoming Helen Keiser-Pedersen.

AT AVON, the idea that would become the seed that grew into his decision to apply to two of the nation's military academies took root. He selected the Naval Academy and West Point, discovering that the process wasn't that simple. First a prospective candidate must *apply to apply.* He did, passed that hurdle, then solicited congressional recommendations from Joe Lieberman and Nancy Johnson, another not-so-automatic requirement. Didn't matter to Andrew, *his mind made up,* he'd already decided that he would attend, never thought getting in would be an issue. It wasn't. Helen wasn't surprised.

Years later, when people, friends, family, would ask Helen why Andrew, really a gentle boy, chose the military, she replied, "It was his secret. If he were still alive, I'd ask him, try to get him to explain." At the time she didn't probe. She had a theory though. At Avon Old Farms there was a set of twins; one went into the Naval Academy, the other chose West Point. Andrew admired them. Helen felt certain they inspired him, maybe they even talked to him. She'd never know. But part of her, part of the explanation, part of the why, she believed, may have had something to do with 9/11. 9/11 influenced him. Andrew was seventeen when the towers fell to the terrorist attack. Helen drove to Avon Old Farms—searched the school—found Andrew.

"You know what happened?" she asked.

"Yes," Andrew said, understanding, even at seventeen, that this was the harbinger of war.

Helen had always felt Andrew's deep understanding of good and evil. What he'd witnessed on television, the attack on the Towers—he understood the depth of its evil. Patriotism, *even without a strong family legacy of military service*, tugged at Andrew.

Beyond his sense of patriotism there existed a strong faith, belief in something bigger, something good. On his own, after Helen let him choose for himself, he never stopped attending Catholic Mass. Right and wrong, the difference ingrained, choosing right, Andrew lived that way, never a fight on the playground, playing field, or classroom. *Andrew just wouldn't allow himself that failing.*

EARLY SUMMER 2002, Andrew, along with hundreds of potential cadets, readied himself for a future at West Point. To secure that future, to punch his ticket, to earn his way into the Academy and become a West Point *Plebe*, to shed the appellation of *New Cadet* Andrew first had to face the "Beast."

Physical, the Beast fed into everything Andrew loved. By summer's end he marched the 12-plus miles from Lake Frederick to Central Area, having tamed the Beast—six weeks of Cadet Basic Training, basic rifle marksmanship, land navigation, and seemingly endless ruck marches. At eighteen, the Beast behind him, a cadre of new friends, men and women who'd shared the challenge, Andrew passed through West Point's Thayer Gate.

Ready, confident, anxious, Andrew, like all plebes an underprivileged commoner, quickly learned that West Point would test him. The Academy would be hard. Good things—things worth doing, achieving—usually are, he'd learned that from Helen. Andrew, for most of his life, life prior to West

Point, had stood out. Over-achiever, always among the best, maybe the best, that's what got him into West Point—but at West Point, the best of the best became one of the many.

———

LONG BEFORE HE BECAME A *FIRSTIE*, a senior at the Academy, maybe while Andrew was still a plebe, *could have been a Yearling*, a sophomore cadet, *probably not though*, on one of her visits, *she went often*, Helen said the quiet part out loud.

"Afghanistan. Iraq. Andrew, you understand the possibility of finding yourself there?" she said, a mother's concern filling her voice. "This early, well you still have time to leave the Academy. I'm not asking you to, just maybe, maybe it's something to think about. You can leave up to the first day of your third year, you know that, right?"

"Mom," Andrew said, "even if I wanted to, I've already made good friends. By then, by that time, the bonds that I'll share with the men and women here, those bonds are lifetime. I can't leave my friends, not now, not ever."

And that was the end of it, the end of any conversation about leaving. Helen never spoke about it again. Andrew was his own man. She was never more proud, never more happy, never more scared. Iraq and Afghanistan, two wars. There was no warning, no blinking orange light, no sign that read slow, danger ahead. Letting go of him had come so quickly. Life changed so fast. She hadn't been ready. Good mothers never are. Soldiers go to war, and in war, soldiers die— violently. Arlington is littered with the graves of young women and men, *the old—not so many*.

———

SUMMER 2003

Andrew met Chris Day during the first weekend of Cadet Summer Training at Camp Buckner, following plebe year.

There's not much that explains the mystery, the attraction that creates a bond between young men, especially soldiers. Strangers brought together by circumstance and choices become best friends, loving each other far beyond the bonds of family, slipping into an easy intimacy.

Andrew and Chris hadn't known each other as plebes, not unusual in a class that numbered north of one thousand. The chance pairing that brought them together during the quiet part of the weekend, two days of team selections, assignments, a ritual reception dinner before training began in earnest, united them.

From there, Andrew and Chris would become lifelong friends.

WEST POINT BROUGHT out the best in Andrew, the mischievous too. He was a prankster, and a sometimes-rebellious cadet. Not a major rule breaker, *plenty of minor infractions*, Andrew tested the limits. Sometimes pushed a little too hard. Helen must have had an inkling, some idea, *maybe not to the full extent*, that Andrew took occasional walks on the wild side.

Indeed he did, even earning the not-so-glorious title of Century Man, a cadet who walked at least one hundred hours of area punishment tours. Would that have surprised Helen? She most likely knew. Oh, he stayed morally grounded, even went to Catholic Mass most Sundays, always wore a small gold crucifix, but Andrew was no choir boy. Chris too. Neither friend had any fondness for the sometimes useless traditional disciplines ingrained in West Point ritual.

BUT…because of their distaste for insensible, often needless discipline, Andrew and Chris became better leaders, disciplining soldiers in their command with respect, never relying on position power. They understood, if rank had its privilege, it had its responsibilities too.

Before West Point, there was nothing that Helen didn't know, could not tell you about Andrew. That was the part of his life she knew best, the part of his life no one could know better. But when a son leaves home, begins another part of life, others come to know him too.

Chris knew the Andrew that lived behind the walls of West Point, the Andrew that loved a woman named Celeste, the Andrew wanting to live up to his own expectations, and the Andrew who sometimes struggled.

After summer training, Andrew and Chris began the daily life of a Yearling, a sophomore cadet. Assigned to different companies, the two new friends caught up with each other most nights and weekends. Andrew, a gym rat, became incredibly physically fit.

While others battled against weighted barbells, *too heavy,* Andrew curled his fingers around the etched grips of a bar dusted with chalk, paused, inhaled, bench pressing beyond his body weight, ten reps smoothly ushered above his chest. Afterward, he relished the ache in his shoulders and chest, reminders that he was becoming bigger, stronger. Andrew wasn't a casual lifter.

Chris, although he lifted too, marveled at Andrew's push in the weight room. *He knew his way around the gym.* Despite a new habit, cigarettes—the two friends had started smoking, they could knock back a few beers too—Andrew excelled at all aspects of physical training, an invincible twenty-year-old, *two invincible twenty-year-olds.*

There was more to Andrew than his physicality. That might have been what most strangers noticed first, but they'd quickly discover the intensity of Andrew's intellect. He possessed a genuine intelligence that intrigued others, surprised them too. *Oh, he's not the dumb jock!*

He read voraciously. Wrote beautifully. He outdistanced everyone in literature courses at the Academy, writing circles around all of his classmates. His intellect carried over into conversation. There, he'd pause thoughtfully before contributing or answering a question. He listened. When he answered, he answered with genuine engagement.

The friendship between Andrew and Chris continued to grow, almost as if they'd known each other, belonged to each other, long before they'd met. They shared a sense of family, passion, and loyalty to friends. And both men lusted for adventure. There were times when they confessed to one another their shared doubts, questioning their own fit for the Army, once even discussing the possibility of leaving the Academy.

They didn't. Instead, they chose warrior paths, becoming infantry officers. That became Andrew and Chris—until life pulled them apart. But distance never changed how they felt about each other—nothing could. Later, when war and deployments insinuated threats into their lives, Andrew and Chris pledged, *if either—well—*then the other would bring him home. A chip neither wanted to cash in—ever—or at least until they were both old men in rocking chairs.

THEY LEFT West Point in early June 2006, just days after graduation. Freed from the harsh West Point disciplines, the trip, lighthearted, adventurous, crowded out serious talk. Unleashed, they reveled in their freedom, setting out across the country. Half the class had two months' vacation, *leave* the military calls it. Half the class, the lower half, earned a month. Andrew and Chris set out for a thirty-day road trip.

Driving from New York, they drove to Michigan, Chris's home, the start of a planned loop around the country, intending to close the circle at Fort Benning where they'd begin Infantry Officer Basic Course training. Knowing that a lot of running would challenge two bulked-up weight lifters, they decided to get into lean, mean, fighting machine condition, avoiding junk food, not easy for nomads and beer lovers visiting friends all over the country.

Something wonderful. Something unexpected happened. The two new soldier officers, not a worry in the world, forgot that they were soldiers. They had time, an us-against-the-world moment might come, but not now.

For now, they slept under the stars in the Dakota Bad Lands, camped at the Hot Springs. Watched—*stared incredulously*—at naked hippies smoking joints, free love, *a rite of passage in the chaotic '60's* apparently remained a time-honored tradition among the refugees from that bygone era. Andrew and Chris drove up to Oregon then followed the Pacific Coastline to southern California, skipped over to Las Vegas, *a short stay*, avoided the gambling tables, hanging onto their cash.

The road trip ended on time at Fort Benning. Andrew and Chris reported for duty, enrolled in the Infantry Officer Basic Course. With the IOBC training completed, Andrew and Chris enrolled in Ranger School. Finished, Ranger school behind them, almost badass, that cognomen usually reserved for Special Forces, *Green Berets*, Andrew and Chris deployed. Chris to Iraq and Afghanistan, Andrew to Afghanistan.

That's the nature of soldiering, military life. Soldiers, best friends, called to different assignments, go separate ways. They stayed close, even living together at times. Despite deployments to two wars at different times their bond, tested, remained unbreakable.

PART TWO
HONORING THE PACT

WITH A BREAK IN DEPLOYMENTS, *BETWEEN THEM*, *THE NUMBER would eventually grow to six*, Andrew and Chris, back in the States, reunited, hit pause—briefly—then qualified for Special Forces School. Once again, the two friends trained side by side. They didn't finish together.

Old targets in need of replacement, *rounds sometimes went through*, didn't always fall, even with a center-mass grouping. At the end of the course, a few too many targets were still standing even though Andrew was certain he'd hit them. Andrew recycled, a forced do-over.

Chris completed the school ahead of Andrew and quickly deployed to Afghanistan, taking command of Green Beret team ODA-3135, splitting his time between Kunar and Nangahar.

Andrew deployed a few months later, in the fall of 2012, billeted initially at headquarters in a disappointing, *to him*, role as a staff officer. The two best friends in a war-torn country together—apart—at times separated by no less than forty-five miles, saw each other just once in early December, just weeks before Christmas, a chance to relax, catch up before going separate ways—again.

THEY TALKED OFTEN, texted too. Small-talk. Soldier-speak.

"How are things with the team?" Chris asked, not long after Andrew became commander of Green Beret team ODA-3126, relieving Captain Seth Neiman, seriously wounded in late November. The team manned a Village Stability Platform, a VSP, outside a village located in Jalrez, Wardak Province.

"Great," Andrew said, relieved of the minutia-laden role at HQ, now in the careful-what-you-wish-for command position he craved. "My guys are badass, some serious dudes. I mean this is what we trained for, right?"

"Yeah, it is," Chris said. "How's Celeste, you guys staying in touch?"

"Talking when we can, texting. You know I think, when this tour is over, I think it's time."

"Time for what?"

"Time to marry her. Settle down. Maybe figure out what I'm going to do too, stay in, get out, find something else to do. Who knows? Anyway, I've got time to figure it all out. When I marry her, looks like I'll be married to a doctor, can you believe it?"

"Don't know what she sees in you—"

"Ha! Thanks. What's going on with you?"

"Not much, still figuring things out. You know what I mean."

"Yeah, everything'll turn out the way it's supposed to."

"I know. Stay safe."

Strange for two friends—Andrew and Chris had lived together or near each other for most of the past ten years—to be just miles apart on overlapping deployments and only see each other once. Not so strange if you understand the nature of war. You go where you're needed, when you're needed. The military calls that *orders*.

Christmas came. The new year rushed toward spring. The brutally cold Afghanistan winter lost its grip. Andrew had been in command of ODA-3126 for more than two months.

The early March days, cold in the morning, warmed quickly. Warmer weather encouraged Taliban activity around the Jalrez VSP. The concept of VSPs—embed a small, almost unprotected, American force into or near villages that were known hotbeds of Taliban activity—put them there as a deterrent against the enemy and a benign influence on the local population.

Andrew's twelve-man Green Beret team, and some regular Army, increased missions and patrols. Sometimes on foot near the village, sometimes mounted, airborne when further away, but always with the intent to diminish Taliban influence.

ODA-3126 often rolled out with the Afghan police and Special Forces soldiers bivouacked near the VSP. The village, like many remote villages, was a hotbed of Taliban activity. *Jalrez was a bad place.*

MARCH 11, 2013

At HQS in Jalalabad, early 0700, ODA-3135, Chris's team, resupplied and ready to roll out, ordered to delay their departure, gathered around Chris, waited for new orders.

"We've been ordered to delay departure. Team 3126 is in a firefight. Bring it in, we can listen in on satellite, SAT-102," Chris told his team, huddling them around the radio.

Chris, his team, listened, heard small arms fire, shouts, reports, fragmented details of a battle, calls for air support. He expected to hear Andrew's voice, surprised when he heard voices he didn't recognize. *Doesn't make sense. Andrew's the team commander. He'd be on the radio. Something's off. I should be hearing a voice I know, Andrew's. I don't know these voices. Reports suggest casualties, no details—no numbers. Got it. Can't broadcast that on SAT. Andrew must be wounded. Gotta be, otherwise he'd be on the radio.*

Hours passed. ODA-3135 wouldn't be responding to the attack. Instead, cleared to leave, Chris ordered his team to mount up, roll out for the forty-five-minute return to VSP Khogyani.

Signal jammers, jammers that prevented Taliban from remotely sending a signal to an IED, *usually by cell phone*, detonating the device when Humvees, trucks, and MRAPs were in their crosshairs, were turned on. That kept the team safe. For some reason, unusual, the jammers blocked the team's comms, cell phones too. Chris lost contact with SAT-102. The battle, a cacophony that had crackled over the airwaves, temporarily muted, left Chris to imagine the worst.

ODA-3135 rolled through the gate at Khogyani. *Signal jammers off.* Tim Egan, classmate to Andrew and Chris had been waiting. His call, *cell phone*, came through to Chris almost immediately.

"Andrew didn't make it, Chris," Tim said.

"You sure?"

"It's confirmed."

"Alright Tim, thanks."

"You going to be okay?"

"Yeah," Chris replied, "Thanks, Tim."

Chris, Andrew too, knew that this could happen, all soldiers do, but the reality hit Chris hard, bludgeoning him into a momentary dead space.

This is . . . I've lost soldiers . . . but . . . this . . . a lot of bad shit goes down . . . but this . . . Andrew? This is different. Even when Dad died, so suddenly, I knew he was sick, never expected he would die, yeah, that blindsided me. My men, soldiers I've lost, wrote letters to their families, I've had to deal with that, even second-guess myself . . . could I have done something different? All of it, every bad thing that's happened in my life, nothing hurts like this. My God, what about Helen, Celeste? We were so close. What? What now?

Of course. Of course! We made a pact, we pledged, if either—well —then the other would bring him home. I have a promise to keep!

MOVING the remains of US military personnel to Dover from Afghanistan receives the military's highest priority. Space for them is made on the first available aircraft. An Air Force 747, already scheduled to bring four caskets to Dover, had room for Andrew and SSgt. Rex Schad, killed just a few feet away from Andrew. Andrew's remains, Rex's too, *intact, identifiable,* would be flown to the States almost immediately.

To honor his pledge, to bring Andrew home to Helen, Celeste, the rest of his family, Chris understood he'd need to act quickly. There wouldn't be much of a final goodbye from ODA-3126, most were wounded. Chris had to get to Bagram, *a four-hour-plus, 225km traverse,* and get there before Andrew's airplane departed. Otherwise he'd have to chase Andrew halfway around the world. *He had to be with him.*

His men, ready to mount up, drive Chris back to Jalalabad, get him to the airstrip there, were willing to risk the trip. Chris knew, even if they remained unscathed, they probably wouldn't arrive at Jalalabad in time. He couldn't ask his men to take the risk.

I need a different plan—think!

While his men helped him pack, stuffing his duffel, Chris had to move through his chain of command, get emergency leave in motion, make certain his men had leadership beyond supper. His command, supportive, moved with a sense of urgency, made certain Chris's team was in good hands and began to do everything possible to make sure Chris connected with Andrew. The issue was transportation. Chris continued to look for a viable option, something that would get him to Jalalabad or closer to Bagram, anything to shave off time. The break came in the form of a favor.

The favor, an offer of friendship, came from Brigade Commander J.P. McGee. The colonel, *today general,* understood the promise men make to each other, *I'll bring you home.* McGee knew Chris. He stepped in.

Grateful beyond words, Chris accepted an offer from

McGee, a ride to Jalalabad airfield on the colonel's personal UH-60 Black Hawk. From there, Chris found an empty seat on another airplane, arriving at Bagram in time, *in a blur, no time to think about anything.* In his combat uniform, the dust of Afghanistan still on his sleeves, Chris boarded the airplane. He slept on the floor, amongst the caskets, near his friend Andrew.

PART THREE

THE AMBUSH

March 11, 2013

    In the dark, VSP Jalrez, Captain Andrew Pedersen-Keel's command, began to wake.

    Specialist Evin Galbreath, the camp cook, ensconced in a guard tower, checked his watch, yawned, still an hour to go.

    Earlier, SSgt. Rex Schad had, like he'd done so many nights, mornings, climbed the tower, visited with Evin, talked about soldiering, home, the day ahead. Evin enjoyed the visits, looked forward to them, a break in the loneliness of solitary guard duty.

    Rex, after leaving the tower, checking on other soldiers, went in search of coffee. He had time, briefing still almost an hour away.

    The sun continued to poke holes through the night clouds. Crimson streaks slipped through. Other men began to stir.

    Andrew, inside his quarters, pushed blankets aside, sat up, and rubbed sleep from his eyes. New mission today. Brief the team at 0700, brief the Afghans that are coming too. 0530 now. He dressed. No rush.

    Airforce MSgt. Delorean Sheridan, a combat controller, pulled on sweats and went in search of his workout partner, Army Special Forces Sergeant Nick Lavery. Along the way, he bumped into another soldier. "Nick's not feeling it this morning," the soldier said. Delorean returned to his quarters, dressed for the mission. Still early, he went in search of coffee.

Warrant Officer Brian Satterlee, Andrew's second, dressed in battle gear, looked at the sky. Night clouds gone, bright sun, clear day. Good day for a mission.

Before the morning would end, Sergeant Lavery would push a soldier away from danger and step in front of him.

8,000 miles away, in the middle of the night, Helen, troubled by a fear-filled dream, bolted awake. ANDREW! Seized by a cold premonition, she scrambled from the bed, somehow without waking Bob.

Downstairs, she hurried to her computer, listened to its soft whirring while it booted up. "C'mon. C'mon! Boot up, please!" A flash of light, ah there you are. She ran her fingers over the keyboard, demanding that the computer tell her something. Pictures! Andrew had sent several pictures just days ago. She searched for those—nothing. How about news, breaking news from Afghanistan. She found nothing. Frustrated, she went back to bed, tried to sleep, light from the computer still flashing behind her closed eyes.

The day began as the Taliban's game—played by their rules—at least for a while. The final score, the win, would belong to the Americans—but not before the Taliban killed, wounded, and maimed Americans, and their own Afghan brothers.

In war, trust is a battlefield paradox.

A soldier needs to trust the man next to him. Soldiers need to trust their leaders. They need to trust their in-country allies too. They need that trust in each other because that's who they depend on when all hell breaks loose.

The Paradox—

Ruthless, their beliefs, their cause, so strong, so uncompromising, committed to opposing everyone and everything in their path, the Taliban exploited trust, using it to kill without regard. All they could see was what looked like them. Nothing, no one, mattered beyond the cause, no gray, only black and white.

The Americans trusted the Afghans, the police and soldiers working with them at Jalrez. They passed onto the base, inside the wire, without issue—daily. The Taliban knew that that trust could be exploited; they just needed one accomplice. They had him, one young police trainee, coerced, threatened, into attacking the Americans.

0700

The Afghans, the police and soldiers embedded with the Americans, *invited—trusted cohorts,* rolled through the wire in armed vehicles, joining the Americans near the motor pool, the site of the pre-mission briefing. They smiled, nodding greetings.

It all made sense to the Americans, *that's where the mission convoy would form up and move out, nothing unusual, the Afghans had joined them on almost every mission.* The Afghans halted their vehicles, stopping just a few feet behind the briefing, a group of Americans and Afghans semi-circled in front of the young American commander. Some left their trucks and joined the briefing. But one stood on the back of a truck, an arm innocently resting over a Russian PKM.

When the briefing began, Andrew positioned himself, standing where he should have been, exactly where he needed to be—in front of his men, his back to the Afghan vehicles.

Ah, look! The Americans. They trust. So unsuspecting. I can do this. Let me wait, pray. Then. Then I will act! I can surprise the Americans. Kill many.

By 0730, the briefing completed, Andrew was about to turn away. Another minute—*no just seconds*—but all the time the shooter needed. In those final seconds Andrew could have dismissed the group, walked away, slipped inside his own vehicle to safety, but something stopped him. Maybe someone had a question. Maybe he wanted to wish his men good luck. He paused, about to say—

I must act now, quickly. This is my chance. Pull the bolt back, be sly, then fire. Go for their leader—yes. Ah—look at him. He doesn't know. Now!

Airforce MSgt. Delorean Sheridan, standing close to Andrew, noticed bursts of movement to his left, his ten-o'clock. Puffs of dust popped from the ground, dancing wildly. *Hell, that's weird, that looks like moving gunfire—Oh Christ—it is—I hear it now, the machine gun blast—recoil.*

Neck on a swivel, Delorean looked behind him, saw the uniformed Afghan—*police uniform*—firing from the back of the truck. Andrew's head bounced forward, his eye blurred in a burst of flesh and bone, the hollow filling with blood as a bullet tore through his head. He fell. He never had time to think of Helen, Celeste, and Chris. *He never had time to fear. Never knew he was dying.*

Delorean, everyone else too, scattered, ran for cover. Delorean slid between two vehicles. He knew what everyone else did. An ambush this close—running meant almost certain death. Fight or flight. *What did they teach us—best chance of coming out of this alive is to fight. Return fire.*

Delorean pulled his pistol. Others must have been positioning to return fire too.

There, an open door on the MRAP, the RG33. Get behind the door, get in the truck, vantage point—the turret—climb up. Who's this? Interpreter. He's good. I'm in. There—there, I see him on the back of the truck, firing. Shoot. Bam! Bam! What? Jammed! My pistol's jammed! Get down. Rifle propped up on the seat—an M4—perfect. Shooter on the move, jumping from the truck—trying to squeeze under. I've got him—clear shot. Pop! Pop! Pop! Pop! Pop! He's down. Pop! Pop! Two more into the truck. Explode dammit! I want that truck gone—gone.

Another soldier moved toward the downed shooter, putting two rounds into the body on the ground.

Delorean ran to Andrew, grabbed him by the shoulder

strap, pulling him away. Outside the wire, gunfire erupted. The Taliban, either encouraged by the chaos or having already planned the attack by using the shooter as the signal, opened fire, attacking the VSP. While the remaining team, those that could, led by Officer Satterlee, wounded himself, engaged the Taliban, Delorean reached SSgt. Rex Schad, grabbed him and dragged him away, establishing a casualty collection point.

—*Evin, still in the tower when the attack began, opened fire.*

—*Rex Schad was killed.*

—*Andrew, shot from behind, died instantly.*

—*Delorean, the Airforce combat controller, led the tactical mission between ground and air.*

—*Warrant Officer Brian Satterlee, despite being wounded himself, led the ground forces counterattack, staying with his men until late in the day when he was medevaced to safety.*

—*Nick Lavery saved the soldier he pushed behind himself, losing a leg in the process, and earning a third Purple Heart. He'd return to active combat 18 months later, the first Special Forces soldier missing a leg to do so.*

—*Late in the day, the Taliban, everything going their way just like they'd planned—until it didn't—having had enough, broke off their engagement, slinking away.*

—*8,000 miles away, Helen readied herself for work.*

PART FOUR

A MOTHER'S HEART

MAY 27, 2006
   West Point, Class of 2006—Graduation Day
   The night before graduation, Thursday evening, Helen, kneeling during the blessing at the end of Catholic Mass, rose and followed the procession out of the chapel. Tears, *happy, worrisome, relief,* the first of many throughout graduation weekend, wet her cheeks. Andrew, an infantry officer now, loosed from four years of academics, thrust into everyday active military life, would go where he was needed, where he was ordered.
   Helen didn't need a compass or a map to navigate her soldier son's future. Two wars, Afghanistan and Iraq. Harm's way, dealer's choice, held all the cards. Deployments, not a matter of if, just when, would send Andrew off to one these wars, maybe both. *Stop! Push those thoughts aside, today is not a time for sadness, worry.*
   After the graduation ceremony, Helen and Barb Day, *Chris Day's mother, Helen's friend,* stood in front of their sons. Behind the men, the statue of three American World War II soldiers, the American Soldier Statue, stood sentinel. Andrew and

Chris, funny that they chose a memorial to the nation's enlisted, had insisted on the site. Helen and Barb pinned the gold bars to the collars of their sons. Cadets Andrew Pedersen-Keel and Christopher Day were United States Army Second Lieutenants, West Point graduates!

Helen stifled more tears, *shed them when no one was looking*, gathered herself and did what she'd always done, she put Andrew first. This day, graduation weekend, belonged to him and Chris too. *Time to celebrate!*

As early as freshman year, Helen, mother of a plebe, everything as new and unfamiliar to her as it was to Andrew, discovered that planning for a West Point graduation began when a cadet walked through Thayer Gate. "Make hotel reservations now, four years in advance; it's that or you'll likely wind up sleeping in your car," people told her. "Graduation party venues too. They fill up just as quickly. Find a place now."

Four years, here it was, graduation day. Two families celebrated down by the Hudson River, rented tent, catered afternoon. Helen had seen the area three years earlier, immediately knew that this, a fairly secluded spot nesting on the river bank, a place, everyone else rented halls and hotels, they'd have all to themselves, was where she wanted the graduation party. Later, when she shared the idea with Barb Day, Barb readily agreed.

Helen and Barb had come together by chance. Strangers connected by the friendship of their two sons, *something the women were unaware of when they met at a buffet table in a bed and breakfast on the Hudson*, they developed a special kinship, came to think of one another as sisters. "My son Andrew is a cadet. You must have a son at the Academy too?" Helen asked.

"I do, Chris, he's just beginning *Yearling,*" Barb said.

Helen looked at Barb, beautiful woman, *and when a woman thinks another woman is beautiful, she is.* Barb, looked back, quizzically. The aha moment over coffee, *our boys know each other?* started a lifelong friendship. The chance meeting turned into the day that the Great Army Sister Friendship was born.

SHIELDED BENEATH THE LARGE TENT, shaded from the late May sun, *just two days before the unofficial start of summer*, parents, friends, party goers, anyone wanting to offer a toast, to speak in honor of Andrew and Chris, clinked a teaspoon against a raised glass. Within the celebration, a collective sigh could be felt too. West Point, the trial, the challenge, the strict discipline, the sometimes doubt, all of that now behind. The party, its helter-skelter momentum gathering inertia, broke the hold the last four years had over everyone.

Helen and Barb, hoping for a quiet moment with Andrew and Chris, confided in each other. "Don't you want to know what the past four years means to Chris?" Helen asked. "I'd like to know what Andrew thinks, now that it's behind him."

"Of course I do," Barb said. "You think we can corral them long enough to get a minute?"

"Maybe."

Good luck with that.

Helen and Barb tried, but were denied their *Hallmark* moment. The newly minted officers, shiny butter bars on their collars, two boys, men now, who'd begun their journey four years earlier, were beside themselves with joy. Lost in the moment, they had no room for reflection. Celebration ruled. The joyful day, lasting into the night, moved from the Hudson to the B&B, the same one in which Helen and Barb became sisters three years earlier.

Andrew and Chris outpaced their parents and friends. *Boys to men*, they partied into the wee hours, heady with relief and accomplishment, reveling *with spirits*, in their newfound freedom, and their accomplishments.

Sometime in the middle of the night, celebration outdistancing the party goers' stamina, Andrew and Chris went looking for a place to crash. When Chris slurred his final *see you later, Lieutenant,* Andrew, alone now, went looking for the most important person in his life.

In the morning, Helen and Bob woke to find Andrew on the floor at the foot of their bed, still dressed, asleep. Helen looked at him, *he always comes looking for me . . .*

She had a few more minutes to watch him, a little more time before he stirred. If there's a *Catch-22* to motherhood, it's wanting a child to grow, then wishing that it didn't happen so fast. Today was the day she'd really be letting go.

This wasn't the first time she watched her son sleep, just the first time in a while. She'd watched over him many nights, peered into the darkness when he was an infant, watched his tiny chest rise and fall, put her hand on him, the warmth of his skin finding her heart. She'd bent over him, kissed him, assured herself that he was okay—breathing. So many nights when she checked on her sleeping son, the infant, the boy, and now the man asleep on the floor of her room.

A lifetime of memories flooded over her, silly, happy, sad. Moments that endeared mother to son, son to mother over two decades came randomly over graduation weekend. While she watched him sleep. When she pinned lieutenant bars to his collar. As others offered their congratulations down by the Hudson. So much to remember, a fast-forward playback, continuous loop, while she watched Andrew at the foot of her bed. So many moments . . .

"*Supper's ready,*" *Helen said.*

Andrew, twelve years old, middle school, pulled a chair out from the table, sat without saying a word.

"You're pretty quiet," Helen said, noticing that Andrew was sort of pouty. He's never pouty, especially when it's time to eat. "Everything okay?"

"Yes," Andrew said, reluctant to say more.

"Yes? I don't think so. Something's bothering you. You want to talk about it?"

"It's just some of the other kids."

"What about some of the other kids?"

"Well, I heard them talking about nerds. Sounded like they think it's not okay to get good grades. I mean it sounded like they use the word to make fun of somebody smart."

"What do you think?" Helen said, understanding her son, knowing his sense of right and wrong. "You think being a nerd is a bad thing?"

"No."

"So, what do you care what they think?"

"I know, but—"

"But what? Nerds are smart. It's the nerds that wind up running the world. Just do your best at everything worthwhile. You'll be okay. You got it?"

"I think so. What's for supper?"

The idea took a while to click, but Andrew understood soon enough. He shrugged it off. Sticks and stones and all that. He didn't have to apologize for who he was or for what he wanted.

There was the lighter side to Andrew too, funny things, silly little episodes that brought a smile to Helen, even made her laugh out loud . . .

"You ready for another road trip?" Helen asked nine-year-old Andrew. "I have to go to a conference in DC."

"I can come?"

"You always do, don't you?"

"*Uh huh.*"

"*Well, there's your answer. Be packed, we leave Friday afternoon.*"

Andrew was a trooper. Easy to travel with. Helen would simply tell him where they were going and for how long. She taught him to do his own packing, figure out how many changes of clothes he'd need, two days, three days, always pack one extra outfit, just in case something spilled. After a few trips, Helen stopped checking his bag.

She'd taught him to fend for himself, wanted him to be independent and to know that she trusted him—but—there was one thing he asked her to keep doing—one task he couldn't match. Lunches. Now lunches were a different thing. Helen made the best lunches. Once, one of Andrew's friends admitted to her that he'd become friends with Andrew because he wanted part of his lunch.

"Promise, Mom, that you'll always make my lunch," Andrew pleaded.

Andrew learned to roll out on his own. Helen never thought about leaving him home. There was no "Billy Joel moment," no "Some Folks Like to Get Away" longing. And for his part, Andrew became, by nine, a well-practiced traveler, comfortable on an airplane, train, long trips in a car. Mother and son clicked, like they could read each other's mind. Andrew loved being included, wanted to be with Helen, was happy to be with her.

Saturday in DC, they stayed at the Washington Hilton, pretty fancy for a nine-year-old. Helen, obligated to attend the conference, left Andrew in the care of a nanny, let her plan the day. She took Andrew to Arlington. The rows of marble headstones left Andrew, a rare moment, speechless.

Later in the day, in a cab on their way to a fine restaurant, Helen and two colleagues in the back seat, Andrew riding shotgun, the cab rolled to a stop at a traffic light. Another car pulled up on the right, window down, the cab and the car just a foot apart. Andrew rolled his window down, looked at the driver and said, mimicking the British accent (just like he'd seen in the commercial), "Pardon me, would you have any Grey Poupon?"

The three women in the back seat laughed out loud. The cabbie looked in the rearview, shaking his head at Helen and smiling. Andrew, suddenly straight faced, turned back, lifted his chin, stiff upper lip, and looked forward, unflinching, playing the part of a British stoic to perfection.

PART FIVE

FIRST DEPLOYMENT

September 2008

Helen, alone, flew into Austin—Bergstrom Airport, renamed in 1943 in honor of Army Capt. John August Earl Bergstrom, killed in the Philippines just three days after the attack on Pearl Harbor. While Helen filled out paperwork for a rental, *Fort Hood and the hotel Andrew was staying in almost three hours away*, off to her left, she overheard fragments of conversation.

A young couple, Helen sized them up, *he looks military, young though, wife, I guess that's his wife, she's young too, still a teenager if I had to take a guess, look like newlyweds, all their belongings in an Army duffel and a green plastic bag—oh my!*

"Hi," Helen said, pushing her hand forward, "Are you kids okay? You look lost."

"I've got to get to Fort Hood, I mean we have to get to Fort Hood. I'm going to be stationed there."

"Where are you two from?"

"Idaho, ma'am."

"Well, Idaho, I'm going that way. I'm going to meet my son, let me drive the two of you," Helen said, listening to the boy, *he was still a boy*, breathe a harrumph of surprise.

"Well, ma'am, ah, that would sure help, but we don't want to put you out—"

"Stop. You're not. You won't. I'm going that way in an empty car."

"I guess it's—"

"You guess nothing. It's decided. Follow me. We can put all of this stuff in the trunk," Helen said, gesturing toward her suitcase, the duffel and the *Hefty* double-ply.

"Yes ma'am, we'll take the ride, grateful ma'am, but let me handle your suitcase."

Three hours later, conversation full of yes ma'ams and one-word answers, punctuated with one longer answer, *Helen asked Idaho what he'd be doing in the Army.* "Infantry, ma'am," he said. "Why join the Army if you don't go Infantry?"

Helen made note of the answer.

Hours later, she pulled the rental into the parking lot of a La Quinta Inn, *the kids staying there too, not a surprise, everyone going to the base stayed there, discount for military,* just three miles from the main gate of Fort Hood. Minutes later, in the lobby, Helen hugged Andrew, *off duty, in civvies, T-shirt tight across his chest, shorts and flip flops, small gold crucifix just above the hollow of his chest,* then introduced him to the young couple.

Idaho, his eyes suddenly wide open, mouth agape, looked at Andrew, recognizing not just another soldier, but by Andrew's appearance, *he moved with ease, brown in-country T-shirt tight across his chest, broad shoulders, neck thick, older,* most likely an officer, immediately stood straight, almost locking his heels at attention.

"Relax soldier," Andrew said, carrying the conversation, putting the young soldier and his even younger wife at ease. "We're both off duty here. My mother tells me you're headed to Fort Hood."

"Yes, sir. I am. AIT, sir."

"Well, it's good to meet you soldier. Good luck."

"Thank you, sir."

Everyone rode the elevator to their rooms. The young couple, their room across the hall from Andrew, said their goodnights.

Inside his room, Andrew and Helen settled in. "Are you all set?" Helen asked, looking at Andrew's duffel and backpack.

"All set, Mom."

"Well, what about the car? You're going to be gone for a year; have you decided what to do with it? Can you leave it here?"

"I suppose I could. I hadn't given it much thought."

Helen and Andrew small-talked their way through the next hour, the conversation turning to the young couple, Helen's chance meeting with them.

"They're so young, Andrew, maybe eighteen, the same age you were when you started at the Academy. Probably not a nickel between them. It's a tough way to start out. Where will she stay if he's here for AIT? Do you know?"

"Maybe she's just traveling with him, Mom," Andrew said. "Maybe she'll go back home once he reports in. They won't have much time together, not with him going through AIT. I hope she goes back home; it would be better for both of them, wait for his PCS orders."

"You know what he said to me in the car?" Helen said, answering her own question. "I asked him what he'd be doing in the Army, he said 'Why join the Army if you don't go Infantry?' That's what he told me, Andrew. I think he's a good kid, but they're so young."

"I think I know what to do with the car," Andrew said.

"What?"

"If I'm right about this kid, you'll see. Why don't you get them, tell them I want to see him."

Helen knocked on the door. Idaho looked surprised to see her standing there. "My son wants to see you," she said, watching concern spread across the young soldier's face, what little self-confidence he had disappearing, his wife's look of surprise.

"Come with me," Helen said, her voice, *unintentional,* sounded more like an order than an invitation. Idaho followed her through the door, his young wife, sheepish, followed the two of them.

Inside the room, Helen stepped away. The kids, *worried whispers,* mumbled to each other. Helen, amused, hid her smile. Andrew pulled the young couple aside. Within a few minutes, satisfied with whatever he'd discussed with them, Andrew beckoned to Helen.

"What did you ask him?" Helen said, her voice low, soft enough so that Idaho and his bride couldn't hear.

"I asked him to repeat what he told you in the car, about Infantry. I like his attitude."

Mother and son looked at the kids in front of them, then at each other, nodded their approval to each other. "I'll give the car to them," Andrew whispered. "If you're right, if they don't have two nickels to rub together, a car could help. If she stays here, gets a job, she'll have a way to get to work. Yeah, I'm going to do it. Let's give the car to them."

Andrew faced the young couple. "I like your attitude, soldier," he said. "So, listen up. I'll be on deployment for the next year. Got a car I need to do something with. I'd like to give it to you," Andrew said. "My car," he said, when Idaho looked like he didn't quite understand.

"For real, sir?" the soldier said, after he found his voice.

"For real, soldier. I'll sign it over to you now."

———

LATER THAT NIGHT, Army Ranger, First Lieutenant Andrew Pedersen-Keel boarded the airplane that would carry him to his first deployment. No matter how prepared, *doesn't matter how rigorous the training, some of it even bordering on brutality, Army*

Special Forces, Navy SEALs, Marine Recon, no matter how ready a soldier believes he or she is, there's an innocence and a question mark before first combat deployments. IEDs, bullets, RPGs, torn flesh, shattered bone, a soldier's final scream, the smell of blood and fear, strips even the most stoical of their innocence, sometimes even their courage. No one experiences those things and escapes unchanged, unscathed. And no one knows, really knows, how they will perform when real bullets fly, when someone, a stranger, is trying to kill you, and you, *you,* may have to take a life. All of that remains a question mark until you live it. First time combat is the big stage, opening night after all the rehearsals.

Captain Andrew Pedersen-Keel, Infantry Rifle Platoon Leader and XO, *promoted in country by General Petraeus,* returned from Maiwand, Afghanistan, one year later. One-hundred-and-fifty foot patrols later. Three lethal air assaults later. Innocence lost. No questions unanswered.

Quiet. Serious. Aged.

PART SIX

THE LAST DAY

MARCH 11, 2013

The day she found out Andrew died, *was killed*, up since 2:00 a.m., Helen busied herself at work. The uneasiness that had pulled her from bed in the middle of the night, *she'd hurried to her computer, logged on and had begun searching for what, she didn't know, just that she had to find something about Andrew, pictures, breaking news, something, anything to assure herself that Andrew was okay*, had followed her into the office, sitting on her shoulders throughout the day.

Whenever she had a minute, a break in the action, no one calling her name, *Helen can you find—Helen can you set up a follow-up appointment for Mrs.— Helen do you have the scan for—Helen can you—Helen—Helen*—she logged on to her personal account, typed keywords into the browser. *Still nothing. Okay, back to work before someone comes looking for me.*

SEPTEMBER 5, 2012

Days earlier, Helen had flown to North Carolina, *part of his plans for a future, Andrew had a home of his own there*, to spend time with Andrew, say goodbye before he left for Afghanistan, help him get ready, this time as a Special Forces Green Beret captain. Although he'd been dubbed officially badass, graduating from Special Forces, he still let Helen take care of his laundry.

They had those few final days in front of them, some stuff to do—*"Where's your laundry?"* Helen asked. *"I'll get everything washed, especially those Special Forces uniforms."*—pack, set up things that would need looking after while Andrew was away, but plenty of time to visit. Helen met all of his friends, roomies, others in Andrew's orbit.

The days, reminiscent of their early years together, except for the few beers they shared, were some of the happiest they'd had together in a while. *Intimate. Relaxed. Fun.* They listened to music. Laundry, most of his gear so new, didn't need washing, done quickly. Helen folded; Andrew packed. They took breaks for lunch. Elliotts Restaurant, great burgers. Dined out at night. No cooking allowed on this trip. Each day, the few that they had, was a celebration.

A few serious moments tried to force their way into the conversation. Helen, not her first rodeo now, knew what to stay away from, knew that Andrew, protective of her, his Mumsie, *he'd spent too much time with the Brits on his first deployment, drove a Land Rover too,* would slough off questions that she might have raised about his deployment.

She risked one question, something important for her to understand. "So, why are you doing this? Why are you going back?" she said.

"I'm going back because I like the people," Andrew replied, his voice lighthearted. "I really believe we can help them, maybe show them a better life, maybe help them live a better life."

They danced their way through the days. Helen looked at books that lined the shelves of a bookcase. They'd, *since he'd become older,* shared the same books, light reading like *The*

History of Constantine. Helen wished the days, a final blessing, two people, a mother and a son, *who got each other*, could have lasted a little longer.

Andrew, *before wheels up*, was anxious for one last night out with his friends. Three days after she arrived, he drove Helen back to the airport. Along the way Helen spotted a sporting goods store. "Stop there. Let me get you another jacket," she said. "Something that will keep you warmer than anything you have." Inside the store, they walked the aisles, sifted through clothes racks. Hanger hooks complaining, screeching, as Helen pushed jackets back, searching, then freeing the one she wanted.

"There, Andrew, that's the one," she said, holding up a jacket at arm's length, pressing it close to him, sizing it. "What do you think? Black bomber jacket. Lined. It's the right one."

Inside the airport they linked arms, walked to Helen's departure gate, really a short flight back to Connecticut. "I love you so much, Andrew," Helen said, "be safe"—her final words to Andrew, words most mothers, fathers too, say to the sons and daughters they send off to war's abattoir.

"I love you too, Mom," Andrew said, suddenly looking younger, *his little boy showing.*

MONDAY! Every day is busy; Mondays are the worst. Sickness doesn't take weekends off. Helen waded through the flood of calls, messages, the numbers grew thick over the weekend. She triaged the callbacks. The day, on little sleep, felt more hectic than most. Helen left work, a bit late, but not late enough to miss the parking lot, Southern Connecticut's notorious traffic jam on I-95, commuters pouring into and out of New York. One accident and she could be there until early evening.

Traffic at a standstill, Helen answered her cell phone.

"Bob, what's up?"

"When are you coming home, Helen," Bob said, the notification team waiting in front of the house. "I thought you'd be home by now?"

"I'm coming, just stuck in traffic. Okay, gotta go, we're moving again," Helen said, brushing off a cold chill, the unusual call from Bob. *Hmm, something must be up. Oh well, I'll be there when I get there.* An hour later, Helen pulled into the driveway. *Car parked in front of the house, that's unusual. I wonder if that's why Bob called. Somebody here? Wow, I'm tired, so happy to be home. Supper, I could use some supper. Let me park. What's this? Why is Bob coming out? He doesn't do that. Geez, what a beautiful spring day, warm for this time of year, still light out. Time change yesterday, Love the longer days.*

"Hey, hon, is everything okay?"

"Come inside. I'll tell you once we're inside," Bob said, touching her elbow, gently, walking her over the threshold. Inside the house, two men, officers, blue trousers, gold stripe running waist to ankle, brass on their collars, oak leaf cluster and a chaplain's cross, hats tucked to their left sides, pinned there by an elbow, silent. The awkward quiet overwhelmed everyone until the officer stepped forward in front of Helen. She understood immediately. Her knees buckled. Bob grabbed an elbow, saved her from collapsing, helped her into the living room.

"Ma'am, are you Helen Keiser-Pedersen?" the major asked, watching Helen nod. "Ma'am, I've been asked . . ."

"What?" Helen said, in disbelief. "Say that again."

"Ma'am?"

"Say that again, please, I need to hear it again. I don't believe it," Helen said.

The major repeated the words, slowly, his voice calm, respectful, honoring Helen's request without question. The suffocating deliberateness of his monologue smothering the last vestige of hope that Helen clung to.

And that was it. Helen's life changed forever. *Her one miracle was gone.*

WANTING the officer and chaplain to leave, Helen wishing they were gone; the officers, held hostage to the moment, made certain Helen would not need medical assistance. They explained what would happen next. "Ma'am," the major said, "A CAO, sorry ma'am that's a Casualty Assistance Officer, he or she will contact you, set a time to come to the house, walk you through everything. The Army is doing everything to return your son to you, to get him home from Afghanistan as quickly as possible."

Almost relieved to see them go, *they can't help me now,* Helen's instincts took over. She was an Army mom called to duty. She responded to the immediacy of the moment. *Calls! I've got to start making calls. I've got to call family, Celeste, quick before she hears it on the news.*

She reached Marianne and Nick, Celeste's parents.

"Helen, sorry doesn't feel like it's enough," Marianne said. "Thank you for getting to us so quickly. We just put Celeste on a train back to Brooklyn. We're leaving now, it's at least four hours from here in Milton. We'll try to get there before she does."

Wanting to be the ones to tell their daughter, Marianne and Nick hung up and left. They'd only just celebrated the weekend with her. The celebration and her good news about medical residency at Virginia Tech, suddenly smothered by the news of Andrew's death. They got to Brooklyn too late. Helen's niece, *impatient,* took it upon herself and called Celeste before they arrived.

Helen finished making calls to family, friends, people who should know—*now.* Others could wait. She made one more call. Helen called the church. Father Jim Shanley hurried himself out of the parsonage and drove the short distance to Bob and Helen's home. Prayed with them. Trying to sustain Helen in the moment, he offered what comfort he could, becoming a lifelong friend.

Bob. He did his best to console Helen. He held her. She could feel him, must know how much he loved Andrew too. He acknowledged her grief, knew he could not take it away, only that he could grieve with her.

Sleep. If only I could. What now? This seems impossible, the most impossible thing in my life, in the entire world. How will I do this, go on without my son? How do others do this? They must. I'm not the first one to lose a son to war. This, this is as old as mankind. This is so—new. Why? Why was Andrew taken from me in a hailstorm of bullets? Did the gunman decide his family's life was more important than Andrew's? Was he threatened into killing the soldiers he'd laughed with in the weeks he'd walked among them? Was he some sort of fanatic? I don't understand.

Andrew. Me. He was more than a son. I was more than a mother. We were friends—a team. Great together, no matter what was in front of us. We always seemed to find each other, even in tough situations, we figured things out. My God, we so lucky.

And that, once her eyes closed, was what Helen went to sleep with. No regrets, just sadness, and a future without Andrew.

EARLY THE NEXT MORNING, before storm clouds released a cold March rain, Army Guard Reserve Officer Corey Holmes stood on the front step to Helen and Bob's house. He wore the Army Dress Blue uniform, creased trousers, knife-edged, blue jacket, ribbons. Polished captain's bars, spotless, reflected what little light the grey morning offered. He paused, took a breath, reminded himself, *no matter what needs to be done, regardless of the schedule, these people have lost their son; patience, respect, kindness, that's the most important thing.*

Bob heard the knock, opened the door.

"Sir, I'm Captain Corey Holmes. I called last night. Good morning, sir."

"Good morning, Captain, please come in," Bob said, stepping aside, ushering Captain Holmes inside. "My wife will be with us in a minute. Sit please."

Corey and Bob remained standing until Helen joined them. After offering his regrets, not wanting to overwhelm, Corey explained as much as he thought he should, at least for now.

"Your son is on his way to Dover," he said. "I'll get you there in plenty of time. Don't worry about where you will stay. Rooms are ready for you at Fisher House. There's no cost to you. You'll have everything you need while you wait for the airplane to touch down."

Everything that needed to happen, *everything that had to happen*, trespassed against the space where Helen might have stolen a moment to grieve. But grief, patient, no expiration or sell-by date, having all the time in the world, waited its turn. Overwhelmed, barely aware of everything that was happening, *Andrew already in the sky*, Helen and Bob sat next to each other inside an official US Army vehicle, a no-frills, cold, uncomfortable six-hour ride. Two journeys, thousands of miles apart, connected by a common thread.

Suddenly, like a bad movie script, the bloated rain clouds loosed a deluge.

Helen listened to rain pelt the roof, wipers swiping at the windshield, tires loudly cutting a swath through the rain-drenched highway. She barely spoke. Cried, *didn't care who heard or watched*, whenever she felt overcome.

Late in the day they arrived at Fisher House—to wait—and wait—hours filled with nothing to do. Awake most of the night, up since early morning, unable to sleep, Helen felt weighed down, wondered how much longer she could hold it together, how much longer she could keep doing this. She told herself what she'd taught Andrew, *there will be times in your life when you will have to do tough things—you just have to make sure you show up.* This was one of those moments.

Close to midnight, the wait was over.

"Ma'am," Corey said, "I have an ETA. The airplane is about an hour out, should touch down around 1:00 a.m. We should head over to the airfield."

Corey led Helen, Bob, other close family members to a waiting bus. They boarded in the rain. The bus roared to life, pulled away from Fisher House. It's a short ride in the dark, rain, wind, cold. Everyone, family, friends, soldiers, anyone who could get there, already waited at Dover to greet the airplane and Andrew's casket. Rex's casket too, and the caskets of four other American heroes.

Soldiers waited on the tarmac, oblivious to the cold and rain. Some knew Andrew and Rex. Some had been friends to one of the other fallen soldiers. Soldiers, those who didn't personally know any of the returning men, duty bound, showed up to honor the dead.

The bus, wet brakes complaining loudly, rolled to a stop. Folding doors clacked open. Helen, Bob, Corey, everyone on the bus, shuffled out into the night. Helen shivered against the cold—the wet. On cue, soldiers showed up with blankets, handed one to Helen and all the families that waited. Bob unfolded a blanket and draped it over Helen's shoulders. Helen stood waiting, surrounded by soldiers. *So many of them. Soldiers. I love them all.*

Out on the runway, the airplane touched down, the screech of the tires, and the roar of its engines, loud over the wind and rain. The airplane's bright landing lights pierced the darkness, wingtip lights flashing as the pilot taxied to the tarmac. Ground crew, orange vests, giant red ear muffs, glowing wands, one in each hand, guided the airplane, positioning it on the tarmac not far from the people huddled against the weather.

The whine of the engines slowed, stopped—quieted. The cacophony of sounds, a contrasting diminuendo lingering for a moment, became a faint echo of sorrow dissolving into the night. Without warning, the rear bay doors of the airplane lowered, revealing the flag-draped caskets. Step by step, a carry team of six members, obeying subdued commands, marched to the rear of the airplane. The whispered command, "Haaalt," stopped the team. They took a moment before moving into the airplane. When they reappeared, carrying Andrew's casket, Helen fell to her knees, the sound coming from her throat, barely recognizable, begging to take her son's place. Bob, Corey, others quickly supported her. The carry team slowly carried Andrew to a waiting vehicle. Soft cries from the many gathered on the tarmac, their gentle murmurs, stifled sobs, muted by the falling rain and wind, disappeared.

Chris Day walked behind the casket, saluting Andrew as the team lifted his remains, then solemnly slipped him inside a waiting hearse. At the Fisher House, Helen and Bob, everyone else, gathered after Andrew was moved to the mortuary. Chris, still wearing his dirty uniform, *twenty hours earlier he'd been in a combat zone in Afghanistan*, his hair shaggy, face covered with the Special Forces signature beard, walked into the reception room. One by one, he embraced the others, tears disappearing into his beard. Two weeks later, Chris would bring Andrew home to Connecticut.

Night slid toward morning. Helen, exhausted, collapsed onto a bed, sinking into the folds of a plush comforter. Cocooned in its soft embrace, she slept.

A day later, Helen and Bob were back home. The house, empty for a few days, felt cold, different, *everything feels different now.* In the following days, Helen and Bob sat down with Corey. He'd remain available to them long after military protocol demanded. Helen had questions. Bob too. There were issues, uncomfortable details she didn't understand, know, or think to ask. But that was the job, the duty, that all CAOs like Captain Corey Holmes understood. What the family didn't ask, the CAO had to bring up, explain. Sensitive issues—things that feel cold-blooded, businesslike, uncaring.

Corey, patient, kind, respectful, went far beyond the call of duty.

———

AT DOVER, mortuary specialists carefully restored Andrew. Likely referring to photographs, they did everything they could to allow for an open casket. Less than two weeks later, on a Friday, Andrew's remains, accompanied by Chris, arrived in Connecticut. Helen, Bob, more family waited at the airport. The Delta pilot delayed the passenger exit until Andrew's remains were placed inside the hearse. A small procession, escorted by Connecticut's Patriot Guard, a rider ahead of the hearse, the hearse followed by the car carrying Helen and Bob, and then the protective line of Patriot Guard riders trailing the small procession, taking Andrew home.

Before the wake, Helen and Bob, in private, had their first look at Andrew. Helen, as if she were tracing the contours of Andrew's face, pressed her fingers against his lips, breathed in, then slid her fingertips along his face and up over his eyes.

Look at him. Eyelashes. His skin so fresh. His beard is gone. Makes him look so young. Sleeping. He looks like he's just sleeping. He looks perfect.

"I'm a lucky mother," she whispered, fingering her rosary. "I got to see my son one last time. So many mothers don't."

St. George's priests, *Helen didn't ask or expect*, on Monday, held a Mass, the celebration blossomed out of love for Helen and Andrew. The offering of support, and a tribute to

Andrew, drew a large crowd. Hundreds of mourners and well-wishers filled the church, and waited outside.

I hope they don't think, expect me to say something . . .

—I won't

—I can't

If I had to stand in front of all these people, something inside of me would break before I could get a word out.

Months from now, maybe longer, *out of obligation and duty*, she'd become good at that sort of thing—talking to crowds. For now, she drew comfort from the outpouring of goodwill. That was all she needed.

Two days later, Andrew, always on the move, had one more journey, his final destination. Arlington National Cemetery, Section 69, Marker 10108. Sixteen days earlier, Andrew woke on a cold Afghan spring morning. The boy who'd been born on the other side of the world, the boy who'd become a soldier, trying to do good.

PART SEVEN

SENSE OF AN ENDING

AFTER ARLINGTON . . .

—*Helen, Bob, and Corey came home to Connecticut.*
—*Chris went back to the war in Afghanistan.*
—*Family and friends went back to work, back to their lives.*
—*The war in Afghanistan continued.*
—*The Army abandoned the VSP at Jalrez.*

IN CONNECTICUT, back in their own living room, Helen and Bob, Corey too, sat. Silent. Exhausted. The first pause since Andrew died.

"That's it?" Helen said, at first softly, then louder a second time. "That's it? Andrew's amazing life is finished? Just like that—that's the end?!"

Bob looked at Corey, then Helen. He shrugged his shoulders, turtled his neck, breathed in, then exhaled like air escaping from a balloon. "It doesn't have to be," he said. "We can do something." Corey nodded in agreement.

Helen, eyes bloated with tears, began to cry openly. "Like what?" she said. "Like what?"

"We can start a charity, or a commemorative race, a foundation, something like that. Others have done it," Bob said. Corey echoed.

And so, they did.

The Andrew Pedersen-Keel Charity (APK Charities) was born— grew, evolved. The money raised goes to a direct assistance program for veterans in need. Helen, Bob, and Corey established an annual 5K road race, the APK 5K, the first Saturday of each November. Later, The Desert Eagles Nest Thrift Store, a store with a little bit of everything for home and family, opened its doors. All proceeds go to the APK Charities Direct Assistance Program.

Helen stayed busy. *Tributes. Different veterans' holidays. Alive Day. West Point commemorations.* The pace didn't allow any grass to grow beneath her feet. She even began, *she wasn't*, to believe that she'd be okay, but getting on with the business of life continued to outwit her. The grief that plagued her, weeds that no matter how many times she tore them up, always grew back. Closure was some cruel myth, a search for the Holy Grail—an endless crusade. She confided in Bob, telling him, "I'm not the person I was."

He remained steadfast in his support. Without him, Helen would have withered.

Work. She'd asked them to wait. She'd be back. "Give me six months, by September," she promised, "I'll be back." She never returned.

Grief counselors. She met a few, engaged with them. No help. She stopped going, *I need to save myself,* and started searching for her own solutions. She keyed the word "Abbey" into the computer browser. Google. *Thousands. Refine the search.* *"Local."*

A link. Benedictine Abbey of Regina Laudis, Litchfield County, Bethlehem, *Bethlehem, really,* and here in Connecticut. She double-clicked. Home page came up. Phone number prominently displayed. She called, surprised when someone, *not a recorded message,* actually answered. Helen explained. A

Benedictine nun, voice soft, contemplative, asked a few simple questions.

"What do you want to do? Why do you want to come here?" she asked, her voice tranquil.

Helen answered the only way she knew how, with the truth.

"I understand," the sister said. "Please, we have many people who want to come here, please send your information to the Abbey on a simple postcard. Also, on the card, write a message, telling again why you want to come here."

Helen sent the card with a simple message that read—**I need help. My son in the Army has been killed.**

The sisters invited her to the Abbey. She stayed. The cloister of women, intelligent, compassionate, loving, helped her move past the sadness. She left the Abbey, *always coming back*, with the strength to navigate her way through a new life, a different life. One without Andrew.

A FEW YEARS PASSED.

"They're having a Christmas party," Corey said. He'd remained part of the small cadre of family and friends, the good sisters from the Abbey, and Bob, people who had closed ranks around Helen in the early days and weeks after Andrew's death, the ones who made up the intimate circle still supporting Helen.

"Who?" Helen asked. "Who's having a Christmas party?"

"The Gold Star Mothers, the Connecticut Chapter."

"What? And no one called me? What's up with that?" she said, pretending to feel hurt.

She went to the Christmas party—became president of the Connecticut Chapter of Gold Star Mothers. The small circle that supported her grew.

Life began to look different. There was work to do. If

Andrew could give his life believing he could do good in another part of the world and trying to help others, Helen could do the same. Others needed care and comfort, the same love and compassion Helen had been given. Helen heeded the call.

"After all," she said. "I'm a soldier mom."

Captain Andrew Pedersen-Keel, June 8, 1984—March 11, 2013

At the Army/Navy Game. From left: Barb Day, Chris Day, Andrew Pedersen-Keel, Helen (Andrew's mother)

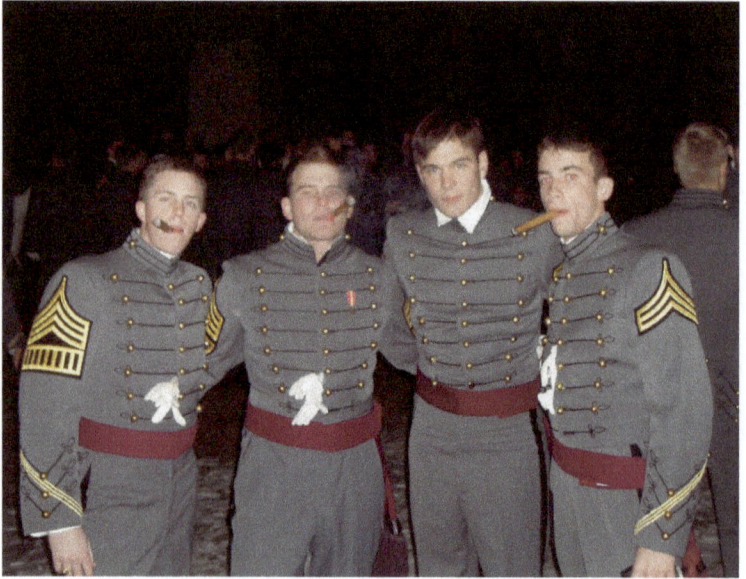

Cadets at West Point. Andrew, 2nd from left. Chris Day to his left.

Graduation Day, West Point

Swearing-in in front of American Infantry Soldier monument

Andrew and Chris travel the country after graduating from West Point

Andrew's daily Yoga routine on trip after graduation from West Point

Swearing in an American soldier reenlisting while in Afghanistan

Captain Andrew Pedersen-Keel and Air Force ground controller Delorean Sheridan

Discussing tactics with Afghan military police before a mission

Jalrez compound

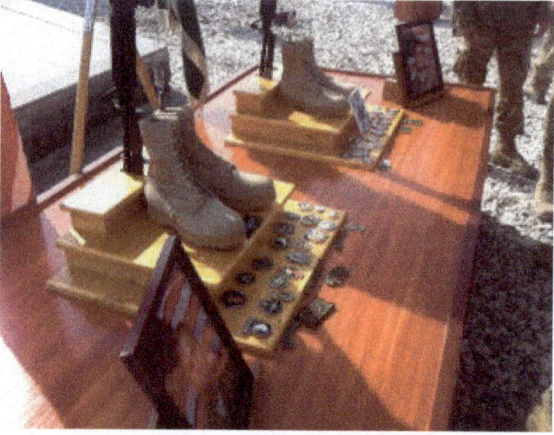

Battlefield memorial to Captain Andrew Pedersen-Keel and SSgt Rex Schad

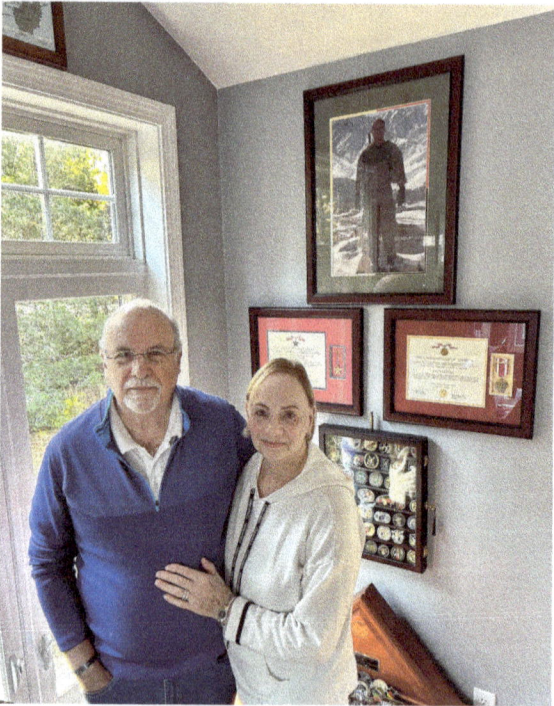

Bob Keiser and Helen Keiser-Pedersen at home with memories of their son Andrew

Every year on the anniversary of the day when Andrew fell, Helen is not the only one to live through grief caused by death. Another mother, a soldier mom like Helen, bows her head too. Colleen Whipple believed she'd been alone when word of her son's death reached her. Her cries that morning, carried on the wind, mingled with Helen's. Rex, Colleen's son, died next to Helen's boy.

There is more to the story. Colleen Whipple and Helen Keiser-Pedersen, two mothers, soldier moms, caught in the same web of tragedy, became entwined forever. There is no her—me—just them, two mothers who lost sons together.

BOOK FOUR:
VOLUME TWO

PART ONE
SOMETHING CLICKED

Rex was alone in a sparsely furnished room, in a building that itself was a rescue. He was eighteen years old, in and out of trouble and running out of chances. But there was more to him than whisky and drugs, more than what the world was seeing. There was something deep and elaborate, like a million-piece puzzle, intricate and complicated. Rex was someone to marvel at—once all the pieces fit together.

A FRIEND, *friend of a friend who had a friend who knew a guy,* had a connection. A clergyman, pastor to a small congregation, had scraped some money together, just enough to buy a small, abandoned building, a vacant hotel on the outskirts of town, Edmond, Oklahoma, where Colleen, *a chance to be close to her aging mom and dad,* had settled.

For the next few years, the area's homeless, once the hotel was refurbished, found refuge with the pastor and his family. But that was before urban sprawl, a strip mall, *they popped up like mushrooms in the forest after a rainy night,* became more important than a shelter for the homeless. The hotel-turned-sanctuary was torn down, but none of that happened before Rex learned something about learning how to breathe on his own.

Rex was the pastor's first asylum seeker, brought to him through the chain of friends who knew Rex and his troubles— and his newest declaration of intent.

"I want to enlist in the Army," Rex said, serious, his announcement raising the eyebrows of many who knew him, most especially his mother, Colleen.

"They will never take you," she told him. "Not if you are doing drugs."

The pastor laid out the terms: no phone, no connection to old friends in the city just a few miles away, no drugs or drink. "That's the deal, if you want to stay," Pastor said. Rex agreed. He stayed under those conditions and the promise to work, *without complaint*, to remake the old hotel into a homeless shelter.

With hammer and crowbar in hand, his body slowly began to forget the bittersweet taste of whisky, and the numbing flush of an opiate high. Encoded in the work, tear down walls, haul trash, cover old paint with new, the message, there's more to life than giving yourself to drugs, *clicked*.

Why? Why this time when other attempts at rehab had failed? Maybe it was the pastor's approach, patient, uncompromising, that kept Rex moving through withdrawal and toward recovery. Maybe it was working with his hands, building something, becoming part of something, something that had meaning. Something bigger than himself. Maybe he really did want to become a soldier. Or maybe Rex had finally had enough. Why does anyone quit using, who can say for certain, but this time sobriety stuck.

MONTHS LATER, after Rex graduated high school, had been working odd jobs, *flipping burgers, groundskeeping at a local golf course*, Colleen, hoping that Rex might have put the idea of the Army aside, even if it was only a temporary hold, took Rex to the University of Central Oklahoma. Rex interviewed well. Colleen wrote a check, covering the application fee. Mother and son, *mother breathing easier*, drove away taking a handful of CLEP exams with them. Why not jump-start the degree with the credits earned from the exams? But Rex had other plans.

"Mom," Rex said, his face a blank, his voice deliberate. "Can we stop somewhere and talk?"

"Okay . . ." Colleen said, looking for a turnoff or a shoulder to ease the car onto, quickly finding a quiet street just a few yards ahead. A little diner too.

Settled in a booth, Rex looked at her, cupping his hands together, supporting his chin, letting out a long slow breath. "I don't want to go to college, at least not now. I want to join the Army."

For a moment, Colleen said nothing.

He's talked about this before. Should I have known this was coming? Yeah—I should have guessed, I just thought with all he's been through, after winning his battle with addiction, re-enrolling in school, graduating —he's so smart. I thought maybe . . . hoped he might go to college, give himself more options—even if he later decided on the Army. Doesn't matter in the end what I want though—does it? This, this is what he wants. I know what to do. I'll do what I've always done. I'll support him, his brother Max too. They are my sons.

"Are you sure about this?" Colleen said, disguising her disappointment. "Because once you go—you don't get to change your mind. You have to follow a lot of rules, some that you won't like. If you get cranky," *she knew her son and how stubborn he could be,* "and tell someone off, it won't go well. If you ever get kicked out, it's not like losing a job, even quitting a job. If you get kicked out of the military it will ruin your life."

"I'm sure," Rex said, and Colleen knew enough about her son to know he'd made up his mind. "I won't quit."

Turned out, Rex was sure. He didn't quit. He made rank quickly, became a great soldier. Infantry. He loved soldiering, and he was good at it. A leader. There's a saying about men in uniform—the uniform wears some men, real soldiers wear the uniform. Rex wore the uniform.

———

EVEN AS A CHILD, Rex had looked after others. Once, Rex, part of a group of children outside in the play yard at pre-school, everyone running, playing, oblivious to their surroundings, looked up, storm clouds darkening the sky. Rex looked for the teacher, didn't see her, knew Oklahoma storm clouds spelled trouble, *big rain*, rounded up all the other children, herding them inside, explaining to the teacher as soon as he saw her that a storm was coming. Surprised, she looked up, and saw the storm quickly moving in on the school, rain drops smacking the ground, puffs of dust exploding. Later, she told Colleen, "I've never seen anything like what Rex had done. I'm surprised that he knew what to do."

For his bravery, five-year-old Rex received a "Certificate for Leaders." It's the kind of boy he was, the kind of man he ultimately became.

His stubborn streak, on display at an early age, did concern Colleen. That lived deep inside of Rex, had taken root at an early age. That, Colleen knew, could get him in trouble in the military. Another schoolyard event, *a different sort of storm this time*, in fifth or sixth grade, reminded her of just how stubborn Rex could be. And if he believed he was on the right side of things, he could be immoveable.

The trouble started on the playground. Rex spotted a Tony Soprano wanna-be, older and bigger than himself, picking on a special-needs kid, a boy unable to stand up for himself. Rex, *the way he saw it, it was his job*, intervened. He stepped in between the bully and the defenseless, younger, smaller boy.

"Leave him alone," Rex said, looking up into the face of the taller boy.

"Make me," the bully said, miscalculating Rex's resolve.

A scuffle, like a lightening flash, erupted. Schoolboy punches thrown quickly, turned into a grappling struggle, both boys rolled on the ground, tumbling over each other while a crowd of grade schoolers gathered around them. *Fight! Fight!* Teachers pulled them apart, escorted them to the principal's office.

"You," one of the teachers said, pointing at Rex, "sit over there near the principal's office door. Wait there and be quiet."

Forty-five minutes later, *the other boy sent back to class*, Rex, having, at least as far he was concerned, waited long enough, left the office unnoticed then slipped out of the school. An hour later he banged on the kitchen door to his grandparents' house.

"What are you doing here?" they asked, looking up from coffee and a newspaper. "Aren't you supposed to be in school?"

Rex explained. His grandfather called Colleen, then the school. They, *the school doors unlocked, left wide open,* had no idea that Rex was gone. Colleen, *Rex in tow*, marched into the school. This time the wait went quickly.

"Listen," she said, "to what my son has to say. He did the right thing."

Rex told his side of the story. He knew he was right and he wasn't about to let it go until they listened. That was all he wanted. If he had something on his chest, especially if he was in the right, he wasn't about to give in or let it go until he fixed it or straightened it out. That stubborn streak, *he never outgrew it,* might have worked in fifth grade, but against Army chickenshit . . .?

PART TWO
YOU CAN'T HAVE THEM BOTH, NOT YET!

NOT LONG AFTER THE VISIT TO THE UNIVERSITY, REX, *HIS mind made up, impatient,* wanted to meet with the local Army recruiter. "I'll go with you," Colleen said. "There are questions," *Colleen, a twenty-year Navy veteran,* "that I'll know to ask."

"I'm coming," Max, *Colleen's second son, Rex's younger brother,* said. "I've been thinking about signing up too."

Days later, Colleen, Rex, and Max met with the recruiter. Colleen sat in the hall while the boys took the Armed Services Vocational Aptitude Battery, ASVAB. The recruiter waited for them to finish, impatiently tapping his thumb against the desk top. Rex and Max finished. The recruiter scored the tests. The boys easily bested the minimum score requirements. The recruiter, *quotas to fill,* gushed over the prospect of signing up two enlistees.

"Not so fast!" Colleen said. "You don't get them both at the same time. Max is only a junior in high school. Seventeen."

Rex enlisted, his plan, MOS 11B, Rifleman. Then Ranger. If soldiering went well, maybe the Army crown jewel, Special Forces, Green Beret, would become part of his future. For now, to get Rex in shape, *his ASVABs were great, physically he might not have been ready*, the recruiter met with Rex every morning for a few weeks, running him around a big mall. The recruiter watched. Rex ran. He got ready. And then, just like that, he was off. In January 2006, Recruit Private Rex Schad reported to Fort Benning, Georgia, for three months of basic training.

Firm, wanting Max to finish high school before making decisions about the military or college, Colleen had a little time. Max, only seventeen, needed her signature to enlist. Holding onto her required permission, thinking she'd quieted the idea of the Army, Colleen bought herself a minute, time to possibly change a mind. She wouldn't give them both to the Army, at least not yet anyway. She was happy when Max graduated high school, took a job in a local garage, and signed up at a local tech school.

REX FIRST, and then Max, proved to Colleen that there is a God. Having lived with two sisters, a brother too, Colleen had witnessed the sisters redefine sibling rivalry. Watching their skirmishes, quarrels just short of bloodletting, she begged off of ever having daughters of her own. "God," she prayed, "if I ever have children, *boys*, give me boys, please!" When she did become pregnant, before ultrasound became routine, she never thought to choose, *in the event of*, a name for a girl. Her prayers were answered.

Rex, born in January of 1987, walked early, talked early too, his three earliest words, mommy, daddy, and french fries. By the time he could chew, Colleen would slip him McDonald's fries broken into small bits. He gobbled them up and pleaded for more. From his car seat, alert, inquisitive, he'd blurt out "French fries, french fries," whenever he spotted the golden arches, which was often, *the fast-food burger joint on the route home*.

Active-duty Navy, Colleen and her husband, active-duty too, stationed in San Diego, lived within view of the ocean. Shore duty, a lot like a day job, gave Colleen plenty of time to take Rex to the beach. The living was easy, idyllic for a toddler. For almost two years, Rex had Colleen all to himself.

"You're going to have," *ultrasound this time*, "a new baby brother," Colleen said, sitting down and trying to explain things to Rex, who gave her the quizzical look of a toddler. But the day Max was born, Rex, with his grandparents, understood what a new baby brother actually meant. Everything had been going fine until Rex saw Max.

"No. No," he said, waving his little hands in the air dismissively. "Let's go home."

Rex and Max, *at times*, were more like strangers than brothers. Different in almost every way. Max rarely caused trouble. Rex caused enough mischief for the both of them. They were both video gamers, Max the more addicted to the PlayStation than Rex, but it had been Rex who tried to sneak, *parental discretion advised*, Mortal Kombat—*Long ago at the beginning of time, there existed only three core immortal and divine beings in the entire universe; the Titans, the Elder Gods, and the One Being. The One Being gained his power by draining it from both the Elder Gods and the Titans, consuming them in the process*, into the car. Colleen marched the nine-year-old back into the video store.

"What the heck are you doing renting this to a nine-year-old?" she growled at the clerk.

"Hey, he told me you were in the car and that it was okay."

"And you believed him?"

Mortal Kombat back on the shelf. The score: Colleen—1. Randy's Video—0.

As they grew, became young boys, teenagers, their differences more defined, *make no mistake though, they always had each other's back*, Max was the quieter of the two. Rex, outgoing, really social, adventurous, a schemer, usually with some plan to make money, always had something in the works, usually a way to game the system or bend a rule. Max, *he kept them organized by author*, might be in his room reading a book. His room was neat, tidy, his shirts sorted by color and sleeve lengths, Max liked things just right. Rex, not so much.

Rex and Max thrived on routine. Colleen, single mom, *Rex Sr. didn't stick around long once Max was born*, organized their lives. She had to. On her own, she needed the structure as much as Rex and Max. Family night. Pizza night. Your turn to cook night. Fixed time for homework. Sports. Life worked for the three of them, especially with some help from Colleen's dad.

Both boys were athletic. Baseball. Basketball pickup games at the end of the street, a cul-de-sac. Wrestling, *until*, deep into a tournament, Rex's next opponent was a girl. He refused. Forfeited the match. Never wrestled again. Stuck to baseball.

Colleen wondered about girlfriends.

Neither Rex or Max had steady girlfriends, but they did go to the high school dances. Colleen explained what a gentleman was, hoped that was enough. She explained too about too much Axe cologne. "Whew, boys," she advised, wrinkling her nose, "less is more." She counseled too, when you go to these dances, ask the girls without dates to dance, be considerate. Rex took her advice. He danced with as many girls as he could.

Colleen saw Rex off to his new dance partner, the Army. What she hadn't seen coming, Max, out of high school and working, waiting for classes to start at tech school, came home after work one afternoon and dropped a bomb. "I enlisted today," he said.

The Army, the country, and two wars, had Colleen's sons now.

PART THREE

COLLEEN WHIPPLE

To know someone's children, to really know them, you need to know their mother. That's how you know who they will become.

Behind her broad smile, flashing eyes, and saucy wit, Navy veteran, single mom, Colleen Whipple, daughter of a career military veteran and a Scottish mother, *she was actually from Scotland, met Colleen's father just after the end of WWII, while he was stationed in Liverpool, three hours from the Scottish border,* is more than anything, a survivor. A capable woman. Strong willed. Independent. Deeply caring. Traits she would pass on to her boys.

Daughter of a career military father, Air Force, Colleen was born on Westover Air Force Base. The winters growing up in New England, Westover was in Massachusetts, were cold and long. The snow, a lot of it, always seemed to be over her little-girl head. Colleen lived the nomadic life of a military family until her father retired.

After high school, she'd navigated her way through a few semesters at Central State. Nearing the end of a third semester, *not feeling it, was the way she put it, not part of the campus party crowd,* she called her dad, spoke with mom, too.

"I can't do this anymore," she said. "I've got plans, not

sure what they are, but what I am sure of is that I don't want to do this anymore. Whatever becomes my plan, it won't include this."

"You've got time before next semester, take a break and then go back," her dad said.

"No, I don't think so."

"Why not?"

"Because I don't want to," Colleen offered, eventually passing the independent gene to Rex.

"Then come to Kansas City, live with us, here, at home, until you figure things out," Mom and Dad said, a no-strings offer.

"That'll work, Dad. Thanks."

Back with family, *until they moved to New Orleans*, Collen worked odd jobs. With a few dollars in her pocket, no responsibilities, free spirited, she traveled, mostly to England and Scotland. By the time her folks left for New Orleans, Colleen had reconnected with a classmate, a casual friend from high school. They rented an apartment together. Turned out that her college classmates didn't have a monopoly on sex, drugs, and rock and roll. Her new roommate liked to party too.

During a visit with her mom and dad, seduced by N'Awlins, Colleen stayed. She quickly found a job, one she loved, working for an off shore oil rigging company. With her hair tucked securely under a hard hat, safety goggles protecting her eyes, her hands sheathed inside Panther leather palm gloves, Galeton's best, she motored a forklift truck, running supplies from a warehouse to waiting cargo ships. Grease spotted her cotton coveralls, stained her hands too, whenever, *can't sign shipping manifests with gloves on*, she pulled off the Galeton's.

The job, a perfect blend of physical activity and paperwork, fit, but it didn't last. Caught in the grips of a recession, *it happens on average every six years, more or less*, an oil glut created a significant surplus of crude oil that led to falling oil prices and downsizing, *layoffs*, in the oil industry.

Colleen, *last to be hired*, first to be fired, suddenly found herself unemployed, which was not part of any plan she had in mind.

For the next week, Colleen stewed over the dismissal. Then, inexplicably, she took a job with the city sanitation department. *Pay's good. Job's physical. It'll work until something better comes along. And, hey, she had her coveralls, gloves, and goggles, tools of the trade, still handy.*

"Pass the bread, butter too, please," Colleen's dad said. "Thanks. So, this sanitation thing. I'm thinking it's probably not what you want to do for a living, not much of a career path, am I right?"

"It'll do for now," Colleen said.

"Have you thought about the military?" he asked, between swallows of dinner.

"I have, Dad," Colleen said, while her mother watched and listened to the exchange. "Actually, I've been seriously thinking about it for a while now."

COLLEEN UNDERSTOOD how her dad felt about military service. The military, any branch, that's an honorable way to serve the country. He had a strong conviction about serving, and an even deeper respect for men and women serving honorably. Once, when Colleen was much younger, during the later years of the Vietnam War, a preacher put Dad's convictions, *his patience for jackasses too*, to the test.

As Colleen remembered things, Dad listened patiently to a sermon that went sideways. The preacher's homily, *going well enough*, asked God to protect our boys, *back then nobody was thinking much about girls in the military*, fighting in the jungles of Vietnam. He should have left things right there, but the good preacher, *like a bad chess blunder*, made a losing move. "And God bless those North Vietnamese too, for they no not what they do," he added.

Colleen's mother froze. *"Oh Jesus, help us . . ."* she whispered.

In the midst of the silent church, heads bowed in prayer, a one-word epitaph shattered the silence. "Bullshit!" Dad said, then defiantly stood, pausing long enough to lock eyes with the well-meaning, *if a bit dumb,* preacher, before leaving the stunned church-goers. No one, *they were all looking,* could mistake his proud, cadenced march toward the exit.

Whispers. *That man's former military, that's for sure.*

On the way home, Dad said, "I don't care if you never go back to church. From now on you don't have to." Mom, Dad's polar opposite, more tolerant, went back without him.

ON MONDAY, instead of tugging on the coveralls and slipping her hands into the familiar pair of work gloves, instead of hanging off the back of a garbage truck, Colleen, with her mother by her side, visited the local recruiting office. Mom waited just outside the office.

The recruiter, *Navy,* asked Coleen what she'd want to do in the Navy.

"Something in the administrative field. I've worked enough dirty jobs that not even a full can of GOJO could get the grease out of the creases in the palms of my hands. That's enough of that."

"I've got the perfect job for you then, Yeoman Clerk, an administrative office job."

After boot camp in Orlando, Colleen enrolled in the Navy administrative school located in Meridian, Mississippi, training to be a keyboard warrior. She'd be active-duty Navy for seven years, never, *wants and needs of the Navy,* getting behind a desk. Stationed on Naval air stations, she worked on the flight line, parked airplanes, worked in supply, other odd duties, but not the administrative jobs she'd trained for.

Didn't matter though. She enjoyed Navy life, met and married a sailor, deployed to Japan, then to NAS San Diego. Loved both duty stations. Rex loved the beach at San Diego. When she became pregnant with Max, she left active duty, she might have left earlier, but the Navy promoted her, made saying no to staying active duty harder. Finally wanting to be more of a mom and less the sailor, she left active duty in '88.

A year later, maybe more, Rex Sr., *must have been something in the water*, decided that a wife and two children were more than he'd signed on for. Colleen handed Rex Sr. a one-way ticket to Chicago. She went home to her parents, living now on an 80-acre farm in Oklahoma.

"This land is your land and this land is my land," Dad said, jokingly mimicking the iconic Woody Guthrie. They had a good laugh. Lucky for Colleen that it was Oklahoma, not the New York Island or the Redwood Forest of California. She stayed. The boys loved the life. Colleen reenlisted, joining the Navy Reserve. Her brother, a Navy officer, swore her in.

In 2005, Colleen, now a Navy Chief, stopped weekend drills. By 2006 she, *with chief's pay*, retired. Her job outside of the Navy had been to raise her two boys into adulthood. Rex, *Max not so much*, had been old enough to feel abandoned when Colleen and Rex Sr. had divorced. There were things, *single mom*, boy things, that she didn't, couldn't know how to teach boys, but she turned to her dad, who eagerly stepped in. Her mission, and she had chosen to accept it, had been to show her boys how to live.

The day the divorce had been granted, she left the court, stopped in at Mom and Dad's, collected her two young sons and walked to her place. She sat of the floor, beckoned the boys, *still toddlers*, to her and said, "We're on the floor, you know what that means, right? That means there's nowhere to go but up from here. It's going to be up to us to get back up.

When I joined the Navy, they had a slogan, *a saying*, 'It's not just a job, it's an adventure.' That's what we're going to do. That's us now. Life is not going to be a job for us, it's going to be an adventure."

Just babies, but Colleen knew, could sense, that in their own way each boy understood. Rex, she knew, certainly did.

PART FOUR

THEY'RE IN THE ARMY NOW

THEY'RE BOTH IN THE ARMY NOW, BOTH MY SONS ARE SOLDIERS.

With two wars, rotations, casualties, enlistment numbers dwindling, and Obama's order to send two additional brigades to Afghanistan, deployments, Colleen knew, were a certainty. What she hadn't gamed out, *could both boys simultaneously deploy,* happened.

By 2009, Rex and Max had married. In the fall of 2009, Rex's soldier wife, Meghan, an interpreter, deployed to different parts of Afghanistan with Rex. Max's civilian wife, Miranda, moved in with Colleen in October of 2009, when Max deployed to Iraq.

I've got two sons and a daughter-in-law in two different wars—and that might be a record for the shortest shelf life of all time as an empty nester. Damn, I was just getting used to it.

Rex and Meghan split their pre-deployment leave between two families and friends. In Oklahoma, they spent a few days with Colleen, made their goodbyes, then headed off together, wheels up and on their way to Afghanistan.

Max left for Iraq a few days later. Colleen flew to Fort Drum in upstate New York to help Max and Miranda pack their belongings into a not very big U-Haul. The plan, drive back to Oklahoma, *they'd already emptied the apartment and turned in the keys,* U-Haul and Miranda in tow, sidetracked when a raging, tree-crushing blizzard came out of the Rockies, raced its way across the country, and blasted the Northeast, delaying Max's deployment. Two days later, after a tearful goodbye, Colleen hit the road with Miranda. Max, wheels up, was on his way to Iraq.

A year later, after twelve months of sleepless nights, a live-in daughter-in-law, and her own plans on hold, Max, Rex, and Meghan returned. Colleen, relieved, welcomed her family home. For a while, *what seemed like a very short while,* her sons were back in the States, out of harm's way. Meghan too.

November 6, 2012

President Barack Obama crushed Mitt Romney, winning the electoral vote 332 to 206, and the popular vote by more than five million, shocking Romney, and many pollsters too.

Max had been in Afghanistan since early October.

Rex and Meghan had been divorced for almost a year.

Meghan was back in Afghanistan.

Rex boarded an airplane, on his way back to Afghanistan.

UNLIKE THE FIRST SEND-OFF, *Colleen and her sons had spent days together just weeks before their wheels-up dates,* there had been no plan to see Max first, and then Rex off to Afghanistan. Colleen spent the week before Rex's wheels-up date, *grand-mother warned her to never ignore a premonition,* restless, uneasy, growing agitated. *Alarmed!*

He visited with so many people when he was here last month. He's never really done that before, hopscotch around the country, Florida, Chicago, before coming home for a last, hurried, visit. This feels like Rex is saying goodbye. I have to go to Georgia, be with him before he is wheels up. I have to . . .

The next morning, early, Colleen knocked, *didn't wait for a come in*, on the open door of her boss's office. "Hey, I need to go to Georgia, to Fort Benning," she said, the tone of her voice letting him know she wasn't asking. "I have to be with my son, Rex. I have to see him again before he leaves for Afghanistan!"

"Go," he said. "You need to be with him, just go!"

Two hours later, the Chevy Corsica, *the first American car equipped with daytime running lights as a standard feature*, loaded, *change of clothes, two, and the dog Maggie, a big black lab, great road-tripper, a gift from Rex, all ninety-pounds of her*, Colleen turned the Corsica east. Maggie kept her head out of the window until they turned onto the interstate. Fifteen hours later, after a two-hour pit stop, *couldn't keep her eyes open*, outside of Birmingham, Maggie, on leash, took care of business. Colleen took a nap.

She checked into a hotel, close to the base, around 9:30 p.m. Minutes later, Rex knocked. They hugged.

"I'm hungry," Colleen said. "What's open?"

"Around here, almost everything's 24/7, but let's hit Firehouse Subs. I know almost everyone who works there. I'm guessing they're open until midnight. You can bring something back for Maggie."

Inside Firehouse, Rex and Colleen took a table, *really no need, the place empty*, off in a secluded corner. An hour later, the crew began clean-up. "Stay, ma'am," the crew chief said. "I'm going to empty the coffee pots, fill your cups—on me?"

Colleen, tired from the long trip, nodded. Rex held his cup out too. The crew, *takes about three hours to close up*, cleaned around them, stored food back into the freezer, washed tables, cashed out, Colleen lifting her feet while one of the workers passed a mop under them.

They, mother and son, talked until the manager had to lock up, around 2:00 a.m. Colleen, a sponge, soaking up as much of Rex as she could, trying to understand how he was feeling, listened. They talked about everything—nothing—vagaries, avoiding conversation about the up-coming deployment. Colleen didn't care what they talked about, only that Rex knew, understood, how much she loved him.

"You'll be gone a long time," she said, yawning, the road catching up to her, hands around a now-tepid cup of coffee. "I'm not going to get to see or talk to you very much, am I?"

"I know, Mom, but only because we're going to be in the mountains. It's a lot more remote than last time. Yeah, it might be tough to get through sometimes."

"Well, email or Skype, and call whenever you can get through. You'll do that?"

"I will, promise."

They laughed at nothing. Talked about a lot of little things. The divorce. Rex admitted that he still had feelings for Meghan. The girl-friend, Colleen had met her once, is not serious. Meghan is deploying again too. Yeah, you mentioned that. Did I? Yeah, I guess I did. We won't be in the same place though. There won't be any women at this outpost. Do you know what it will be like? Pause . . . Not really. Just that it'll be rough this time, different than last time. That's all I know.

There was more, but that's all Rex would say, all he would allow himself to say. He knew the dangers, knew the risk, but soldiers don't burden loved ones with their fears. Rex wouldn't go there.

Colleen had hoped for more, not about how it might be, just more conversation. A few more minutes of this intimacy with her son, but the night was over.

"I'll have more time tomorrow," Rex said. "I need to get back to the base. I still have things to take care of, make sure everything is set, but we can spend most of tomorrow," *Tuesday, November 06, 2012, the significance lost upon them both,* "together."

They left Firehouse. Colleen walked back, *just ten minutes away,* to the hotel. Before they said their goodnights Colleen, *worried,* turned to her son. "Rex, I know these deployments don't get any easier, but understand, I'm here for you, for anything you need, now or when you get back. You know that, right?"

"I know, Mom."

Colleen, exhausted, slumped onto the hotel bed and closed her eyes, worry, *too much of it on her mind,* making sleep almost impossible, until it wasn't.

Months later, much of the worry made sense. By January, Hamid Karzai, careful what you wish for, made it public that he wanted American troops out of Afghanistan. Rex couldn't give Colleen the mailing address of the remote FOB, a VSP, outside a village located in Jalrez, Wardak Province. A dangerous place. The few times they did Skype, lines creased her young son's face. Dark circles, a raccoon's mask, surrounded his eyes. Colleen began to understand how bad things might get.

She slept until Maggie, *LaQuinta Hotels allow pets,* nudged her awake. "When did you get up here? We have, *two queen size beds,* a bed of your own, and by the looks of that pile of blankets—did you do that canine circle and scratch thing before jumping in with me? Is that what you did? Now I suppose you need to get outside too, don't you?" Colleen said, yawning, stretching herself fully awake, Maggie doing a dance, her best imitation of a whirling dervish while Colleen pulled on her jeans. "Okay, okay, give me a minute, let me get dressed."

She met Rex later that afternoon. Maggie with her. He showed her Savannah, the old Savannah. They ate lunch at a Scottish pub. Picked up some incidental items from a few places. The few hours they had left, before he had to be on the tarmac with his squad, flew. Maggie with them every step of the way. Conversation dwindled—and then just like that, Rex had to get back on base.

They hugged. Colleen held him. "This isn't like last time," Rex said, his eyes welling up. Colleen, *I've never seen him so serious,* pulled him closer, holding him tighter, longer, squeezing him, not willing to let him go until she had to.

"Okay, well . . ." she said, holding back her own tears, choking back a cry, unable to find the right words any words, while Rex gently pulled himself away, then reached down to rough Maggie with an affectionate abuse, the big dog groaning with pleasure. He stood, smiled at Colleen, and walked away.

Colleen checked out of the hotel, walked back to Firehouse Subs, Maggie on leash, resting against her leg. Not hungry, *Maggie felt differently*, Colleen finished a coffee, loaded Maggie into the Corsica, and drove away. Not even 50 miles away, she stopped, pulled out her cell, wanting to leave Rex one last message.

"Hello," Rex said, surprising Colleen.

"Hey, I thought you'd already be wheels up, didn't think I get you. What's going on?"

"Hurry up and wait is what's going on. We've been sitting in this airplane for over an hour, just stuck here on the tarmac."

"Yeah, well that's the military for you."

"Yeah, that's the military," Rex said, while they both laughed.

Now, not just once but for the second time in two years, Max, Rex and Meghan deployed to a combat theater simultaneously.

There is no rule against family members serving together in combat; that there is, that's a myth.

PART FIVE

ONE LAST TIME

JUST DAYS BEFORE CHRISTMAS, REX EMAILED. THE MESSAGE unnerved Colleen. She'd talked with him about the lingering effects of multiple tours. The few times they did get to Skype, she could see changes in him, his voice more serious, the worry etched on his face. *This is bad. I know it is. What isn't he telling me?*

Rex, she knew, was in a dangerous place. She worried, avoided, *for the most part*, the news broadcasts, just checked every few days. For months, leaked incident reports, bad news, grabbed by rogue reporters looking for a story, populated the major cable networks. A casualty listed here, another there, a story's opening line, "In a remote region of Afghanistan, three soldiers died today." *Is that, could that be where Rex is?*

In other news . . .

TIME ZONES GET CONFUSING, but it must have been March 10th in Afghanistan, Rex got a good connection and managed to Skype with Colleen. He looked tired. Disheveled. Older. Said he was fine. They caught up. He had to go. *Got to get ready, we're going out in the morning.* They promised to talk when he got back in.

Colleen, later that night, had dinner with her dad. "I talked with Rex today," she said. "He looked tired, Dad, but he sounded okay. We didn't talk long; he was getting things ready for a mission."

No one could know that that would be the last time Colleen would talk to her son.

IN THE MOUNTAINS OF AFGHANISTAN, in the Jalrez region, on the VSP, commanded by Special Forces Captain Andrew Pedersen-Keel, inside the wire, Rex did what he almost always would. He spent the night awake. Like a wraith, he walked around the FOB, stopping to talk with soldiers on perimeter watch. He visited with men on guard duty in the one tower, its outline silhouetted against the night sky. He listened. Encouraged. Offered what advice he could. Soldiering was the most important part of his life. His men, the men in his squad—he'd die for them.

Mission Briefing 0700

Rex placed his Kevlar on the front seat of an MRAP, his red hair cropped short. He kept his long gun with him. Captain Keel stood in the middle of a group of soldiers, waiting to brief the squad and team leaders on the final details of the morning mission. Rex moved closer to the captain, to his right, just a few feet separating them. His eyes clear, he focused on Andrew, the man who would lead the mission. He looked at a few members of his squad, offered a nod of reassurance. He'd found his place in the world. He belonged here. Maybe he thought, *don't worry Mom, I've got this.* No one will ever know.

Afghan police and soldiers, embedded with the Americans, rolled through the wire in armed vehicles, joining the

Americans near the motor pool, the site of the pre-mission briefing. They always did. *Nothing. No indication that all hell was about to break loose.* The captain called the men together. No one worried.

It all made sense, this is where mission convoys always formed up, the easiest place to get everyone together. The Afghans halted their vehicles, stopping just a few feet behind the briefing. A group of Americans and Afghans semi-circled in front of the young American commander. Some left their trucks and joined the briefing. But one stood on the back of a truck, an arm innocently resting over a Russian PKM.

When the briefing began, Rex moved closer to the captain, listening. The briefing completed, men beginning to move out, Rex, to the right of Captain Keel, was about to turn away.

Airforce MSgt. Delorean Sheridan, standing close to Andrew, noticed movement to his left, his ten-o'clock. Puffs of dust popped from the ground, dancing wildly. *Hell, that's weird, that looks like moving gunfire. Oh Christ! It is—I hear it now, the machine gun blast—recoil.*

Neck on a swivel, Delorean looked behind him, saw the uniformed Afghan—*police uniform*—firing from the back of the truck. He saw Andrew's head jolt forward, his eye blurred in a burst of flesh and bone, the hollow filling with blood as a bullet tore through his head. He saw Rex, *a bullet tearing through his head too*, fall forward.

He wouldn't have had time to think of Colleen, Meghan, Max. He wouldn't have had time to fear or feel pain.

Delorean, everyone else too, scattered, ran for cover. Delorean slid between two vehicles. He knew what everyone else did. An ambush this close—running meant almost certain death. Fight or flight. *What did they teach us—best chance of coming out of this alive is to fight. Return fire.* Delorean pulled his pistol. Others must have been positioning to return fire too.

There, an open door on the MRAP, the RG33. Get behind the door,

get in the truck, vantage point—the turret—climb up. Who's this? Inter-
preter. He's good. I'm in. There—there, I see him on the back of the
truck, firing. Shoot. Bam! Bam! What? Jammed! My pistol's jammed!
Get down. Rifle propped up on the seat—an M4—perfect. Shooter on the
move, jumping from the truck—trying to squeeze under. I've got him—
clear shot. Pop! Pop! Pop! Pop! Pop! He's down. Pop! Pop! Two more
into the truck. Explode dammit! I want that truck gone—gone.

Another soldier moved toward the downed shooter, putting two rounds into the body on the ground.

Delorean ran to Andrew, grabbed him by the shoulder strap, pulling him away. Outside the wire, gunfire erupted. The Taliban either encouraged by the chaos, or having already planned the attack by using the shooter as the signal, opened fire, attacking the Americans. While the remaining team, those that could, led by Officer Satterlee, wounded himself, engaged the Taliban, Delorean reached Rex, saw the savagery of the wound, *understood the hopelessness of first aid,* and carried him off the battlefield.

IN A DIFFERENT TIME, zone, eight thousand miles on the other side of the world, Colleen, after a particularly tiring day, pulled into the driveway of her home. Maggie, cooped up all day, would be ready for her, ready for a walk, her nose glued to the ground, sniffing out fresh scents along the route. Colleen wasn't sure who enjoyed the walks more, her or Maggie.

Damn, I forgot to stop and pick up food for Maggie. Don't go in, she
won't understand if you don't take her out. Go to the store now. Don't
even turn off the car, back out, get it done. Now what the heck is that?
Three guys in a van, white shirts, ties. When did these Mormon mission-
aries get vans—they're usually walking.

Fifteen minutes later, *the store close by,* Colleen, back home, pulled into the driveway for a second time. This time she turned the car off and pulled the keys from the ignition, noticing the van for a second time. *Something's different. They moved, parked right across the street now, in front of that empty house that's up for sale. Are those, yes—they are, Army Berets. Putting on jackets, Army Dress Blue. They're coming this way. Oh shit! Oh No!*

Colleen turned away, pulling the big bag of dog food from the back seat, pushing the door shut with her hip, turning to face the men standing behind her, close, just inches away, almost on top of her.

"No!" she said, holding the bag of dog food in front of her like a flak jacket. "No! I don't want to hear it. No! No! No!" she shouted, struggling to breathe while the men froze, shocked into silence.

"Okay. Okay," Colleen said, gaining control of herself. "Which one is it?"

"Ma'am, maybe we should go inside," the ranking officer said.

"No! No, you tell me now, do you understand, you tell me now! Just name him, which one of my sons is it?"

Colleen, a twenty-year veteran, familiar with the routine, knew the words, the obligatory spiel that no matter how filled with kindness, no matter how softly the words are spoken, shatters lives.

"Rex, ma'am. Your son Rex has been killed—"

The bag of dog food slipped from Colleen's arms, smacking the pavement and exploding, showering the shoes of the men in front of her. Colleen collapsed, dropped to the ground. A woman, Colleen's neighbor, *the one who'd just sold the house*, had been moving a few remaining boxes into a car, saw what looked like trouble and rushed across the street. She barged in between Colleen and the soldiers, helped Colleen up, threw her arms around her, protecting her. Then, *looking at the soldiers, understanding their intent*, she embraced Colleen.

"I'm okay," Colleen said. "I'm okay, I want to go inside . . . calls . . . things . . . I need to do," leading the team inside.

"I have to make a phone call," Colleen said, once everyone came in.

"Yes, ma'am, of course, but ma'am, may I ask who you're going to call?"

"I have to call my son, Max, Rex's brother. He's in Alaska at Fort Wainwright."

"No ma'am, not yet. Don't call him yet. The Army is taking care of that, he is already being notified."

"Are you telling me I can't call my son?" Colleen snarled. "Is that what you're telling me?"

"Not exactly, ma'am, just not yet, not until the Army officially notifies him."

"Alright, that's fine for now, so now get out of the way. I'm calling my father. I need him here. Rex and my dad were very close. He has to hear this from me."

Her father, gray hair thinning, tall, still in his work coveralls, long sleeve Dickies, *he'd sold the farm after a heart attack, but before Mom died,* lived just a few miles away now, arrived quickly. Everyone sat. The officer in charge began to explain everything. *Here's how Rex will be flown back home, Dover. We will make arrangements to get you to Dover, to greet Rex's remains. Everything that is going to happen will be explained, taken care of—*

"Okay, stop," Colleen said, interrupting the officer, having listened long enough. "I need to speak with my other son, Max. Will the Army let him come home?"

Before anyone gave her an answer, the chaplain, part of the notification team, and a sergeant, excused themselves, went back outside to the van, presumably to make some calls. They returned quickly.

"Max, *Specialist Whipple,* your son, is in H.Q., in the office, being informed. He will be granted leave, I can tell you that much for certain," the chaplain said.

"Okay, but I need to talk with him."

"Yes, ma'am, as soon as we get permission, as soon he's out of the office."

"His father, I need to tell his father, he has to be notified too."

"We've located him, ma'am. He is being notified."

"Okay. Okay, that's good."

In Alaska, off duty, at home, off-base housing with his wife Miranda, Max answered the phone. Called back to base, worried now, *what the hell could have gone wrong, did I screw something up, is something missing, is a vehicle off line? What? Geezus, by the look on everyone's face, haven't seen this much brass in one place in a long time. For me? Shit, this has to be bad. Think, what the hell could be wrong? Somebody must have stolen something, that's gotta be it, gotta be. Christ, I hope no vehicle is missing.*

Two hours later, Max felt like a kid in trouble sitting outside the principal's office. In the space of that time, Colleen called her employer. Her dad called Colleen's sisters and brothers. Colleen called Rex's girlfriend. As soon as she hung up, she knew she'd made a mistake. The girlfriend, not understanding her place, not understanding the solemnity of what had happened, posted the news on Facebook. Colleen, *the ping on her phone alerting her,* read the post, "My Rex is gone!"

"Dammit! Why did she do that?" Colleen shouted. "Now everyone, Max too, will see the post. Everyone will know Rex has been killed before I even talk to Max. This is not how Max should hear about this. What is up with his command? Why won't they tell him? Why are they keeping this a secret? Why?"

She went through the contact list on her phone, tapped Max's number. Max's wife answered. "I just saw the post on Facebook," Miranda said.

Command, waiting and waiting, this is not right. They're making the situation worse. The girlfriend, Rex had said it's going nowhere, that he wasn't serious about her. He admitted that he still had feelings for Meghan. This girl, I wanted to respect her, and she couldn't respect the privacy of the family. What a mistake I made calling her.

With kindness in her heart, Colleen would later pay for an

airline ticket for the girlfriend to fly out to Oklahoma and attend Rex's funeral. Colleen's dad graciously opened his home to her, allowed her to stay with him. Her thanks? She grew angry when Meghan's parents attended the funeral.

"Young lady," Dad, never one to hold back, *remember the church incident*, said, "listen and listen good. They have every right to be here."

Weeks later, having access to Rex's Facebook account, she began posting things about Rex, looking for what—sympathy for herself, maybe more, portraying herself as more to Rex than she'd been. When Colleen posted otherwise, she blocked Colleen from Rex's Facebook page. Colleen turned to an organization that helps prevent acts of Stolen Valor. They took some action, and eventually had Rex's Facebook page frozen.

FINALLY—COMMAND informed Max. Colleen reached him too. "Max, say something. Max, are you okay?"

"I'm here, Mom. I . . . I . . ." But before he could say more, one of the officers interrupted him.

"Go," Colleen said. "Call me back when you find out what's going on."

PART SIX

BRINGING REX HOME

DELAY. GETTING A FALLEN SOLDIER HOME FROM THE battlefield takes some time, even when the remains are intact, identifiable. Home is not Dover Air Force Base. That's a stop, a first stop on a final journey, beginning with the ceremonial Dignified Transfer, a solemn, respectful, deplaning of the fallen soldier meant to provide some comfort to the family, and a tribute to the soldier.

Then, after remains are received at the mortuary, the callous, but necessary processes, autopsy, positive identification, and preparation of the remains, especially those that may have a chance to later be viewed by family, begin.

COLLEEN DECIDED NOT to meet Rex's remains at Dover. Thinking that it was best for Max to have Miranda by his side, Colleen gifted one of her two, *supplied by the Army*, airplane tickets to Miranda. She gave the other to Rex's dad.

For the next five days, Colleen waited. Unnerved, unable to sleep. Wanting Max by her side, wanting him home, she, *after dark*, sat outside—all night. *Awake*. Staring at the stars. Smoking, filling a sand-filled bucket with the crushed stubs of the cigarettes. That first night, before she silenced cell phones, disconnected land lines, unplugged the television too, she talked with Max and Miranda deep into the night, until they boarded the airplane to Dover.

Cocooned inside her home, she waited, breaking her own rule, no smoking in the house. During the day, she couldn't sleep or stay still. She paced, looped around the hallways of the house, wearing a pathway into the carpet.

One visitor. A day or two into her seclusion, at dawn, shrouded in a cloud of half sleep, she heard a knock on the door, faint, just sharp enough to rouse her from the chair. When she opened the door, a neighbor, a slight woman, *thread-bare pajamas*, ninety-four, bent over a walker, stood there. Barely able to walk, she'd shuffled across the street.

"I just saw it on the news," she said. "Your boy Rex was killed. I'm sorry."

"Oh my God," Colleen said, wondering how the woman had scuffed her way across the street. "Thank you. Come in. Thank you. Thank you."

Colleen made coffee. Mrs. Kennedy stretched her delicate, thin-skinned fingers around the cup. She clicked her nails, *without polish, shaped and manicured,* against the cup. She stayed, talking aimlessly, for about an hour, taking only a few sips of the coffee. Colleen was glad for the company, a stranger without the history of family.

———

By the second or third day, Colleen and the CAO grew increasingly uncomfortable with each other. For Colleen, at odds with the officer in charge, still rankled by his callous insistence that she not call Max, *he's my son—my son dammit,* working with him was just a bridge too far. Master Sergeant Alice Torres took over. The officer moved on, serving as CAO to Rex Sr.

Torres, professional, smart, compassionate, *night and day*, handled everything without intruding. She ran interference with reporters, patiently explained everything to Colleen, everything that would likely happen, everything that could and probably would go off the rails. Colleen, in turn, explained the family dynamics, an ex-husband, things could get dicey there, maybe not. "I'm not sure," *Rex had been living with her*, "about the girlfriend, not certain what to expect there," Colleen volunteered.

"Not a problem, ma'am. I'll take care of it."

"We're not always considered normal," Colleen cautioned. "We laugh at funerals. The family is close knit, loving, but full of drama too."

Warned, MSgt. Torres handled everything, right down to who sat where in church. Rex's dad, his side of the family, practicing Catholics, *they could have used more practice*, wanted the funeral service in a Catholic church.

But Rex, *just in case I'm killed*, had music picked out, music he'd decided he wanted played at his service, cool stuff, the Rolling Stones, other rock and roll that he liked, listened to. The Church, *it's 2013 people, not anno domini 590, CE if you prefer*, said no to that sort of "secular" music.

Torres moved everything to a non-denominational church. Mick Jagger rocked. Jesus probably would have approved.

MAX AND MIRANDA landed in Dover, staying at the Fisher House. Max met Helen Keiser-Pedersen, the mother of the captain killed alongside Rex. Later, bused to Dover AFB, they all waited for the airplane carrying a brother and a son back home.

Five days later, Max and Miranda, with Rex, landed in Oklahoma. Until Rex, *throughout their entire history*, the family had never waked a body, everyone was cremated. Colleen wanted to see Rex one last time. *I want that one last minute with him. This time it'll be different, it has to be.*

Dover had worked their magic restoring Rex. At the Baggerley Funeral Home, *final preparations,* the director contacted Colleen. "Rex still has a beard, ma'am," he said. "Do you want him clean shaven?"

"God, no!" Colleen said. "That's him, that's who is, and that's the way he is going to meet the Lord."

Later, in a viewing room at the funeral home, *a last goodbye,* Colleen, Max, Miranda, Rex's dad, Colleen's father, semi-circled in front of Rex's open casket. Max broke down, nearly collapsing. Colleen, *he seems so at peace,* looked down at her son. *He does . . . he looks as if he's just asleep, that's all, just sleeping. I'm glad. I'm glad I got to see him one last time, to say goodbye.*

TEN DAYS after Rex had been killed, outside of the Edmond Life Church, the Westboro Baptists, *a hate group, known for protesting at funerals of US military killed in action,* tried to stage a "Thank God for Dead Soldiers" protest. Dissuaded quickly by the Patriot Guard, they fled.

Inside the church, *Alice Torres had coordinated everything, everything the family told her they wanted, everything they changed their mind about,* the family drama on hold, the service, solemn and dignified, went on without incident.

Uninvited press crowded into the back of the church. Strangers showed up too, but none more bizarre than a woman no one knew or had seen before. She carried a huge bouquet of flowers, placed them near the casket, took pictures —but then at the end of the service, she collected the flowers, the bouquet she'd provided, and left, disappearing, never to be seen again.

Strangers outnumbered family and friends. *Where are you when soldiers are alive?*

PART SEVEN

THE AFTERMATH

COLLEEN STAYED AWAY FROM WORK A WHILE LONGER. THE bosses told her to take all the time she needed. "Your job is always going to be here," they told her.

"That's good," Colleen said. "I still have to tie up a lot of the loose ends."

At the end of April, more than a month after Rex had been killed, Warriors Walk in Georgia held a memorial for Rex, planting and dedicating a tree in his memory. Before she left, boxes of Rex's gear, his battlefield belongings, personal effects, shipped by the Army, arrived. Colleen found herself unable to go through them. Max opened the boxes, searched through the contents, and sealed the boxes again. Colleen put the boxes in what had once been Rex's room and closed the door.

After the memorial in Georgia, Colleen returned to work. Max, still waiting for the result of a medical board evaluation, he'd been, *non-combat*, injured, had to return to Fort Wainwright. At work, Colleen snapped at colleagues, coming close to going off on a bona fide, certifiable troublemaker, an opinionated, caustic, small-minded woman with the social skills of a paperweight.

Normally mild tempered, Colleen had always tolerated the woman, but now the woman picked the wrong day to get all up in the middle of Colleen's business. Flushed with anger, she brushed past the woman, almost bumping shoulders, wishing she had—warning her off. Collecting herself, Colleen marched into the supervisor's office.

"I'm taking some time off," she said, leaving, not returning for two months.

Max, still waiting on the medical board's decision, came home on leave. Rex's unit, A Company, 3rd Battalion, 69th Armor Regiment, would be redeploying stateside, would be back just days after the country celebrated Independence Day. Max figured they should be there. Colleen agreed. Max flew directly from Fort Wainwright. Colleen picked him up at the airport in Atlanta. They met up at Fort Stewart in time to welcome Rex's unit home.

Men who'd served with Rex, who knew him, remembered him fondly, talked to Colleen. Surprising Colleen, Army Lieutenant Garcia unpacked a hand-made box etched with unit information and Rex's name. The box contained gifted mementos from Rex's squad.

"Ma'am," the Lieutenant said, "this is for you. Your son was a good soldier, ma'am."

Max talked with the officer too. Colleen met with the SSgt. who took charge of Rex's squad, and the injured dog handler.

In the immediate months following Rex's death, more memorials than Colleen can remember, soldiers honored Rex. She met so many men who knew Rex. Men who served with him. The faces blur.

Rex is buried at Fort Sill National Cemetery.

GRIEF STILL AMBUSHES COLLEEN, randomly. Something, a song, a place she may have sat together with Rex, Max too, a park, a store she'd taken them to as children, a favorite meal, reminds her that Rex is gone.

Once, a Christmas not that long ago, *small store*, gift shopping, looking for something special, music filled the store. The song, instrumental, reminded Colleen of Rex. Overwhelmed, she placed the few items she'd picked out on the counter in front of the shopkeeper.

"I'll be back for these," she said.

"Like, back tomorrow, next week?" the shopkeeper said, puzzled.

"In a few minutes. I just need a few minutes," Colleen said, whispered, then hurried toward the door, out to her car, waiting until the tears stopped.

Not a day passes without some memory of Rex claiming a minute. The hurt, *closure is a myth*, just as cutting, the wound just as fresh as the moment she learned Rex had been killed. Going back to work, Colleen realizes now, years later, had been a mistake. Barricaded inside her cubicle, she could overhear conversations, whispers about Rex. She cried silently.

The weeping redbud trees, *300 of them*, planted at Warriors Walk, dedicated to Rex and all the other soldiers, not happy in the Georgia heat, began to wither and die. Soldiers and volunteers began swapping out the redbuds for crepe myrtle, a classic southern tree. Everyone was given a chance to rescue a redbud before it was, *ahem*, retired. If you could get one home alive, replant it, *your own Warrior's Walk*, there was a chance it would thrive.

Colleen wondered if retrieving Rex's tree was worth the fifteen-hour drive. *What if it dies before I even get it home?*

"What do you guys think?" she asked, skeptical.

"I guess we could do it," Max said. Miranda, *a raised eyebrow*, seemed to agree. They made plans to leave in the morning. Colleen, over breakfast coffee, *no one seemed too excited about going*, shared a dream she had during the night.

"In a dream I had last night," she said, "Rex said, 'Geez Mom, it's just a fucking tree!'"

Max laughed out loud. "Well, that settles that," he said. "We're not going to get 'a fucking tree.'"

Everyone laughed.

THERE ARE OTHER DREAMS. Some more real than others. But none more real than the one Colleen woke from after feeling Rex close, wanting to touch him. In a crowded room she could see Rex, his back to her, walking away. *Rex*, she called. *Rex, wait.* But he wouldn't turn around. *Rex! Rex*, she called again, louder this time. He turned.

I'm sorry. I'm sorry, Mom, he said, and then he was gone.

Rex and Colleen on his wedding day

Rex, Colleen, and best man Max

Graduation Day from Infantry Training. Colleen, Rex, and Colleen's mother,

Home from first deployment

SSgt Rex Schad with his squad in Afghanistan

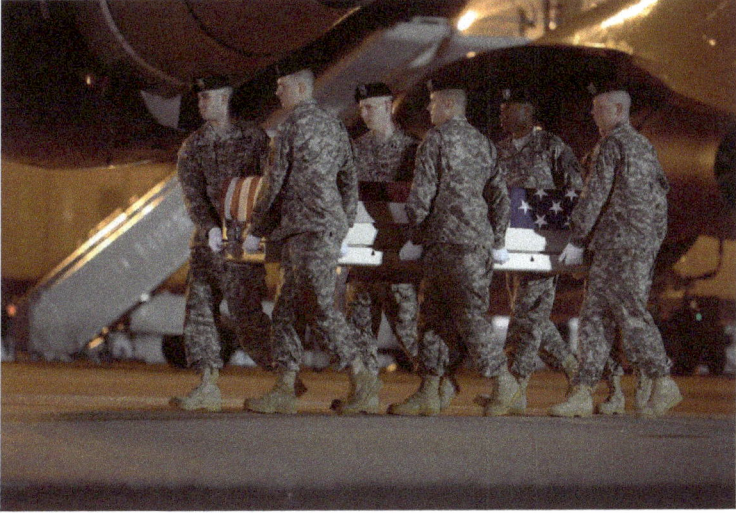

Dignified Transfer of SSgt Rex Schad at Dover AFB

Final service for SSgt Rex Schad, Edmonton, Oklahoma

SSgt Rex Schad, January 29, 1987—March 11, 2013

BOOK FIVE

PART ONE
REPORT TO WORK!

AUGUST 5, 2011

Navy SEAL Lieutenant Commander Mark "Oz" Ozdarski returned to Virginia Beach—home. He'd hopscotched from a routine air commute to and from DC. Happy to be back, wanting to eat a meal at his own table, he walked through his front door in time to sit with his wife and children. After putting his young son and daughter to bed, tired after an early start, all-day meetings, and quick turnarounds in an airplane, he turned in early.

Barely settled into a deep sleep, jarred awake by the hair-raising dance of a Command Pager, his adrenaline surging, Oz read the unmistakable message displayed on the LED strip—"REPORT TO WORK!" an all-hands recall. Thirty minutes. Be in the team briefing room. Thirty-one minutes and you're late. Thirty-one minutes and you're dismissed. Thirty-one minutes and the team moves on without you. He didn't know—yet—what had happened or how bad the rest of the night might be. Details are not part of "REPORT TO WORK" messages.

He grabbed his go bag, kissed his sleeping children goodbye, kissed his wife too. He could be gone for a day, a week, until Christmas—longer. He'd done this before, understood—the mission would be explained behind the closed doors of the Naval Special Warfare Development Group (DEV-GRU). He could be wheels up in four hours—on his way anywhere in the world. That's the life of a Navy SEAL. That's what Mark had signed up for.

On site in 20 minutes, he waited. Thirty minutes after bolting from his bed, inside the briefing room, the long night ahead—not a mission he'd expected—turned into one of the worst days of his life. EAGLES DOWN. This time, he'd be leaving his family to take care of another.

Weeks would pass before he returned home.

AUGUST 6, 2011—Afghanistan

On the outskirts of a village in the Tangi Valley, a place as dangerous to Americans as Vietnam's A Shau Valley had been in that war, Army Rangers hunted for a local Taliban commander, a bad guy with bad intention. They found him hiding out in what Rangers and SEALs affectionately called a camel-shit hut, a mud and camel dung, thatched roof, hovel. The Rangers moved in to capture him. Taliban fighters, trying to flee, were engaged by the Rangers on the ground, and by air attack. Some, including the target himself, Qari Tahir, escaped, then hid nearby, waiting, looking for an opportunity to attack the Americans, or disappear. The commander of the Rangers, wanting to seal off escape, called for reinforcements.

LITTLE MORE THAN a day had passed since SOC (SEAL) Brian Bill and the rest of a SEAL Team squadron had returned to their district FOB in Wardak province. Twenty-four hours earlier, a nighttime raid on a fiercely defended Taliban target had been a success. The savagery of the raid, more violent than expected, had earned the SEAL Team some down time. The squad owned the next 24 hours. Time to decompress, a much-needed day off after the brutality of the raid.

Day off. Ha!

War doesn't work on predetermined shifts. SEALs don't tuck a card into a time clock slot and punch out.

Downtime, *everyone understood*, meant that the SEALs had no scheduled missions. But Quick Reaction Force or QRF duty was a 24/7 sort of thing. The squad could be called, *they would be*, to respond in an instant.

When the call for the QRF came in, SEALs, a few sleeping, some lifting weights, playing cards, others on computers, skyping with girlfriends, wives, kids, geared up. Petty Officer First Class John Douangdara strapped a K9 tactical vest around the chest of Bart, a trained military working dog. The big dog pushed his head into Douangdara's chest, an anxious whine muffled by the dog handler's own tactical gear. Douangdara snapped the clips of the K9 vest together, listening for reassuring clicks. Bart was geared up—ready. In less time than it takes to grill a burger, *rare*, the SEALs boarded an armed CH-47D helicopter, call sign EXTORTION-17, responding to the Rangers' request for reinforcements.

Flying out from the FOB, the intent—take up a position, *high ground*, on a ridge two klicks, *maybe less*, out from the village. The pilot circled the ridge, *come in on a different approach, don't be predictable*, the team had been here before. SEALs, others flying with them, *60 to 90 seconds from exiting*, unbuckled. The ramp opened. The most dangerous times of flight, the most exposed to ground fire, are the seconds during takeoff and landing. Ninety feet above the ground now—*less!*

Taliban hidden in the dark blindly fired RPGs, *several*, at EXTORTION-17. They got lucky. One hit the helicopter, exploding into one of the CH-47D's rotors. The helicopter spun wildly. Men, Brian among them, *the ramp now open*, thrown into the air, plummeted from the aircraft. The remaining men on board, some of whom may have died while the helicopter was still in the air, went down with the helicopter. There were no survivors.

PART TWO

A DIFFERENT MISSION

MARK STOOD AMONG THE GROUP OF NAVY SEALs GATHERED inside DEVGRU headquarters—watching—listening. Every tactical event around the globe is tracked 24/7. Notice of an incident is almost instantaneous. When the Command Pagers sounded off, their loud vibrations waking dozens of men, their wives, girlfriends, EXTORTION-17, in the sky just moments earlier, lay scattered across the Afghan countryside—still smoldering.

Inside the room, Navy SEALs, *a small, tightly knit band of brothers living in the same communities just outside the Naval bases where wives know each other, kids go to school together, play together,* listened to the unimaginable. *EAGLES DOWN!* A QRF aboard a CH-47D, call sign EXTORTION-17, had been shot down. There were no survivors. Thirty-eight are dead. Thirty-nine, when you counted Bart. Twenty-two are Navy. Seventeen are SEALs.

Ready to fly into harm's way, *his blood up*, Mark, in disbelief, began to understand what might be expected of him and others in the room. The *hot* mission he'd anticipated, maybe in on the hunt for another bad guy, *just three months earlier, the team had killed Osama Bin Laden,* dissolved, replaced by shock and sadness that settled over everyone. This mission, a sacred call of duty, a *family affair, one that had to be kept in the family,* would be like no other.

The SEALs in the room would need to move faster than any QRF.

———

WHAT CAME NEXT? Only those in the room know for certain. Some of what happened may always remain classified. Some of what was said, for SEALs only, can only be surmised, guessed at, a sort of "what happens in Vegas stays in Vegas" kind of thing. But someone had to take charge, orchestrate the simultaneous notification of twenty-two families, select the Casualty Assistance Calls Officers (CACOs), the men and women who would tell the families that their Navy SEALs had been lost.

It might have sounded like this:

So, listen up, once you're read in, have the names, first question, do you know or have a connection to the deceased? If you do, can you deliver the news to the primary next of kin (PNOK)? Are you able to do it? Anyone responding in the affirmative, you're up. Everyone got it? If you're good, get the particulars—then go get your Dress Blues on—and get there —fast. This is not a one-off. We have twenty-two families' primary next of kin that have to be notified, and they have to be notified before the media sinks their teeth into the red meat of a mass American military casualty incident. This is a race against everyone and everything that can spread this information. The only thing faster is the Navy wives' network —their call chain. Once one person knows, everyone will know. Your mission is to get to the PNOK first—notify them with dignity and respect. Compassion. It's our mission to make sure they don't get blindsided by the media or any other source. You may be grieving. You may have been close to the men that have been lost. There will be time to grieve later.

For now—Move Out!

SEAL Team CACOs are assigned based upon their intimacy with the deceased individual, someone they know personally, a friend, someone in the same unit, or training class, a thread, some connection. Mark knew several of the men, wished, *wanted*, to be CACO to all of them. He also knew Brian Bill. Not intimately. They'd probably only exchanged a handful of words, passing each other in the corridors of DEVGRU. *That was enough.*

Mark would notify Brian Bill's primary next of kin, his mother. Patricia Parry.

OKAY, I've never done this before, no formal training—so? Doesn't matter. This is no different than any mission down range. Alright then— game this out. Not knowing what I don't know—what can go wrong? If I can have a support team—I can—who do I want, maybe need, in my back pocket? I've got every animal in the zoo to choose from: chaplain, JAG, media jockeys, Public Affairs Officers.

Game theory. C'mon. Who? PNOK listed is Patricia Parry, Brian's mother. I read through Brian's package; not married, no children, biological dad is not listed as PNOK. Stepdad is listed. If I wind up face to face with the biological dad before the mother—could get ugly. I can't tell him anything. Where am I going? Connecticut, never been to Stamford before. Address is in the package. Okay got it. Closest airport?

What? What's the most likely scenario once we get there? Am I going to get blindsided by CNN? Fox? That seems probable given a mass casualty incident. What about a corpsman? Should I bring along a corpsman? I mean what if someone needs emergency medical care?

The mom. Okay, what do I know about her? Where will she most likely be? Working? Home? (Didn't game in vacation). When I do get to her how will she react?

AND—I've got to be first. Can't have the media get to the family. They won't know anything, but they'll tell her anyway—that her son was killed. Not kind, not caring. Media wolfpacks wanting a scoop. Circling. They'll rip her to pieces.

Mark chose the members of his team, a senior communications specialist, Senior Chief Karl Parssons, and two Seabees, construction guys, *a long story*. Later, to deal with the story-starved media, he added a Public Affairs Officer. They boarded a predawn flight, a sleek Pilatus Airplane, a turboprop, one of many in the Navy's private fleet, landing in White Plains, New York, about thirty to forty minutes out from the address in Stamford, depending upon commuter traffic.

In the passenger seat, *nondescript airport car rental,* the drive easy against the commute into New York City, Mark navigated. They got there quickly, quicker than expected.

"We're not far out. Look for the next left. There. Turn. Left again. Now right. There. Turn now. Keep going, it's on one of these next streets. There it is, there's the house, up on the right. That's it," Mark said, looking at a spacious ranch style home, sprawling gardens, manicured lawn. "Roll past, park further down the street. Let's not pull into the driveway. Don't want to alarm anyone, give us a minute too."

Fifty feet beyond the driveway, Senior Chief Parssons pulled the car to the curb. The men pushed open the doors. All four stepped into the already hot, *one of the hottest on record*, August morning. Mark and the senior enlisted men wore the heavy, wool, dark Dress Blue uniforms, white shirt and tie. The most junior member of the group wore the Navy *crackerjack*. Everyone straightened their uniform, donned covers.

"We good?" Mark asked.

A chorus of whispered "yes sirs" answered.

"Let's form up two by two. When we reach the door, I'll knock. Alright, let's do this."

Their footfalls, dress shoes tapping a soft cadence, barely echoed into the quiet neighborhood. *Quiet! Saturday morning. Streets are empty. Gated community explains that. No through traffic. Not a car anywhere. Not even a lawn mower running, no one out for a walk, no dogs barking. I'll take it. No onlookers gawking at four men in Navy dress uniforms. No one asking questions.*

There, that's the driveway. Door. Knock or ring the bell? Knock. Five taps, knuckles striking the solid wood front door. *No answer. Knock again. Wait. Okay, last time. Wait . . . wait. Okay, it's early, maybe they sleep in? Working? On a summer Saturday morning? Nah. Out for breakfast? Geezus, I hope no one has got to them already. So now what? I cannot tell this mother over the phone. Where is she?*

Mark sent two of the men to the back door. He peered through a window, a glass door. When it became obvious to him, *and before someone called the police,* Mark gathered the team. "Alright, she's not home. No one is. Let's go back to the car, check the package. Maybe she's at work."

Mark reviewed the information. "She works at Stamford Hospital," he said. "It's on Palmers Hill Road. We passed it on the way here. Let's mount up, see if she's at work."

A hospital receptionist stopped the team, *four guys in dark navy blue suits, almost black,* at the hospital entrance.

"Excuse me," she said. "What's this? What's going on? Can I help you?"

"Look," Mark said, not, *but getting close,* yet concerned, "I'm here to see one of your staff, Patricia Parry. I need to find her."

"What's this all about?"

"I cannot," *now annoyed,* "tell you," Mark replied, his voice controlled, even, authoritative. "Ma'am, I need to find Patricia Parry. Is she here? Do you know? Is she at work?"

"Well," *elevating things to a game of one upmanship,* "I can't tell you that."

Been here before. This lady's not going to budge. She thinks it's a game of chicken, a who-is-going-to-blink-first contest. What's the rule of engagement here? "Don't take a no from someone who cannot say yes." The solution has to come from me.

"Okay," Mark said, calmly. "I get it. You've got rules that you have to follow, I appreciate that, and I appreciate that you want to protect her. I can't tell you what this is about, only that it's important information that has to come directly from me. It cannot be relayed, and it's time sensitive. I think," *go for it, make her part of the solution,* "you can help though."

"How?"

"The hospital must have emergency contact information for her. Can you call her?"

———

MOMENTS LATER, Pat, *in a car with her older son, returning from vacation,* answered her cell phone. *"Hello this is Pat,"* she said.

"Mrs. Parry?"

"Yes, this is Pat Parry."

"Mrs. Parry, this is hospital administration. Are you on duty today, are you here in the hospital?"

"No, I'm on vacation, why?"

Mark listened intently, getting one side of the conversation. The receptionist's answers, *pieces coming together,* gave him a solid idea of what Pat was asking. He continued to listen, began to understand. He fought the temptation to rip the phone out of the woman's hands.

"There are some people here," she said.

"Who are they, do you know?"

"I don't know who they are, they won't tell me."

"Maybe you should let me talk to them."

"Are you sure," *pause,* "okay," she said, handing the phone over.

Mark, happy to take the phone from her, cleared his throat. "Ma'am," he said, his voice hardwired for situations, confident, calm. "Mrs. Parry, my name is Lieutenant Commander Mark Ozdarski, with the Navy. May I speak with you in private?"

"I'm driving. Can you tell me what this is all about?"

"No, ma'am, not over the phone. Where are you ma'am? I can come to you."

"I'm at the Cape, Cape Cod, on vacation."

Now what? I've lost a brother, many brothers. I'm tasked, trusted, to tell this mother of one of those brothers that her son was killed. I've got orders. Procedures. I'm supposed to do this in person. That's the drill. But I can't get to her, not yet and she must certainly . . . she knows. She has to. Oh Christ, I cannot screw this up. But I can't do this right anymore. I can only do this wrong. NO! No . . . this is a no-fail mission. Do—not —screw—this—up! Do everything in your power to do this right. Make good calls. Use good judgment. Think. Solve the problem. This is the most important mission of your life—stop, dammit. Stop. There's no time for self-doubt. I know what the rules are, so how do I bend them to fit the mission? Think! Think through all the options—play out the scenarios— the what-ifs.

—Should I ask her to wait at the Cape?

—Should I meet her on the road—close the gap?

—Do I wait for her at her home?

—Do I risk letting her find out, the press, news, someone else who knows?

This last has me worried the most.

"Ma'am, I can come to you, be there in an hour by airplane."

"We've already begun the drive back. Today was the last day of our vacation."

"I can meet you on the road then, halfway."

"That . . . no . . . I'll be home in two hours, can you just wait for me there?"

"Yes, ma'am. I can do that, that will be fine," Mark said, his voice tinged with finality, knowing that Pat, *she's the mother of a deployed Navy SEAL,* must certainly realize what this is all about.

"Ma'am, I'll meet you at your home," Mark replied, then left the hospital.

Back at the house, long before Pat would pull into the

driveway, parked so that they could not be seen from the house, car doors open, the men waited on one of the hottest days of the summer. "We'll watch from here," Mark said. "When we see the car, move out, let's meet them as soon as they arrive."

With time on his hands, *the first break since the pager went off*, nothing to fill the space, nothing to soak up the grief, Mark began to understand the extent of the tragedy, feel the sadness. The loss weighing heavily on his shoulders pushed its way into his warrior heart. He closed his eyes, slowly rolled his chin from side to side, shaking his head in disbelief.

So many killed, all heroes, believing they could make a difference, secure freedoms for a people living without them. Heroes willing to give their lives for others—gone—extinguished in the flash of one $138 unguided rocket propelled grenade fired blindly into the darkness. Just in SEAL seniority, two-hundred and fifty years of combined combat experience. In total, thirty-eight lives.

STOP!

This is no different than being on the ground in a firefight, ambush, members of my team getting shot up. You suck it up. You do what needs to be done. Detach. Stuff it. Save the grieving for later. Right now—DO THE JOB!

"Sir," Senior Chief Karl Parssons asked, looking over from the driver's seat, shaking Mark loose, "you good?"

"Huh? Yeah, yeah, I'm good," Mark replied, glancing at Karl. "Just a lot to process, even if we didn't know these guys it would be a lot to take in. Just a lot."

Before Karl could say more—

"There, pulling into the driveway, *two cars*, there they are," Mark said.

The cars rolled to a stop, parking one behind the other. Mark, the team, slowly entered the driveway. They stopped far enough away, deliberately wanting to give Pat and others with her some space—just a little more time. When the doors of the first car swung open, Pat and her son climbing out, Mark and the team stepped out of their car, straightened their uniforms once again, donned covers, and waited. Michael, Pat's husband, Brian's stepfather, *more a father than anyone*, stepped out of the second car. Doors thudded shut, slapping at the quiet, the sound echoing over the quiet street. Mark saw a woman standing near the driver's side, knew, *some things don't need explanation*, she had to be Pat Parry.

There are words, formal military etiquette, but are those the right words for this? Maybe. Maybe not. Is there a way to explain away pain? I don't know. All I know is I have to try. That's my mission. Go to her . . . now.

———————

PAT HAD SEEN the car parked not far from her driveway, almost amused by the sight of four men, Navy Dress Blues, crammed into a small compact sedan. She watched them pull into the driveway. She watched them park, climb out of the small car. She watched them put their covers on and look at each other. She watched them, led by the officer, walk toward her.

In the few seconds, before the men would reach her, her cell phone sounded off. "Hello," Pat said, recognizing her younger brother Jeff's voice, fearing he might have already heard something on the news. But Jeff, full of excitement, began to tell her about a pair of pants he just bought.

"They're great!" he said, "I got them for Brian. I'm sending them over to him."

"Jeff, stop! Stop! Have you heard—seen—the news today?"

"No. Why?"

"You need to check the news and call me back," Pat said, ending the call before turning back to the men walking toward her. As the team closed the distance, an officer, a SEAL, in the lead, she searched his face, a pleading half smile, a tilt to her head, the faintest glint of hope in her eyes. . .

I know this has to be about Brian. We heard the news this morning, a helicopter shot down. There's no other reason for these men to be here. But maybe Brian has been hurt, it could be that—it doesn't have to be the worst that can happen . . .

She knows, Michael and Christian know too, that something has happened to Brian. That's what's coming. Now all that's left is to wait to hear what the officer has to say. She reminds herself to breathe, waiting to hear out loud what she has suspected since she heard the news early that morning.

She won't remember later if Jeff, *her younger brother, Brian's godfather*, ever called back.

MARK KNOWS that she knows something bad has happened. How can she not? It's already all over the news. A Navy SEAL showing up at the hospital looking for her, calling her. Willing to come to the Cape if she'd not been on her way home, and now here at her home, with three others. Of course, she knows.

Mark reached her, stood in front of her, hiding his emotions behind a barricade, a bulwark of two decades of military bearing.

"Ma'am," he said, his voice clear. "Are you Patricia Parry?"

"Yes," Pat said, quietly. "Yes, I am."

"Ma'am, I'm Lieutenant Commander Mark Ozdarski. May we go inside? I want to explain what has happened."

"Yes, please come in," Pat said, graciously.

Inside the house, Pat's husband Michael and her son Christian stepped into another room, giving Mark and Pat a private moment.

"Ma'am," Mark said, knowing that what he has to say hurts more than the words he'll say out loud, "Brian was on a mission last night . . ."

PART THREE

HERE'S BRIAN

AUGUST 23, 1979

"It's time," Pat said to her husband, *not husband Michael, but Scott, the one before Michael,* just seconds after he walked in from work.

"Nah, can't be," Scott said, not noticing the look of incredulity on Pat's face, "You can't be in labor yet."

Pat, who'd carried two children already, who had been carrying this one, Brian, through the hottest months of summer, knew, *the mule kick of a contraction gave it away,* that it was time. In fact, not only was it time, but she was running out of time, and didn't have time to argue. If the topic had been up for debate, *it wasn't,* she might have suggested that Scott, *since he knew so much about giving birth,* should have been the one to carry the child for the past nine months. AND—unless he knew how to deliver a baby, he might want to listen, get her and the kids in the car, get the kids to her mother's, and get her to the hospital.

Her stare must have warned him off; he quit protesting and listened. Pat piled Christian and Amy into the car. "Drive," she commanded, "back," *they'd spent the day at the swimming pool,* "to my mother's house. Go now. This baby isn't waiting much longer. We'll drop the kids off. Then get me to the hospital!"

Minutes later, in her mother's driveway, it was how fast can she get Christian and Amy out of the car and get going to the hospital, *sorry Mom, no time for chit-chat*, Pat ushered the kids out of the car. She moved quickly, felt like the car was still rolling, waved and off they went.

Inside the hospital, Brian, helping his mother make a point, impatient, ready to make some noise, announced with a loud cry, "I'm here world!"

PART FOUR

SINGLE MOM

FOUR MONTHS AFTER BRIAN WAS BORN, JUST DAYS AFTER Christmas, Scott convinced himself that three children, a wife, and all the obligations that came with a family, made life too complicated, too hard. It wasn't something new, something that started with the addition of a third child. He'd been wavering for a long time. If he'd hadn't been a coward, he'd have run out on Pat and their children long before Brian was born. And now, even when he ought to have explained, Scott slunk away, disappearing in a haze of deceit, leaving Pat to fend for her children and herself, and wonder, *for a minute,* where he might have run to.

Surprise, *at least for a minute,* became worry. With her world suddenly spinning in the opposite direction, all she knew was that she had children to take care of, to keep safe. Scott's gone, he walked out on Pat, Christian, Amy, and Brian. He walked out on car payments, the mortgage, and everything else, too.

Okay, that's done. Life goes on. It doesn't give me any other choice, neither did Scott. Hungry kids, babies that need a safe place to live. I've got to . . . what other option is there, go home for now, move back to Stam-ford, live with mom and dad until I get things straightened out. I'll be okay. I can do this. Easy? No! Who said anything about easy?

Single mom now, *she would be for seven years*, Pat fought back, won, regained her footing. Personally. Professionally. Financially. By that first summer, Christian, *new school*, was re-enrolled in kindergarten. Amy turned three. And—Brian mastered crawling. He could scamper away on all fours, disappear in a flash, laughing when Pat would catch up with him and scoop him off the floor. He'd quickly begun pulling himself up to stand on wobbly legs too.

One warm summer morning, back turned, busy at the kitchen sink, Pat, startled by a knock on the back door, turned to find a neighbor with Brian on her hip, smiling.

"I found him outside," she said. "He was just sitting near the road, laughing, playing."

"What? He was right here, how—" Pat said, surprised. "Thank you."

"You're welcome. You might have your hands full with this little guy!"

"Tell me about it."

Weeks passed. Doors secured; Pat hoped that she need not worry. Busy again, Brian playing near her feet, Christian and Amy okay, she looked down. Gone. *Where on earth did he go this time?* She walked through the rooms. No Brian. Upstairs? *I've looked everywhere else; he's got to be up here.*

"There you are," she said, finding Brian almost hanging out of a second story window, giggling when Pat snatched him away.

Summer alone. Three kids, all just about two years apart, nobody over five. Life was hard. Crazy. Happy.

For the next seven years, *don't let anyone tell you it's the dads that do it all,* the single mom shuffled her three children to after-school clubs, games, Scouts, swim team, tennis lessons, all while building her own nursing career. She sat with them, helped with homework, made sure it was done. Kissed the cuts to make them better. Nursed their colds.

She learned things, did things a dad might do with a son, like the time Brian joined a kids' hockey team.

"I'll need all the equipment," Brian said.

Pat, not all that familiar with hockey, visited the local sporting goods store. Skates, *kids size thirteen*, stick, helmet with full cage, gloves, pads, mouth guard, special hockey socks, and, *oh yes*, a gear bag to carry it all in.

Walking out of the store, she turned back. "How do I put all of this stuff on him, make sure he's wearing it right? I don't know anything about hockey. How am I going to get him dressed?"

"Bring him to the store," the shop owner said. "I'll show the both of you how it all works."

Pat did it all, until she didn't have to, after she met Michael Parry.

PART FIVE

FINDING HIS OWN WAY

EVEN BEFORE MICHAEL, BRIAN WAS GROWING UP VERY physically active. Pat, oldest of seven children, had, like all her brothers and sisters, belonged to a swim club. She enrolled Brian into the same club. He joined the swim team. A few years in, the club began an organized water polo team—competitive. The coach, tall, thin, demanding, pushed Brian and other players to learn the basics, master the fundamentals. Water polo, well let's just say, "it ain't golf!" It's physically demanding. It's all-out war in the water.

"How was practice?" Pat asked, casually, one afternoon after Brian's workout, not expecting to hear the response Brian offered.

"Mom," he said, excitedly, "you don't understand. Coach showed me a move today, sort of how to take an opponent out of play, legally. Mom, he pinned me to the side of the pool."

"Really? Was he tough, he wasn't mean?"

"No, but, Mom—he didn't even use his hands!"

Water polo, one of Brian's first serious physical challenges, stirred something inside of him. He loved the physicality.

The team called themselves the "Seals."

OF ALL OF HER CHILDREN, Brian, *tennis, soccer, hockey, swim team,* may have been the most physically active. Maybe the most mischievous too. Not long after Michael and Pat married, blending families, Michael installed an outdoor hot tub. Brian would submerge, staying under for an unnerving amount of time.

"Michael, make him come up!" Pat pleaded, nervously. "He's going to drown!"

Brian surfaced, laughing, not even breathing heavy.

"How did you stay underwater so long?" Pat asked.

"I figured out that I could breathe by catching a gulp of air from the bubbles," Brian said, matter-of-factly.

"Where did you learn that?"

"I don't know. I just figured it out. Kinda cool, huh?"

Michael and Brian, *fly fishing one of the links in their chain,* bonded easily, Michael awed by Brian's graceful cast. What takes most fly casters years to perfect came naturally to Brian. He'd snap the rod back and forth, using a delicate wrist motion, letting the heavy line do all the work. He'd watch the line propel the nearly weightless fly through the air in a graceful curve, its energy coming from the flick of his wrist. On the back cast, Brian would whip the tip of the rod behind him, arching it gracefully overhead, letting the weighted line follow.

"That cast? It's a thing of beauty," Michael said, more than once. "But he's impatient, won't let that fly rest on the water. I wish I could just get him to let that fly lay on the water a bit longer. Let it float along on slow currents, let the fish see it as a real water bug. Oh well."

His only real issue—he started fly fishing at such a young age, maybe eight years old— waders came up to his neck. Another fisherman looked at him, turned to Michael and said,

"You know, if he falls, he'll drown in those waders." *Kidding? Yes?*

"DOOGIE HOWSER." That's what Pat's colleagues nicknamed Brian. For a give back to the community service program, something the Catholic school required, Brian told the school he wanted to volunteer at St. Joseph's Medical Center, where Pat worked as a nurse manager. The school quickly, *sounded like a really good plan, fit right with what the school wanted*, signed off.

Not so fast. To make it work, he had to be supervised. Who else but Pat? She came in after hours, after Brian finished with hockey or soccer practice, to supervise him. He'd go from room to room, fill water pitchers, clean off trays, supply fresh cups, talk with patients, ask how they were feeling. *Doogie Howser!*

He announced, *to Pat*, one afternoon that he wanted to go to the Philmont High Adventure Scout Ranch. He had it all planned out, how to get in shape, how to get accepted, and he went. And—that was Brian. Once he decided on something, something that was meaningful to him, something he wanted to do, he had a way of figuring out how he'd do it, he had his own schemes.

In high school, his interest in the military, more than a passing curiosity, grew. Posters depicting different military images began to wallpaper his bedroom. Pat, *surprised, no one in the family really had a deep military legacy*, took notice.

Pat's father, *graduation present*, took Brian and a friend, co-captains of the high school hockey team, to a SEAL demonstration at Westchester County Airfield, *the same airfield Mark Oz would use years later.* The SEALs didn't disappoint. A helicopter roared in over the airfield. A SEAL Team, in full tactical gear, simulated a fast-rope insertion/extraction. On the ground, SEALs took up tactical positions, rescued a hostage, withdrew, fast-roped, disappeared inside the heli-copter, and sped off.

The demonstration wowed the crowd, sealed, *pun intended*, the deal. Seventeen-year-old Brian was captivated. Back home, after the show, he burst through the door.

"Mom!" he shouted. "I got the name of a man who was a SEAL. I'm going to call him!"

"Why would you do that?"

"To see if he does any training." *He did.* "If he does, I want to see if I can train with him."

And Brian did train with him. Then, in a minute, *high school finishing up*, college looming, Brian made his choice.

Norwich University, a private military school near Mont-pelier, Vermont, the oldest military school in the United States, *no matter what other schools they considered*, seemed to stand out for Brian. Pat sensed it immediately. He embraced the university's military traditions during the visit. He "Yes Sirred" and "Yes Ma'amed" everyone he met, standing at attention, braced like a West Point cadet while he spoke.

He applied. The university saw in him the things they were looking for. Norwich was where Brian wanted to be. When it came time to pick a major, Michael suggested a broad general education. Brian shocked everyone, choosing the school's most onerous degree program, Electrical Engineering.

Brian flourished at Norwich. He joined the Northfield Ambulance Service, and the Montpelier Cold Weather Rescue Team. But—during a summer break he announced to Pat that he was resigning from both.

"But, Brian," Pat said, more than surprised, "You love both."

"I do, but I'm an Electrical Engineering major! Do you know how hard that is? I've got to study."

Pat had to laugh. You had to be there—it was funny. Brian graduated with a degree in Electrical Engineering. A professor, head of the school's EE degree program, never, *ha!* doubted it for a moment, congratulated Brian. The university had, for Brian, been the best choice. For most of his young life, Brian knew what he wanted, knew what he'd need to learn, understood who he had to become. Norwich nurtured his drive, burnished the few jagged edges of youth, fed and honed his drive and passions.

Once though, if he'd had his way, a moment of youthful spontaneity, herd instinct, maybe both, he momentarily flirted with the idea of leaving the university before graduating. *It went like this*—

A friend, John, *it wasn't Brian's idea*, also a student at Norwich, influenced by his dad, a man who was involved with the Navy Underwater Demolition Team (UDT) training, preamble to the SEALs, left the university and enlisted in the Navy with the intent to become a SEAL.

Becoming a SEAL had become the sweet song of Siren, a lure that Brian could not resist, but the half-bird, half-woman creature was no match for Pat. When Brian announced that he could do the same thing, join the Navy, get into Basic Underwater Demolition/SEAL training school (BUD/S) school, become a SEAL, *never crossed his mind that most never make it through the training*, finish his degree while on active duty, Pat's voice, like Orpheus, was louder, a contrapuntal response, drowning out Siren's song. "Yeah, I don't think so. Finish school—then go do whatever you want," Pat offered, and that, as the saying goes, was that.

Brian settled for learning how to SCUBA dive during his senior year.

Home after graduation, restless, just a few weeks into summer, he came to Pat, announced that he'd decided to enlist in the Navy, with the caveat, a guaranteed ticket into BUD/S, the Navy's precursor to SEAL training.

Pat, not surprised, supported, *not without concern, she didn't want to see his dream crushed*, Brian's decision. Surviving BUD/S, one of the most mentally challenging and physically demanding training qualifying prerequisites in the world, would not be easy. The pass/fail rate leaned heavily toward the latter. Pat knew it. She knew that Brian had been privately dreaming of and preparing for BUD/S in earnest. His decision hadn't been a whim. He'd thought about becoming a Navy SEAL, planned it, prepared for it for most of his life. He would tell anyone who'd listen exactly what getting through BUD/S and then SEAL training would take. Brian knew what he was getting into.

Some folks questioned Pat's unapologetic support. To the doubters, she'd simply say, "What mother doesn't want to support her child's dreams, and in this instance, for something so honorable? This is what he wants to do. This is what will make him happy."

He left for boot camp in July, less than two months before 9/11.

PART SIX

BOOT CAMP. "A" SCHOOL. BUD/S.
FRIENDS LOST.

BUT FOR THE TERRORIST ATTACKS ON THE TWIN TOWERS, something that left everyone in uniform, *no matter how long or short a time*, wondering what now, Brian, *nothing out of the ordinary*, breezed through boot camp.

After boot camp, Brian left for "A" school to receive technical training in his selected military occupational specialty (MOS). You'd think something to do with electrical engineering, but given a chance to select a specialty, *first choice, second, third*, the Navy, *Brian's pattern analysis must have been fairly good*, approved his request to attend Parachute Rigger School.

"Why on earth did you decide on that?" Pat asked, when Brain told her what he'd decided.

"Because it's the shortest of almost all the schools. I just want to get on to BUD/S," he said, not telling Pat that the course is pass/fail and for the final test, the rigger jumps with a chute that he or she has personally packed. If it opens, **you've passed the course!** Brian left for BUD/S not long after Christmas 2001.

Many Americans, still numb, celebrated quietly.

IN BUD/S Brian met Marc Lee. Marc had originally entered BUD/S Phase I in an earlier class. Pneumonia forced him to suspend his training. He later joined the class that Brian had been assigned to. The two trainees, *Tadpoles,* hit it off, bonding together with an unplanned intimacy that throws strangers together, making them inexplicably friends for life.

But the lingering effects of pneumonia weakened Marc. His stamina compromised, unable to match his desire to the physical demands, Marc *rang out.* Brian also sickened in BUD/S, refused to go to medical, *if he had, he'd have been disqualified,* was pulled from the class and medically rolled into another.

Re-entering BUD/S, more determined than ever, he moved through "Hell Week" Phase I, then rolled into Phase II. Out to prove he belonged, he passed every test, every step of Phase II, on the first attempt, an achievement rarely accomplished. FIRST TIME, EVERY TIME!

Brian successfully completed SEAL training. He chose, *probably thinking it would be easier for Pat and Michael to visit,* the East Coast as his duty station.

In 2004, Brian and Marc Lee, both now stationed on the East Coast, reconnected, even sharing an apartment. Brian, *probably a private conversation over a few beers,* suggested that Marc take another run at BUD/S. Marc agreed. And this time, Marc Lee, Navy SEAL, succeeded.

On August 2, 2006, just three months into his first tour, against all odds Marc became the first Navy SEAL to be killed during Operation Iraqi Freedom when he was shot during a fierce firefight while on patrol against insurgents in Ramadi. Everyone believed that Marc and an extraordinarily beautiful woman named Maya were engaged and planned to marry when Marc returned. What they didn't know, *Brian did,* is that they, *before Marc deployed,* eloped instead, telling no one except Brian.

BRIAN, *so that they wouldn't be left wondering*, had told Pat and Michael if they hear, *on the news*, about something, a mission gone wrong, if anything bad really happened, he'd call to let Pat know that he was okay. So, when he called from Iraq, Pat's heart almost stopped, even though the plan was, "I'll call to let you know I'm okay."

"Brian," Pat said, answering the phone, "is everything okay?"

"I'm okay. But Marc has been killed. I'm flying back to the states, to New York, to get Maya, take her to California."

"We'll come," Pat said.

"Don't, Mom. I won't have time for you. I'm here for Maya, for Marc, and his mother. I have to concentrate on them."

"We know, Brian. We know," Pat said. "It's okay, we don't expect you to devote time to us. You're there for Marc, we understand. Marc and Maya, they're your job right now. Marc's mother, too. We expect you to do your job, but we just want you and Maya, Debbie," Marc's mother, "to know we support you . . . we love you. We knew Marc. Marc has been in our home."

In California, Brian visited Pat and Michael briefly at their hotel. They said their hellos, hugged. Brian lay down on the bed, just to rest for a minute, and fell asleep almost immediately. While he, *for a few hours*, slept, Pat looked down at him, watching over him, watching him sleeping peacefully—safe—secure. Relieved of the dangers of a combat zone, Brian slept soundly.

Days later, Marc was buried at Fort Rosencrans National Cemetery near San Diego, the West Coast Arlington. Brian returned to Iraq.

Marc's death, *hitting close to home*, worried Pat. She grew more concerned. The suddenness of Marc's death left its footprint. Sadness, fear too, settled over Pat. Michael, too. Brian did his best to reassure them that he'd be fine. "Different work," he said. "Mostly nighttime ops, safer than daytime missions. I'll be okay."

Pat reluctantly accepted the explanation, the reassurance. *Look at him. He looks so invincible. Three deployments already, he's always come home. He comes back each time. He'll come back again. I have to believe that.*

PART SEVEN
DEVGRU

BRIAN DID RETURN. *CHANGED*. HE LET PAT KNOW THAT HE'D requested transfer to a different unit, the Naval Special Warfare Development Group, abbreviated as DEVGRU, the SEALs' elite worldwide counterterrorism unit.

It's hard to become a SEAL, even harder to make it into the DEVGRU. The dropout rate is 80% going through BUD/S. DEVGRU is BUD/S on steroids. SEALs wanting to join DEVGRU must first spend five years in one of the regular SEAL teams. That's just a ticket to admission, a chance to enter the grueling DEVGRU training and selection process.

DEVGRU candidates driven to physical exhaustion must push beyond. The emotional stress, deliberate, is meant to mentally bankrupt even the most stoic. And in the end, if you get that far, only SEALs select their DEVGRU dance partners. Brian, *of course he did, he'd been training for it for most of his life*, made it through and over every hurdle, and into the ranks of DEVGRU SEALs. He was part of the big dance now.

DEVGRU is not the classic military unit embedded into a war zone for year-long deployments. It is, without saying more, *classified secrets*, akin to a permanent QRF, wheels up, *anywhere in the world*, within four hours, on the toughest, most dangerous missions. If you think you know what it's like because you watched a movie or television series, forget it, you're clueless.

Brian thrived in this new SEAL world, a world he didn't, *couldn't*, talk about or provide Pat with much detail about, except to tell her, "I'm working with the greatest men on the planet, the most skilled, the most kind, the most—*humble*."

What Pat learned was that these were men, *warriors all*, spent a lot of time together. They are more than the greatest cadre of elite warriors willing to lay down their lives, and put it all on the line, without hesitation. They are family.

They live within thirty minutes of their respective DEVGRU commands, in *Leave it to Beaver,* throwback neighborhoods. Everyone knows everyone. They gather for the holidays. Build decks together. Become godparents to each other's children. Block parties. Military holiday picnics.

Brian loved it. Fit in perfectly. He purchased a house within the thirty minutes, *times up to get there,* on-site-response standing order. He rode a Harley, but moved a piano into his home; his guitar rested against the bench. He always took classes, *SEAL ranks are populated with a large number of college graduates,* searching out the best courses, courses that would make him a better SEAL, more of an asset to his team. Learning never took a back seat to his lust for adventure. Adventure never took a back seat to learning.

He summited mountains, had a goal, made a plan, *he always had a plan, a scheme*, to summit Mt. Elbrus in Russia, studied Russian, and planned the trip, *because it will cost me less*, to coincide with the end of a deployment.

AND HE BROUGHT MORE lost SEALs, friends, brothers, home.

During a 2010 deployment, he called, "I'm okay, but I'm

coming home with Adam Brown. John, John Haas is coming with me."

"Brian," Pat said. "I'm so sorry."

"He's a SEAL, a friend, a brother, a teammate. His family will need help."

Adam, a man who'd beat all the odds against becoming a SEAL, including drug addiction and jail time, had been serving in Afghanistan with Brian and John. Adam, engaged in a firefight, was hit by enemy fire, but before he died his action saved several others pinned down by the enemy fire.

Brian and John stayed with Adam's wife, Kelly, and their children for over a month. They brought Kelly and the kids to the White House, helped Kelly move back to the family home in Arkansas, then—returned to Afghanistan.

Adam had operated out of the East Coast like Brian. He'd lived, SEAL neighbors, near Brian. Once, after helping Adam put down a new hardwood floor in his home, Brian called Pat.

"Mom," Brian said, excited. "I helped Adam put down a new floor. First time either of us did that."

"You sound pretty excited about it," Pat said, a little surprised at the enthusiasm in Brian's voice.

"Yeah, it came out great. So, now that we know how to do it, I'm going to do the same thing in my house."

ADAM WAS KILLED on March 17th. The body count was growing. Pat worried.

PART EIGHT

THE STRENGTH OF THEIR WOMEN

Sometime in 2007, during one of her visits to Virginia Beach, not long after Brian was ensconced into DEVGRU, he pulled a book, Gates of Fire, *from a crowded bookcase in his home. He opened the book to page 426. "Mom," he said, "There's something I want to read to you."*

"Okay," Pat said, quizzically, "What is it about?"

"It's the story of the Battle of Thermopylae. There's a passage on this page that explains how Leonidas chose the 300 to defend against the millions of Persians. He said, 'I picked them because of the strength of their women.'"

———

AUGUST 6, 2011

". . . the helicopter Brian was on went down. Shot down. Brian was killed. There were no survivors," Lt. Commander Mark Oz said, telling Pat, finishing, *with reverence*, what he'd started out to do early that morning. His words sent a chill into the room on one of the hottest days of the year.

"I understand," Pat said softly, her voice trembling.

"Ma'am, I'll be your Casualty Assistance Calls Officer,

your CACO. You are my sole concern. I'm here to take care of you. I'm here to manage the process and keep you informed. I'll be with you for as long as you need and want, today, tomorrow, and for the rest of time. I'll communicate everything I can. Whatever I know and find out, you will know. No secrets. We do this together."

"Okay," Pat said, stunned, processing. "May I tell my family now?"

"Yes, ma'am. That's up to you from here on out. My duty was to tell you first. The other men with me are part of the team that will help coordinate everything, staring with getting Brian home to you. *Ma'am, I'm sorry.*"

Pat called the others into the room. Mark stepped back, waited. Watched. Michael, Christian too, stepped into the room. Sadness swept in with them like a wind blowing into their faces. Michael inched close to Pat, his hand on her shoulder. Christian stared at the floor then at the men in uniform. Pat, *Leonidas. The 300. The strength of their women. I understand. I understand now why Brian told this story to me. . . it's what he tried to tell me. I have to be brave, show strength. It's what he wanted,* wiped tears away with the back of her hand.

"Now what?" she said.

Mark hesitated. Swallowed. Cleared his throat. Began. "Ma'am, you know that Brian was part of DEVGRU. This, his death, and the death of the others, this is going to hit the media soon. The information is already out. One of my responsibilities will be to control the information that gets to the media. Information about Brian. About you. About your family. As I said, there were no survivors, a lot of men were lost. This is a big story for the media. I can't control what gets leaked or said elsewhere," *Mark, within days, added a Public Affairs Officer to the CACO team,* "but I can control it here. I'll make sure this is done right. Your son is a hero—he will be treated with the respect and dignity owed to a true American hero—I promise you that."

Pat looked on, silent, the onslaught of information already overwhelming.

"Ma'am," Mark asked. "Do you have any questions?"

Pat hesitated, unsure how to respond. She wanted to raise her head and yell . . . *Do I have any questions? I don't know anything about how all this is supposed to work. So, let's see, Brian, my son has been killed. There are four men here. One of them is telling me about the media, and a process, and Brian is a hero. I . . . I don't know . . . what . . . what happens . . . how any of this really works. Do I have questions? At least a million, but what am I supposed to ask? What happened to Brian? When will we have Brian's body? Funeral arrangements? Who does that? He's going to be buried at Arlington, right? That's what we are expecting. I don't know what to ask, I just want to know what comes next. Seems like everything is up to the military right now. They need to do whatever needs to be done to get Brian home, to get all those men home. What do we do besides wait? Seems like that's what it is right now, a waiting game. Grieve and wait. Wait and grieve.*

"Have you recovered Brian yet?" Pat said, the only question out of the many that she could think of asking.

The CACO team stayed for a while, long enough to make certain that Pat, everyone, would be okay, then left to find a hotel. Within hours, family began to gather in Stamford. Who, *no one knows for certain*, called whom? But they came. They would stay until Brian was buried at Arlington. The CACO team would stay too, longer than almost anyone. Pat needed them all.

———

OVER THE NEXT one or two days, waiting held center stage while some questions were answered, answers to others still unknown. Recovery of the men killed had been quick; it had to be. Bodies could not fall into the hands of the Taliban. Identifying the men took longer. Everything, every step, every *next*, depended upon that macabre function. *DEVGRU SEALs do not wear dog tags.* Pieces of clothing. Body parts. Dental records. Eventually DNA.

Collected remains, intact or otherwise, *a casket for each man lost,* were flown to Dover. Some of the men, like Brian, his body recovered, were identified quickly. Others would take much longer, in some instances—*years.* Comingled remains, ashes that could not be separated, were interred in a single grave.

At Dover, arriving caskets, empty or not, were labeled. It was there that Pat, Michael, and other family members would wait for Brian.

"We'll get you to Dover," Mark said, just as he promised. "Do you want to fly?"

"NO WAY!" Pat said, unable to fathom the idea of getting onto an airplane. "Drive us. I'm just not getting on . . . I'm just not going to do it . . . I won't fly. DRIVE ME!"

Mark and the team did just that, ensconcing Pat and Michael in a huge black SUV, chauffeuring them to Dover. They arrived early in the day, checked in, *not the Fisher House, too small for the hundreds of family members,* to a hotel large enough to accommodate the families and friends of the thirty men killed during EXTORTION-17.

In the lobby, waiting, *always waiting,* Pat and Michael sat. Families, most already at the hotel, began to crowd the lobby. Pat, a stranger to everyone, felt awkward, uncomfortable in the midst of so many strangers. Her own family arrived, Jeff, Amy, others.

While they waited, Michael turned to Pat, placed a hand over hers. "I know what we are going to do for Brian," he said. "We are going to start a scholarship in his name."

Pat, surprised, quickly agreed.

"It's time," someone announced. "Time to make our way to the airport."

Pat, Michael, and Jeff walked back to the SUV. Navy Chief Logan Johnson held the doors open. Many in the crowd moved into waiting buses. The short ride to the airfield took only a few minutes. Lt. Commander Mark Oz and the rest of the team made their own way.

Inside a large ballroom at the "Landings" hundreds of family members and friends milled about. Pat avoided conversation with all but Michael and members of her CACO team. Jeff, shielding Pat, *deliberately or not*, graciously engaged with many of the people introducing themselves— wanting—trying to talk with Pat. He met and spoke with a SEAL who'd attended Norwich with Brian, then with mothers, sisters, fathers, children, lifting the burden of conversation from Pat.

Another mourner, President Barack Obama, traveling in a "White Top," one of the Presidential helicopters, touched down at Dover. He first made his way to the Landings to meet with families, engaging personally with as many as he could. He met with family members, offering his condolences, and his personal gratitude for their sacrifice and service, before taking a motorcade down to the tarmac.

Two C-17s, one of the military's largest transport airplanes, holding the remains of the thirty men killed, sat sentinel on the tarmac. Inside the airplanes, first one, then another, and another, the President paused by each casket, silently paying his respects to each man.

Families moved to the tarmac. The President left the airplanes. Honor guards began the dignified transfer of the fallen. Before the day ended, Pat, Michael, and Jeff, back in the SUV, Logan Johnson at the wheel, returned to Connecticut.

Along the way, Pat's cell phone sounded off. A woman introduced herself as the Gold Star Ombudsman. *What is a Gold Star Ombudsman? Now what, what could this be all about? Why is she on the phone with me? Gold Star Family, I know what that means. I guess that's what Michael and I have become, a Gold Star Family, but what does she want?*

"We are here to support you, to help in any way we can. Do you need toiletries?"

Why in the world is someone asking me if I need toilet paper? Is that what she's asking? I mean Michael and I are here in this SUV, somewhere in New Jersey, all I want to do is get home, sleep in my own bed. And someone is asking about toilet paper!

"I don't understand what it is you're asking," Pat said, mystified, but it all became clear over the next few weeks. Pat's home turned into an Airbnb. She suddenly had a house full of people, a lot of people. Soap. Toilet paper. Toothpaste. Clean towels. COFFEE! She could easily have run out of everything. The Gold Star Ombudsman, Gold Star Families, the organization, supplied Pat with all the things she needed to have a house full of people for weeks. Everyone around her, the CACO team, family, clergy, SEALs, Brian's friends, set up a mini command center inside Pat's house, mapping out and planning memorials and services.

Outside, Mark Oz had, *for a lot of reasons,* set up an around-the-clock security detail. Media hounds, sure, they were a problem. But he had a media guy handling that. What then? The *what then* is this. DEVGRU is exposed now. DEVGRU killed Bin Laden just a few months earlier. DEVGRU families, especially those far away from SEAL communities, are, *even here on American soil,* at risk for retaliation. If Taliban terrorists can find you, they'll attempt to exact revenge—anywhere in the world.

PART NINE

WHAT COMES NEXT

HOME IN CONNECTICUT, EVERYTHING BEGAN TO OVERWHELM Pat. All she wanted to do was sleep. And she did. She stopped eating too, losing weight, but the thought of eating seemed impossible. Family took over. Family ran her house—at least for now—and waited. Waited and wondered. Questions. What comes next?

At Dover, after the dignified transfer, with most of the families gone home to wait, to learn, to hear about their son, father, husband, autopsy and identifications began. Life, not just for Pat, but for thirty families, was on hold until everything the military needed to do was completed. It's a waiting game with little anyone can accomplish beyond what the military, *at least for now*, authorizes. Time to grieve and wait. Wait and grieve.

In between bits and pieces of news, in between all of the chaos, Pat, Michael, and the rest of the family rose each day, anticipating the completed identification of Brian's remains. While they waited, Pat, surprised by a shocking question, felt stunned.

"Ma'am," Petty Officer Logan Johnson asked, "how much

of Brian needs to be recovered for you to accept that we have found him?"

What? What did he just ask me? Who wants to answer a question like that? What—what do you want me to say? What should my answer be? Ten percent—twenty—fifty—one hundred? Do I want to hear you say we believe he may have been burned in the crash? I don't want to hear that. Do I want to hear you say part of him was recovered? I don't want to hear that either. I can't imagine anyone wanting to hear the answers to these questions.

Even though I'm a nurse, I've worked in the emergency room—seen it all, I thought if this ever happened, that I would say, yes. Tell me. I want to know everything. I want to see his remains. I can take anything. But now, no, that's not what I want. I don't want to know. I don't want my last memory of my son to be a terrible image of his broken body. I want to remember him happy—alive—vibrant . . .

"I won't answer that question," Pat said.

Long before the final autopsy report, the Navy assured Pat that, *standing near the open rear ramp, Brian was tossed from the helicopter,* his remains had been recovered. Later, much later, Pat agreed to read the autopsy report. Scared, afraid of what she might read, she read anyway, understanding more about her son's death. There were photos in the report too. Pat never looked at them. She never allowed anyone else to look at the photos either. They remain sealed. It was hard, *it was for the best,* to hold the image of Brian the way she last saw him— happy, handsome—full of life.

Closed casket.

But Pat had a special shirt, short sleeved, green, buttons down the front, *one that Brian wore a lot,* that she wanted buried with him. The Navy had already advised Pat not to look in the coffin, advised the staff at the funeral home to follow the same protocol. Pat gave the shirt to Logan. He took care of it. The how of it doesn't matter. The shirt, *a favorite,* is with Brian.

THE DAYS, like the lyrics of the song, did *dwindle down to a precious few*. By the middle of August, the wait, what had felt endless, ended abruptly. The autopsy, *at least Brian's*, complete, final identification confirmed, Brian was on his way home, a short stay before his final trip back to Virginia, his final resting place at Arlington. A hometown funeral would be Pat's one last chance to have Brian here in Connecticut. Everything would go from pause to fast-forward. Brian arrived in the middle of the week, on Wednesday, then by Friday, August 19th, family, friends, officials, politicians, *the important people*, joined Pat and Michael inside St. Cecilia Church in Stamford for Brian's funeral. Norwich University sent cadets.

Before then, Pat's one chance to eulogize Brian met with resistance. Logan Johnson stepped in, listened politely to the priest. "We here at St. Cecilia," the parish priest opined, "discourage a eulogy. The Church sees the funeral mass as a time for celebrating the life of the deceased, but the focus should be on Christ, who conquered sin and death, and on the resurrection and hope offered through faith. A eulogy detracts from this focus and could potentially detract from the spiritual meaning of the funeral mass."

"Father, excuse me, but Brian was killed in war fighting for our country. Are you going to deny the family a eulogy?" Logan said, convincingly.

"No," the priest said, matter-of-factly, "You may have a eulogy, but only after the Mass is finished."

Jeff and two of Brian's friends, SEALs, delivered eulogies.

The church objected to any secular music inside the nave, a quarrel Pat didn't feel like fighting. Logan took care of that too. He took care of many of the small things—seating arrangements, transportation, relaying Pat's requests, *the casket carried not wheeled*.

The president of the Gold Star Mothers met with Pat before the funeral, presenting her with a Gold Star pin. *Is that what I am now, a Gold Star Mother? It is, isn't it . . . I'm a Gold Star Mother now . . .*

———————

So many things came next. On every form, every box on every document, anything, everything that needed to be assigned, everything legally bequeathed, Brian had designated to Pat. Her name filled in all the blank spaces. Things to take care of. Brian's house? His truck? His personal effects at Command? So much to do . . .

But all of that needed to wait. Brian was on his way to Arlington.

For Pat, two weeks of just putting one foot in front of the other ended abruptly. The days ahead gathered with momentum of the wildest of tornados. *Friday, August 19th, the funeral in Connecticut. Monday, August 22nd, leave for Virginia Beach. Tuesday, August 23rd, SEAL teammates throw (would have been his 32nd) a birthday party for Brian. Friday, August 26th, Brian and eleven other SEALs are buried at Arlington. A thirteenth casket holding comingled remains is last in queue.*

PART TEN
LIFE GOES ON

By the end of August, back home in Connecticut, Brian laid to rest with his brothers, the benign chaos, the din that had taken up necessary residence inside Pat and Michael's home, quieted. The demands of everyday life, put on hold, grew impatient. Grownups had jobs. Children had school. Pat and Michael had careers they had to go back to. The ordinary, *for now*, pushed the extraordinary aside.

Punctuating the last few weeks, *Brian's death, the Stamford ceremony, Arlington, and everything that went with it*, a hurricane, the first of the season, made landfall in North Carolina on August 29th, trekking its way north like a runaway freight train. Its path nicked Connecticut, but Hurricane Irene bore down on New York and New Jersey. Amy, *remember her, she's Pat's daughter*, seven months pregnant, *moving from Brooklyn to a new house in New Jersey*, stayed with Pat and Michael, waiting to close on the new house. But the new home in New Jersey, in harm's way, flooded by Irene, became an afterthought. Amy moved in, *in toto*, with Pat and Michael.

Days after Irene continued north and mercifully out to sea, Pat and Michael went back to work.

BACK AT THE HOSPITAL, running into colleagues, *Oh Pat, I'm sorry—Pat, how are you doing—Pat, is there anything I can do—if there's anything you need,* left Pat feeling awkward, uncomfortable. The expressions of condolence, *it was easier to be strong without them,* all well-intended, only threatened fragile emotions.

She wouldn't, couldn't, let her guard down, give in to her sorrow publicly. That's not how she'd acquit herself. That's not, *she believed,* what Brian would have wanted. Her position at the hospital, Clinical Research Nurse, gave her the cover of a private office. Outside of her door, the clinical demands of working with patients participating in a trial didn't afford others the time or space to ask about Brian. Pat, lost in her work, didn't have, *at least here at the hospital,* much time to dwell on Brian. Work actually allowed some return to normalcy. In time, Pat, becoming more like herself again, relaxed around others.

NOT LONG AFTER returning from Arlington, after weeks back at the hospital, life outside of home and work became a roller coaster, a hang-onto-your-hat ride of events. Brian was nominated and selected the USO Sailor of the Year. Pat was asked to ring the opening bell at the New York Stock Exchange in honor of Brian. Pat and many other EXTORTION-17 family members attended a Navy Seal Foundation benefit dinner in New York City. Pat met several of them, including Deb Cox, who introduced herself.

"You're Pat Parry," Deb said, holding out her hand without reservation, catching Pat off guard, surprising her.

"I am," Pat said. "And who are you?"

"I'm Deb Cox. My son Heath, Heath Robinson, was killed with Brian."

"I knew him," *the brotherhood that existed between SEALs extended to their families too.* "Heath lived near Brian. I knew they were close."

The cascade of events, honors bestowed upon Brian blossomed, someone or some organization always wanting to pay tribute to Brian or honor Pat. The queue seemed endless. There's the Gold Star Mothers' annual trip to Israel. Pat goes. SEAL mothers' Spa Weekend. Pat goes to that too. Gold Star Mothers' national and local events.

Pat attended the ceremony at Norwich University, Brian's alma mater, when they added Brian's name to their memorial wall. SEAL Command initiated an annual Memorial Day ceremony to honor SEAL Team members of DEVGRU. Pat attended, attends annually, considers her inclusion in the annual celebration of the men and women of this special unit an honor.

During the 2012 celebration, during a tour of the Team Room, Pat's escort turned to her.

"You missed the toast to the team," he said. "I'll get you a drink."

"That's okay," Pat said. "I really don't drink."

"You do now!" her SEAL escort said.

Everything, *wonderfully well-intended,* took on a life of its own. Pat, grateful for all of it, had her own private way of coping too. And then came *the firsts.*

Brian always tried to come home each Thanksgiving. Most of the family, *Pat and Michael's home large enough,* usually gathered in Connecticut, at Pat and Michael's. But this year, the first without Brian, forty relatives, spouses, children, brothers, sisters, Pat's mother, crowded themselves into the Parry house. Pat and Michael rented an event tent, heated it, enclosed their outdoor patio, and ensconced everyone there.

For the next few years, celebrating Thanksgiving at Pat's became an unspoken tradition. Family came together. Early in the morning, those that could, went for a run. Later, before the meal, they'd read the names of the fallen and lift a glass in their honor, their memory.

The first Christmas followed, then Easter, Brian's birthday. There are a lot of firsts.

PART ELEVEN
NEW BEGINNINGS

LIFE LOOKED DIFFERENT AFTER BRIAN WAS KILLED. WOULD become different. Was different. There's the good, the bad, and the, sometimes, ugly.

The Ugly—Conspiracy theories surround EXTORTION-17. They should not. Not all the remains, *comingled*, were individually identifiable. Some next of kin had nothing to grieve over. There will always be unanswered questions. So many, *no survivors*, men, not just SEALs or Americans, were lost, thirty-eight in all, and a brave combat canine.

The Bad—To others, even family, there may be a limit to support. Pat, and the other families, walk a fine line between honoring and remembering the fathers, sons, husbands, and brothers lost in EXTORTION-17. But that's part of the tragedy, isn't it? Losing Brian is hard, not just on Pat, but on everyone. And it's painful to talk about, to remember, but it would be more painful if Pat let herself forget.

Someone once said to Pat, "You talk about Brian a lot."

"Why shouldn't I?" Pat, forced to reply, said. "Don't you talk about your kids? Should I not talk about my son because he died?"

Amy, her relationship with Brian marginalized by some,

usually someone thinking they knew Brian well, grew annoyed by their unearned intimacy, their claims of some special connection. "He's my brother," she complained to Pat. "I knew him. Not these strangers."

A few years later, Christian died—suddenly.

THE GOOD—As months, then years, distance Pat and Michael from the day EXTORTION-17 was shot out of the sky, more good memories of Brian crowd out the tragedy. Pat and Michael surround themselves with those memories, remembering Brian in wonderful ways—and that sustains them.

Brian's death wasn't the end; his sacrifice was a beginning.

The day after Pat and Michael learned that Brian had been killed, while they waited for his body to arrive at Dover AFB, Michael had turned to Pat, placed a hand over hers and declared, promised, to start a scholarship in his name. *A promise made and kept.* Thirty-eight recipients at Norwich University, Brian's alma mater, the place where he burnished his skills, the place that gave life to his passions, have received sixty-four undergraduate scholarship awards.

Fifty-four recipients, ensconced in university's College of Graduate Studies Program, have received fifty-six scholarships.

In memory of Brian, Pat and Michael have been able to give more, *over two million in scholarships and gifts,* to others. More, Pat would tell you, than they ever would have imagined, or ever would have been capable of.

They funded a second scholarship program at New Mass Boston in memory of Christian.

WHAT IS LIFE WITHOUT BRIAN? Is his laughter missed? His touch? His strength? What else, *he succeeded at everything he cared about*, might he have accomplished? No one will ever know, but, "Life," Pat will tell you, "just keeps on going. There is always something else to do, someone, somewhere to help."

———

LEONIDAS CHOSE the 300 to defend against the millions, picking them because of the strength of their women. Brian became who he was because of the strength of a woman, *his mother*.

Eight-year-old Brian Bill fly fishing

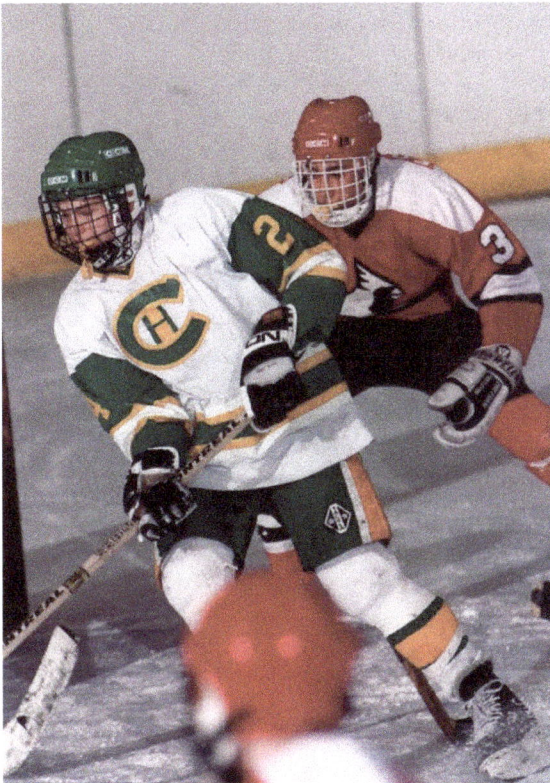

A young Brian Bill on the ice

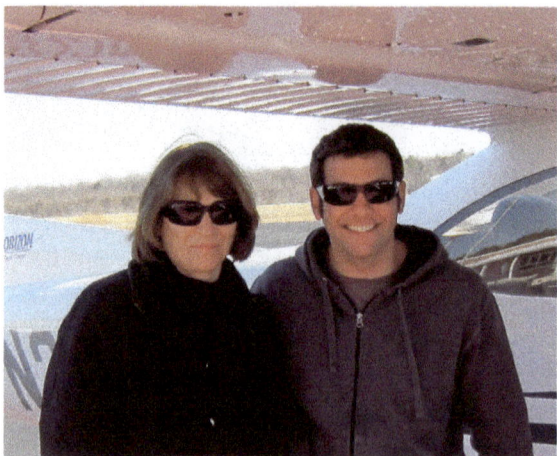

Pat Parry and her son Brian Bill

*SEAL Commander Mark "Oz" Ozdarski—CACO Team
Leader*

Years later, Mark "Oz" and Pat Parry, Brian Bill's mother. Mark delivered the keynote address at the annual Brian R. Bill Memorial Gala.

Chief Special Warfare Operator, Navy SEAL, Brian R. Bill. August 23, 1979—August 6, 2011

Grief is the last act of love we give to our loved one. Where there is deep grief there is great love. Grief is a great rite of passage, it is a hero's journey of courage, of sacred battles, sorrow, love, joy, and loss. Through the darkness of grief, we can see the light of love which transcends death.

And with the pain can come gratitude for the gift of time we had the love that was shared and the power to become a better person because they loved us.

— *CHAPLAIN ROBERT ORR*

GLOSSARY OF TERMS

AFT: Afghan time.

AIT: Advanced Individual Training (training after boot camp in the soldier's selected military occupational specialty).

ALIVE DAY: The anniversary of the date when a veteran almost lost his or her life in combat.

AL-QAEDA: A radical Sunni Muslim terror organization founded by Osama bin Laden.

ANGEL FLIGHT: In the armed forces, this term is used to describe taking deceased military personnel home. The angel describes the United States Air Force planes, known as C-130s, used for this duty. The call sign of these planes is given the highest priority in terms of air space.

BAMC: Brooke Army Medical Center is the United States Army's premier medical institution.

BLUE STAR FAMILIES: A Blue Star Family is the immediate family of a US military member who is serving during war. They are authorized by the US government to hang the Blue Star Banner from their residence for others to see.

GREEN-ON-BLUE: A slang term to describe attacks by Iraqi or Afghan security forces on US personnel.

BUTTER BARS: The brass collar insignia for a second lieutenant, resembling sticks of butter.

CACO: The Navy or Marine Corps provides a Casualty Assistance Call Officer (CACO) to notify primary next of kin of a deceased SEAL, sailor, or Marine. The PNOK are notified in person by a uniformed CACO. A chaplain accompanies the CACO when possible. Following notification, CACOs assist the next of kin with burial arrangements, applications for benefits and entitlements, contact with benevolent and philanthropic organizations, obtaining reports of investigation, as well as other pertinent issues.

CAO: After primary next of kin have been notified of the death of an Army soldier, an Army Casualty Assistance Officer (CAO) will meet with the family to provide as much information as available regarding the circumstances of the member's death and will answer any questions. The CAO will also ensure that the survivors' immediate needs are being met during this difficult time. The CAO will immediately begin the process of providing any assistance available in making funeral or memorial arrangements as appropriate.

CHU: Containerized Housing Unit.

CSH: Combat Surgical Hospital.

DFAC: Basically, a cafeteria. While the Army and Air Force both officially use the term DFAC ("Dining Facility"), Marines refer to it as the "chow hall."

DEVGRU: The Naval Special Warfare Development Group (NSWDG or DEVGRU) is the Navy's dedicated counterterrorism, hostage rescue, and direct-action special missions unit, staffed by Navy SEALS. According to a media report in 2010, its present name may have changed and subsequent designations may be classified.

DIGNIFIED TRANSFER: The process by which, upon the return from the theater of operations to the United States, the remains of fallen military members are transferred from the aircraft to an awaiting vehicle. A solemn Dignified Transfer is conducted upon arrival at Dover Air Force Base, Delaware, to honor those who have given their lives in the service of our country.

DOVER: Dover Air Force Base, or Dover AFB, is a United States Air Force base under the operational control of Air Mobility Command, located two miles southeast of the city of Dover, Delaware. Soldiers wounded or killed in action are flown from their place of deployment to Dover.

DOWN RANGE: Military slang for being deployed overseas, usually in a war zone. Used more frequently by Iraq and Afghanistan veterans.

FISHER HOUSE: A foundation that builds comfort homes where military and veteran families can stay, free of charge, while a loved one is recovering from wounds or injuries, or where families can await the return of a soldier's remains, usually of a soldier killed in action.

FOB: Forward Operating Base, a relatively small outpost often meant to help control dangerous territory.

GOLD STAR FAMILIES: A Gold Star Family is one that has lost an immediate family member in the line of duty of military service.

GOLD STAR MOTHERS: American Gold Star Mothers (AGSM) is a private nonprofit organization of American mothers who lost sons or daughters in service of the United States Armed Forces.

HAJI: Arabic word for someone who has made the pilgrimage to Mecca; derogatory military slang used to mean the enemy in Iraq and Afghanistan.

HIGH SPEED SOLDIER: Generally, a soldier who thinks ahead and shows a good amount of dependability.

HUMVEE: HMMWV, "High Mobility Multipurpose Wheeled Vehicle."

IED: Improvised Explosive Device.

IFAK: Individual First Aid Kit.

KEFFIYEH: A Keffiyeh (also called shemagh) is a traditional square cotton scarf worn by people of the Middle East.

KEVLAR: Kevlar is the registered trademark name for the fiber produced by DuPont. It is found in most protective gear, including helmets, gloves, pants, and jackets. Many US soldiers use "Kevlar" as a slang term for the modern American military helmet.

KIA: Killed in Action.

LNs: Local Nationals.

LZ: Landing Zone.

M249: A light machine gun, individually portable, mounted or unmounted.

MEV: Medical Evacuation Vehicle.

MK19: An American 40mm belt-fed automatic grenade launcher.

MRAP: Mine-Resistant Ambush Protected light tactical vehicles.

NCO: Non-Commissioned Officer is a subordinate officer (such as a sergeant) in the Army, Air Force, or Marine Corps appointed from among enlisted personnel. Nominally lower rank than commissioned officers (second lieutenant and above).

NT: A notification team is composed of a field-grade officer of equal or higher grade than the member about whom they are making notification, a notification officer (the title varies among branches), and at least one other person. If possible, additional people include a chaplain and medical personnel capable of delivering assistance to the next of kin. Their duty is to notify the primary next of kin of a deceased soldier lost in the line of duty as quickly as possible.

OCS: Officer Candidate School.

PCC: Pre-Combat Check, generally carried out by the officer or NCO in charge of the unit readying to roll out on a mission.

PCS: Permanent Change of Station orders.

PNOK: Primary next of kin.

RANGER: Any soldier who graduates from the elite Ranger School is called a Ranger. While most Rangers serve in a variety of units alongside non-Rangers, some are assigned to the 75th Ranger Regiment, an elite light-infantry airborne formation that conducts raids within enemy territory.

RPG: Rocket-Propelled Grenade.

SAT-102: A 24/7, always monitored, American channel for all in-country coverage in Iraq and Afghanistan.

SAW: Squad Automatic Weapon.

SEAL: The United States Navy Sea, Air, and Land (SEAL) Teams are the US Navy's primary special operations force and a component of the Naval Special Warfare Command. SEALS conduct small-unit special operation missions in nearly any environment.

SPECIAL FORCES: The United States Army Special Forces (SF), popularly known as the "Green Berets," are a special operations force of the United States Army. The Green Berets' original mission was to train and lead partisan units behind enemy lines; they have since incorporated other missions such as counterterrorism, counterinsurgency, and security force assistance.

TALIBAN: A fundamentalist Muslim movement whose militia took control of much of Afghanistan from early 1995 and soon set up a radical Islamic state. The movement was forcibly removed from power by the US and its allies after the attacks on September 11, 2001, but fought a sustained guerrilla war against the US-supported Afghan government. The Taliban returned to power in 2021, following the US withdrawal from Afghanistan.

THE WIRE: Generally, the accepted term for the secure base perimeter.

UDT: Underwater Demolition Teams, or "frogmen," were amphibious units created by the United States Navy during World War II. They were predecessors of today's SEAL teams.

WIA: Wounded in Action.

ALSO BY RON FARINA

BOOKS

Who Will Have My Back: Stories of Love and Care for Those Who Have Served and Sacrificed

Out of the Shadows: Voices of American Women Soldiers

At the Altar of the Past

ESSAYS

Keeping Promises

War Torn

SHORT STORIES

A Place More Kind Than Home

Names In a Can